James F. Cooper

Historical Stories of American Pioneer Life

James F. Cooper

Historical Stories of American Pioneer Life

ISBN/EAN: 9783337716806

Printed in Europe, USA, Canada, Australia, Japan

Cover: Foto ©ninafisch / pixelio.de

More available books at **www.hansebooks.com**

HISTORICAL STORIES

OF

AMERICAN PIONEER LIFE

AS TOLD IN THE FAMOUS LEATHERSTOCKING TALES

THE LAST OF THE MOHICANS
THE PATHFINDER   THE DEERSLAYER
THE PIONEERS   THE PRAIRIE

BY J. FENIMORE COOPER

THE WALTER SCOTT OF AMERICA

ADAPTED TO YOUNGER READERS

BY

"THE BEST KNOWN WRITER OF JUVENILE BOOKS IN AMERICA."

EMBELLISHED WITH TEN MAGNIFICENT LITHOGRAPHS

AND NUMEROUS ORIGINAL DRAWINGS IN THE TEXT

Entered according to Act of Congress, in the year 1897, by
W. E. SCULL,
in the office of the Librarian of Congress, at Washington.
All rights reserved.

ALL PERSONS ARE WARNED NOT TO INFRINGE UPON OUR COPYRIGHT BY USING EITHER THE MATTER OR THE PICTURES IN THIS VOLUME.

CONTENTS AND LIST OF
WATER-COLOR REPRODUCTIONS.

	PAGE
THE DEERSLAYER.	17
Hetty and Hist in the Iroquois Encampment.	
The Peril of Deerslayer.	
THE LAST OF THE MOHICANS.	64
Cora a Prisoner to the Hurons.	
Hawkeye and the Bear take the Fox Prisoner.	
THE PATHFINDER.	113
Pathfinder Shoots at the Target.	
The Pathfinder Rescues Mabel.	
THE PIONEERS.	189
Leatherstocking to the Rescue.	
The Young Hunter Saved the Sleigh from its Danger.	
THE PRAIRIE.	236
Mahtonee Surprises the Sleeping Sentinel.	
The Pawnee and the Palefaces.	

INTRODUCTION

AND

LIFE OF THE AUTHOR.

ITHOUT doubt, Leatherstocking is the one great original character with which America has enriched the world's literature. James Fenimore Cooper presented this imposing character, this realistic impersonation of the early pioneers, in five volumes composing the "Leatherstocking Tales."

To read these stories is not only a pleasure which no one should deny himself, but a duty every one owes to his education in the early history of his country. While the characters are fictitious, they are the true historic types of the times they represent—more real than any history could present.

The five stories are here condensed, by leaving out long and tedious details, into one volume, especially adapted to the reading of young people. The following sketch of the author and his writings is an appropriate introduction to the work.

THE LIFE OF JAMES FENIMORE COOPER.

Our first American novelist, and up to the present time perhaps the only American novelist whose fame is permanently established among foreigners, is James Fenimore Cooper. While Washington Irving, our first writer of short stories, several years Cooper's senior, was so strikingly popular in England and America, Cooper's "Spy" and "Pilot," and "The Last of the Mohicans," went beyond the bounds of the English language, and the Spaniard, the Frenchman, the German, the Italian, and others, had placed these books beside their own classics and were dividing honors between him and Sir Walter Scott; and it was they who first called him the Walter Scott of America. Nor was this judgment altogether wrong. For six or seven years Scott's "Waverly Novels" had been appearing, and his "Ivanhoe," which was first published in 1820, —the first

11

historical novel of the world,—had given the cue to Cooper for "The Spy," which appeared in 1821, the first historical novel of America. Both books were translated into foreign languages by the same translators, and made for their respective authors immediate and lasting fame.

James Fenimore Cooper was born in Burlington, New Jersey, September 15, 1789—the same year that George Washington was inaugurated President of the United States. His father owned many thousand acres of wild land on the headwaters of the Susquehanna River, in New York, and while James was an infant removed thither and built a stately mansion on Otsego Lake, near the point where the little river issues forth on its journey to the sea. Around Otsego Hall, as it was called, the village of Cooperstown grew up. In this wilderness young Cooper passed his childhood, a hundred miles beyond the advancing lines of civilization. Along the shores of the beautiful lake, shut in by untouched forests, or in the woods themselves, that rose and fell unbroken, except here and there by a pioneer's hut or a trapper's camp, he passed his boyhood days, and slept at night in the solemn silence of nature's primeval grandeur. All the delicate arts of the forest, the craft of the woodsman, the trick of the trapper, the stratagem of the Indian fighter, the wily shrewdness of the tawny savage, the hardships and dangers of pioneer life, were as familiar to Cooper as were the legends of North Britain and the stirring ballads of the highlands and the lowlands to Walter Scott. But for this experience we should never have had the famous "Leatherstocking Tales."

From this wilderness the boy was sent, at the age of thirteen, to Yale College, where he remained three years ; but he was too restless and adventurous to devote himself diligently to study, and was dismissed in disgrace at sixteen. For one year he shipped before the mast as a common sailor, and for the next five years served as a midshipman in the United States Navy, making himself master of that detailed knowledge of nautical life which he afterward employed to so much advantage in his romances of the sea.

In 1811 Cooper resigned his post as midshipman, and married Miss Delancey, with whom he lived happily for forty years. The first few years of his married life were spent in quiet retirement. For some months he resided in Westchester County, the scene of his book, "The Spy." Then he removed to his old home at Cooperstown, and took possession of the family mansion, to which he had fallen heir through the death of his father. Here he prepared to spend his life as a quiet country gentleman, and did so until a mere accident called him into authorship. Up to that date he seems never to have touched a pen or even thought of one except to write an ordinary letter. He was, however, fond of reading, and often read aloud to his wife. One day while reading a British novel he looked up and playfully said: "I could write a better book than that myself." "Suppose you try," replied his wife; and retiring to his library he wrote a chapter, which he read to Mrs. Cooper. She was pleased with it, and suggested that he continue, which he did, and published the book, under the title of "Precaution," in 1820.

No one at that time had thought of writing a novel with the scene laid in America, and "Precaution," which had an English setting, was so thoroughly English that it was reviewed in London with no suspicion of its American authorship. The success which it met, while not great, suggested to Cooper that as he had not failed with a novel describing British life, of which he knew little, he might succeed with one on American life, of which he knew much. It was a happy thought. Scott's "Ivanhoe" had just been read by him,—it suggested an American historical theme, and he wrote the story of "The Spy," which he published in 1821. It was a tale of the Revolution, in which the central figure, Harvey Birch, the spy, is one of the most interesting and effective characters in the realm of romantic literature. It quickly followed Scott's "Ivanhoe" into many languages.

Encouraged by the plaudits from both sides of the Atlantic, Cooper wrote another story, "The Pioneers" (1823), which was the first attempt to put into fiction the life of the frontier and the character of the backwoodsman. Here Cooper was in his element, on firm ground, familiar to him from his infancy, but the book was a revelation to the outside world. It is in this work that one of the greatest characters in fiction, the old backwoodsman, Natty Bumpo—the famous Leatherstocking—appeared, and gave his name to a series of tales, comprised in five volumes, which was not finally completed for twenty years. Strange to say, this famous series of books was not written in regular order. To follow the story logically the reader must read first the "Deerslayer," next the "Last of the Mohicans," followed by "The Pathfinder," then "The Pioneers," and lastly "The Prairie," which ends with the death of Leatherstocking.

The sea tales of Cooper were also suggested by Walter Scott, who published "The Pirate" in 1821. This book was being discussed by Cooper and some friends. The latter took the position that Scott could not have been its author, since he was a lawyer, and therefore could not have the knowledge of sea life which the book displayed. Cooper, being himself a mariner, declared that it could not have been written by a man familiar with the sea. He argued that it lacked that detail of information which no mariner would have failed to exhibit. To prove this point he determined to write a sea tale, and in 1823 his book, "The Pilot," appeared, which was the first genuine salt-water novel ever written, and to this day is one of the best. Tom Coffin, the hero of this novel, is the only one of all Cooper's characters worthy to take a place beside Leatherstocking, and the two books were published within two years of each other. In 1829 appeared "The Red Rover," which is wholly a tale of the ocean, as "The Last of the Mohicans" is wholly a tale of the forest. In all, Cooper wrote ten sea tales, which, with his land stories, established the fact that he was equally at home whether on the green billows or under the green trees.

In 1839 Cooper published his "History of the United States Navy," which is to this day the only authority on the subject for the period of which it treats. He also wrote many other novels on American subjects, and some eight or ten, like "Bravo," "The Headsman," and others, on European themes; but it is by "The Spy," the five Leatherstocking tales, and four or five of his sea tales that his fame has been secured and will be maintained.

In 1822, after "The Spy" had made Cooper famous, he removed to New York, where he lived for a period of four years, one of the most popular men in the metropolis. His force of character, large-heartedness, and genial, companionable nature, notwithstanding the fact that he was contentious and frequently got into the most heated discussions, made him unusually popular with those who knew him. He had many friends, and his friends were the best citizens of New York. He founded the "Bread and Cheese Lunch," to which belonged Chancellor Kent, the poets Fitzgreen Halleck and William Cullen Bryant, Samuel Morse, the inventor of the telegraph, and many other representatives of science, literature, and the learned professions. In 1826 he sailed for Europe, in various parts of which he resided for a period of six years. Before his departure he was tendered a dinner in New York which was attended by many of the most prominent men of the nation. Washington Irving had gone to the Old World eleven years before and traveled throughout Great Britain and over the Continent, but Cooper's works, though it was but six years since his first volume was published, were at this time more widely known than those of Irving; and with the author of the "Sketch-book" he divided the honors which the Old World so generously showered upon those two brilliant representatives of the New.

Many pages might be filled with the pleasant records of Cooper's seven years in Europe, during which he enjoyed the association and the respect of the greatest literary personages of the Old World. It would be interesting to tell how Sir Walter Scott sought him out in Paris, and renewed the acquaintance in London; how he lived in friendship and intimacy with General Lafayette at the French capital; to tell of his association with Wordsworth and Rogers in London; his intimate friendship with the great sculptor Greenough, and his fondness for Italy, which country he preferred above all others outside of America; of the delightful little villa where he lived in Florence, where he said he could look out upon green leaves and write to the music of the birds; to picture him settled for a summer in Naples; living in Tasso's villa at Sarento, writing his stories in the same house in which the great Italian author had lived, with the same glorious view of the sea and the bay, and the surf dashing almost against its walls. But space forbids. Let it be said that wherever he was, he was thoroughly and pronouncedly an American. He was much annoyed by the ignorance and prejudice of the English in all that related to his country. In France he vigorously defended the system of American government in a public pamphlet in favor of General Lafayette, upon whom the public press was making an attack. He was equally in earnest in bringing forward the claims of our poets, and was accustomed at literary meetings and dinner parties to carry volumes of Bryant, Halleck, Drake, and others, from which he read quotations to prove his assertions of their merits. Almost every prominent American who visited Europe during his seven years' sojourn abroad brought back pleasant recollections of his intercourse with the great and patriotic novelist.

Cooper returned to America in 1833, the same year that Washington Irving came back to his native land. He retired to his home at Cooperstown, where he spent the remaining nineteen years of his life, dying on the fourteenth day of September, 1852, one day before the sixty-second anniversary of his birth. His palatial home at Cooperstown, as were also his various places of residence in New York and foreign lands, was always open to his deserving countrymen, and many are the ambitious young aspirants in art, literature, and politics who have left his hospitable roof with higher ideals, loftier ambitions, and with a more exalted patriotism.

Though other fashions in fiction have come and gone, and other novelists have developed a more finished art, no one of them all has succeeded more completely in doing what he tried to do than did James Fenimore Cooper.

If we should visit Cooperstown, New York, the most interesting spot we should see would be the grave of America's first great novelist; and the one striking feature about it would be the marble statue of Leatherstocking, with dog and gun, overlooking the last resting-place of the great author. Then we should visit the house and go into the library, and sit in the chair and lean over the table where Cooper wrote. Ostego Hall is a shrine to the memory of Cooper and Natty Bumpo, the greatest hero of American fiction. And we turn away determined to read again the whole of the "Leatherstocking Tales."

THE DEERSLAYER
A STORY OF HUNTERS AND INDIANS.

BY JAMES FENIMORE COOPER.

ANY years ago, when these United States were colonies of England, there lived on the shores of Otsego Lake, some sixty miles west of the Hudson River, a trapper and hunter whose name was Tom Hutter.

I might say he lived in the lake instead of on its shores; for his house was built on piles in the lake, and, as it was entirely surrounded by water, and hard to get at, the hunters and soldiers there abouts called it "Muskrat Castle." Besides the castle, Tom Hutter had also a floating house—or rather a house built in a scow—which could be pushed or rowed or towed to any part of the lake he desired, according as he wished to be near his traps or hidden from sight in the thick tree growth along the shores. This house-boat was generally called the "Ark."

Tom Hutter had two daughters; one was twenty and beautiful; the other was sixteen and "not just right in her head." Tom was very fond of his daughters, and very watchful for their safety in this land of Indians and dangers.

Into this beautiful region in which lies Lake Otsego, and in which lived Tom Hutter and his daughters, Judith and Hetty, there came, one fine June day, two hunters. One was about twenty-six, handsome, stalwart, careless, reckless, and unscrupulous. His name was Harry March, nicknamed, because of his heedlessness and quickness, "Hurry." The other was a brown and sinewy young fellow of twenty-one; his name was Nathaniel, or "Natty," Bumpo. He had been brought up among the Delaware Indians, and was called by them, because of his skill as a hunter, "Deerslayer." He was gentle, true-hearted, fearless, cool, and strong, and as honest as the day is long.

There were rumors of war between the French of Canada and the

English of the Colonies; this meant that the Indians would take sides either with the French or the English. The authorities paid money for Indian scalps, on a proof of their destruction, and, as the French Indians, or Iroquois, were known to be camping about the lake, Hurry and Tom Hutter determined to steal out by night, surprise the Iroquois, and make some money by the sale of their scalps. The Deerslayer would not agree to this; he was too noble to take part in such mean business; he did not object to fighting Indians in war, but he was opposed to stealing on sleeping Indians and murdering them for gain; for women and children, as well as warriors, were counted fair game by the scalp-hunters. So, that night, Hurry and Tom started out on their expedition, while Deerslayer, though he accompanied them, refused to join in their "business." Instead, he held the canoe away from the shore, to be ready to help the men should they get into trouble—which they did speedily.

HURRY HARRY AND DEERSLAYER.

For, just as they were at their horrid work, they were surprised, overpowered, and captured by the Indians, and Deerslayer, when he tried to help them, found he was but one against a host.

So he acted upon Tom Hutter's desire to get away at once and defend his daughters in the ark, as he could do the prisoners no good.

At once he paddled off toward the ark, having first secured the Indian canoes so that these could not be used to approach the scow, and hurried to the daughters of the trapper with the tidings of the disaster that had fallen upon their father. In the effort to secure the canoes, he had been compelled to shoot an Indian—the Wolf—who attempted to frustrate his design. He was so averse to bloodshed, however, that he had given his enemy more than a fair opportunity of overcoming him, and after mortally wounding him had ministered to his dying wants as tenderly as if he had been his nearest friend.

Neither of the girls spoke as Deerslayer stood before them alone, his countenance betraying all the apprehension he felt on account of the two absent members of their party.

"Father!" Judith at length exclaimed, succeeding in uttering the word, as it might be by a desperate effort.

"He's met with misfortune, and there's no use in concealing it," answered Deerslayer, in his direct and simple-minded manner. "He and Hurry are in Mingo hands, and Heaven only knows what's to be the tarmination. I've got the canoes safe, and that's a consolation, since the vagabonds will have to swim for it, or raft off, to come near this place. At sunset we'll be reinforced by Chingachgook, if I can manage to get him into a canoe; and then, I think, we two men can answer for the ark and the castle till some of the officers in the garrisons hear of this war path, which sooner or later must be the case, when we may look for succor from that quarter, if from no other."

"The officers!" exclaimed Judith, impatiently, her color deepening and her eye expressing a lively but passing emotion. "Who thinks or speaks of the heartless gallants now? We are sufficient of ourselves to defend the castle; but what of my father and of poor Hurry?"

"'Tis natural you should feel this consarn for your own parent, Judith, and I suppose it's equally so that you should feel it for Hurry, too."

Deerslayer then commenced a succinct, but clear narrative of all that occurred during the night, in no manner concealing what had befallen his two companions, or his own opinion of what might prove to be the consequences. The girls listened with profound attention, but neither betrayed that feminine apprehension and concern which would have followed such a communication when made to those who were less accustomed to the hazards and accidents of a frontier life. To the surprise of Deerslayer, Judith seemed the most distressed, Hetty listening eagerly, but appearing to brood over the facts in melancholy silence rather than betraying any outward signs of feeling. The former's agitation the young man did not fail to attribute to the interest she felt in Hurry quite as much as to her filial love, while Hetty's apparent indifference was ascribed to that mental darkness which in a measure obscured her intellect, and which possibly prevented her from foreseeing all the consequences. Little was said, however, by either, Judith and her sister busying themselves in making the preparations for the morning meal, as they who habitually attend to such matters toil on mechanically even in the midst of suffering and sorrow. The plain but nutritious breakfast was taken by all three in somber silence. The girls ate little, but Deerslayer gave proof of possessing one material requisite of a good soldier—that of preserving his appetite in the midst of the most alarming and embarrassing circumstances. The meal was nearly ended before a syllable was uttered; then, however, Judith spoke in the convulsive and hurried manner in which feeling breaks through restraint, after the latter has become more painful than even the betrayal of emotion.

DEERSLAYER AND HIS DYING ENEMY, THE WOLF.

"You have been fighting the savages, Deerslayer, singly and by yourself!" she said. "In your wish to take care of us—of Hetty—of me, perhaps, you've fought the enemy bravely, with no eye to encourage your deeds or to witness your fall had it pleased Providence to suffer so great a calamity!"

"I've fou't, Judith; yes, I *have* fou't the inimy, and that, too, for the first time in my life. These things must be, and they bring with 'em a mixed feelin' of sorrow and triumph. Human natur' is a fightin' natur', I suppose, as all nations kill in battle, and we must be true to our rights and gifts. What has yet been done is no great matter; but should Chingachgook come to the rock this evening, as is agreed atween us, and I get him off it unbeknown to the savages, or, if known to them, ag'in their wishes and designs, then may we all look for something like warfare afore the Mingos shall get possession of either the castle, or the ark, or yourselves."

"Who is this Chingachgook? from what place does he come, and *why* does he come *here?*"

"The questions are nat'ral and right, I suppose, though the youth has a great name already in his own part of the country. Chingachgook is a Mohican by blood, consorting with the Delawares by usage, as is the case with most of his tribe, which has long been broken up by the increase of our color. He is of the family of the great chiefs; Uncas, his father, having been the considerablest warrior and counselor of his people. Well, this war having commenced in 'arnest, the Delaware and I rendezvous'd an app'intment to meet this evening at sunset at the rendezvous rock at the foot of this very lake, intending to come out on our first hostile expedition ag'in the Mingos. But, Judith, do you know the ar'nd on which your father and Hurry went ag'in the savages?"

"I do; and a cruel errand it was! But what will you have? Men will be men, and some even that flaunt in their gold and silver, and can carry the king's commission in their pockets, are not guiltless of equal cruelty." Judith's eyes again flashed, but by a desperate struggle she resumed her composure. "I get warm when I think of all the wrong that men do," she added, affecting to smile—an effort in which she only succeeded indifferently well. "All this is silly. What is done is done, and it can not be mended by complaints. But the Indians think so little of the shedding of blood, and value men so much for the boldness of their undertakings, that did they know the business on which their prisoners came, they would be more likely to honor than to injure them for it."

"For a time, Judith, yes; I allow *that*, for a time. But when that feelin' dies away, then will come the love of revenge. We must indivour— Chingachgook and I—we must indivour to see what we can do to get Hurry and your father free; for the Mingos will no doubt hover about this lake some days, in order to make the most of their success."

"You think this Delaware can be depended on, Deerslayer?" demanded the girl, thoughtfully.

"As much as I can myself. You say you do not suspect *me*, Judith?"

"*You!*" taking his hand again, and pressing it between her own with a warmth that might have awakened the vanity of one less simple minded and more disposed to dwell on his own good qualities. "I would as soon suspect a brother! I have known you but a day, Deerslayer, but it has awakened the confidence of a year. Your name, however, is not unknown to me ; for the gallants of the garrisons frequently speak of the lessons you have given them in hunting, and all proclaim your honesty."

"Do they ever talk of the shooting, gal?" inquired the other, eagerly, after, however, laughing in a silent but heartfelt manner. "Do they ever talk of the shooting ? I want to hear nothing about my own, for if that is n't sartified to by this time, in all these parts, there's little use in being skilful and sure ; but what do the officers say of their own—yes, what do they say of their own ? Arms, as they call it, is their trade ; and yet there's some among 'em that know very little how to use 'em!"

"Such, I hope, will not be the case with your friend Chingachgook as you call him. What is the English of his Indian name?"

"'Big Sarpent,' so called for his wisdom and cunning. Uncas is his ra'al name, all his family being called Uncas, until they get a title which has been 'arned by deeds."

"If he has all this wisdom, we may expect a useful friend in him, unless his own business in this part of the country should prevent him from serving us."

"I see no great harm in telling you his ar'nd, a'ter all ; and, as you may find means to help us, I will let you and Hetty into the whole matter, trusting that you'll keep the secret as if it was your own. You must know that Chingachgook is a comely Injin, and that there is a chief that has a daughter called Wah-ta !-Wah, which is intarpreted into Hist-oh !-Hist, in the English tongue, the rarest gal among the Delawares. Well, Chingachgook, among others, took a fancy to Wah-ta !-Wah, and Wah-ta !-Wah took a fancy to him. But a sartain Briarthorn, as we call him in English, took it most to heart, and we mistrust him of having a hand in all that followed. Hist-oh !-Hist went with her father and mother two moons ago to fish for salmon on the western streams, and while thus empl'y'd the gal vanished. For several weeks we could get no tidings of her ; but here, ten days since, a runner that came through the Delaware country, brought us a message, by which we l'arn that Hist was stolen from her people—we think, but do not know it, by Briarthorn's sarcumventions —and that she was now with the inimy, who had adopted her and wanted her to marry a young Mingo. The message said that the party intended to hunt and forage through this region for a month or two afore it went back into the Canadas, and that if we could contrive to get on a scent in this quarter, something might turn up that would lead to our getting the maiden off."

"And how does that concern *you*, Deerslayer ?" demanded Judith, a little anxiously.

"It consarns me as all things that touches a fri'nd consarns a fri'nd. I'm here as Chingachgook's aid and helper ; and if we can get the young maiden he likes back ag'in, it will give me almost as much pleasure as if I had got back my own sweetheart."

"And where, then, is *your* sweetheart, Deerslayer?"

"She's in the forest, Judith, hanging from the boughs of the trees,—in a soft rain—in the dew on the open grass—the clouds that float about in the blue heavens—the birds that sing in the woods—the sweet springs where I slake my thirst—and in all the other glorious gifts that come from God's providence!"

"You mean that as yet you've never loved one of my sex, but love best your haunts and your own manner of life?"

"That's it—that's just it. I am white—have a white heart, and can't, in reason, love a red-skinned maiden, who must have a redskin heart and feelin's. No, no ; I'm sound enough in them partic'lars, and hope to remain so—at least, till this war is over. I find my time too much taken up with Chingachgook's affair to wish to have one of my own on my hands afore that is settled."

Deerslayer kept his appointment and met his friend the Mohican, at the place appointed. Then they went back to the ark for a consultation with Judith, but while there Hetty slipped away from them, and, paddling off in a canoe, started on an effort to save her father from the Iroquois. Judith and Deerslayer were greatly disturbed over this, but the night was dark, and Hetty had so completely escaped them that they could not pursue her, but, instead, rowed the ark toward a point which they hoped Hetty would approach.

Sure enough, they came upon the poor child, standing on the shore of the lake where she had landed from the canoe. Her sister called to her and begged her to come back.

"Oh! Hetty, what is it you do?" she said. "Remember, 'tis drawing near midnight, and that the woods are filled with savages and wild beasts!"

"Neither will harm a poor, half-witted girl, Judith. God is as much with me here as He would be in the ark, or in the hut. I am going to help my father and poor Hurry Harry, who will be tortured and slain unless some one cares for them."

"We all care for them, and intend to-morrow to send them a flag of truce to buy their ransom. Come back, then, sister ; trust to us, who have better heads than you, and who will do all we can for father."

"I know your head is better than mine, Judith, for mine is very weak, to be sure ; but I must go to father and poor Hurry. Do you and Deerslayer keep the castle, sister ; leave me in the hands of God."

"God is with us all, Hetty—in the castle or on the shore—father as well as ourselves ; and it is sinful not to trust to His goodness. You can do nothing in the dark, will lose your way in the forest, and perish for want of food."

"God will not let that happen to a poor child that goes to serve her father, sister. I must try and find the savages."

"Come back, for this night only; in the morning we will put you ashore, and leave you to do as you may think right."

"You *say* so, Judith, and you *think* so; but you would not. Your heart would soften, and you'd see tomahawks and scalping knives in the air. Besides, I've got a thing to tell the Indian chief that will answer all our wishes; and I'm afraid I may forget it if I don't tell it to him at once. You'll see that he will let father go as soon as he hears it!"

"Poor Hetty! What can *you* say to a ferocious savage that will be likely to change his bloody purpose?"

"That which will frighten him, and make him let father go," returned the simple-minded girl, positively. "You'll see, sister; you'll see how soon it will bring him to, like a gentle child!"

"Will you tell *me*, Hetty, what you intend to say?" asked Deerslayer; "I know the savages well, and can form some idee how far fair words will be likely, or not, to work on their bloody natur's. If it's not suited to the gifts of a redskin, 'twill be of no use; for reason goes by gifts, as well as conduct."

"Well, then," answered Hetty, dropping her voice to a low, confidential tone; for the stillness of the night and the nearness of the ark permitted her to do this and still to be heard. "Well, then, Deerslayer, as you seem a good and honest young man, I will tell *you*. I mean not to say a word to any of the savages until I get face to face with their head chief, let them plague me with as many questions as they please; no—I'll answer none of them, unless it be to tell them to lead me to their wisest man. Then, Deerslayer, I'll tell him that God will not forgive murder and thefts; and that if father and Hurry did go after the scalps of the Iroquois, he must return good for evil, for so the Bible commands, else he will go into everlasting punishment. When he hears this, and feels it to be true, as feel it he must, how long will it be before he sends father, and Hurry, and me, to the shore opposite the castle, telling us all three to go our way in peace?"

Then she disappeared into the forest. To follow would have been useless, since the darkness, as well as the dense cover that the woods everywhere afforded, would have rendered her capture next to impossible; and there was also the never-ceasing danger of falling into the hands of their enemies. After a short and melancholy discussion, therefore, the sail was set, and the ark pursued its course toward its habitual moorings, Deerslayer silently felicitating himself on the recovery of the canoe, and brooding over his plans for the morrow. The wind rose as the party quitted the point, and in less than an hour they reached the castle where all was found as it had been left. Judith occupied a solitary bed that night, bedewing the pillow with her tears, as she thought of the innocent and hitherto neglected creature who had been her companion from childhood; and bitter regrets came over her mind, from more causes than one, as the weary hours passed away, making it nearly morning before she lost her recollection in sleep. Deerslayer and the Delaware took their rest in the ark, where we shall leave them enjoying the deep sleep of the honest, the healthful, and fearless, to return to the girl we have last seen in the midst of the forest.

Hetty made a bed of leaves in the forest, and next morning walked straight to the Indian encampment.

While making her way slowly through the bushes, the girl suddenly found her steps arrested by a human hand, that was laid lightly on her shoulder.

"Where go?" said a soft, female voice, speaking hurriedly, and in concern. "Indian—red man—savage—wicked warrior—that-a-way."

This unexpected salutation did not alarm the girl. It took her a little by surprise, it is true, but she was in a measure prepared for such a meeting; and the creature who stopped her was as little likely to excite terror as any who ever appeared in the guise of an Indian. It was a girl not much older than herself, whose smile was as sunny as Judith's in her brightest moments, whose voice was melody itself.

She was dressed in a calico mantle that effectually protected all the upper part of her person, while a short petticoat of blue cloth edged with gold lace, that fell no lower than her knees, leggings of the same, and moccasins of deerskin, completed her attire. Her hair fell in long, dark braids down her shoulders and back, and was parted above a low, smooth forehead in a way to soften the expression of eyes that were full of archness and natural feeling. Her face was oval, with delicate features; the teeth were even and white; while the mouth expressed a melancholy tenderness, as if it wore this peculiar meaning in intuitive perception of the fate of a being who was doomed from birth to endure a woman's sufferings relieved by a woman's affections. Her voice was soft as the sighing of the night air, and had procured for her the name of Wah-ta!-Wah; which, rendered into English, means Hist-oh!-Hist.

In a word, this was the betrothed of Chingachgook, who, having succeeded in lulling their suspicions, was permitted to wander around the encampment of her captors. This indulgence was in accordance with the general policy of the redman, who well knew, moreover, that her trail could have been followed in the event of flight. It will also be remembered that the Iroquois, or Hurons, as it would be better to call them, were entirely ignorant of the proximity of her lover—a fact, indeed, that she did not know herself.

"Where go?" repeated Wah-ta!-Wah, returning the smile of Hetty, in her own gentle, winning manner; "*wicked* warrior that-a-way—*good* warrior far off."

"What's your name?" asked Hetty, with the simplicity of a child.

"Wah-ta!-Wah. I no Mingo—good Delaware—Yengeese friend. Mingo cruel, and love scalp for blood—Delaware love him for honor. Come here, where no eyes."

Wah-ta!-Wah now led her companion toward the lake, descending the bank so as to place its overhanging trees and bushes between them and any probable observers; nor did she stop until they were both seated, side by side, on a fallen log, one end of which actually lay buried in the water.

"*Why* you come for?" the young Indian eagerly inquired; "*where* you come from?"

Hetty told her tale in her own simple and truth-loving manner. She explained the situation of her father, and stated her desire to serve him, and, if possible, to procure his release.

"Why your father come to Mingo camp in night?" asked the Indian girl, with a directness which, if not borrowed from the other, partook largely of its sincerity. "He know it war time, and he no boy—he no want beard—no want to be told Iroquois carry tomahawk, and knife, and rifle. Why he come night time, seize *me* by hair, and try to scalp Delaware girl?"

"You!" said Hetty, almost sickening with horror; "did he seize *you*—did he try to scalp *you*?"

"Why no? Delaware scalp sell for much as Mingo scalp. Governor no tell difference. Wicked t'ing for paleface to scalp. No his gifts, as the good Deerslayer always tell me."

"And do *you* know the Deerslayer?" said Hetty, coloring with delight and surprise, forgetting her regrets at the moment in the influence of this new feeling. "I know him, too. He is now in the ark, with Judith, and a Delaware who is called the Big Serpent. A bold and handsome warrior is this Serpent, too!"

Spite of the rich, deep color that nature had bestowed on the Indian beauty, the telltale blood deepened on her cheeks, until the blush gave new animation and intelligence to her jet-black eyes. Raising a finger in an attitude of warning, she dropped her voice, already so soft and sweet, nearly to a whisper, as she continued the discourse.

"Chingachgook!" returned the Delaware girl, sighing out the harsh name in sounds so softly guttural as to cause it to reach the ear in melody. "His father, Uncas—great chief of the Mohicans. *You* know Serpent?"

"He joined us last evening, and was in the ark with me for two or three hours before I left it, Hist." Hetty could not pronounce the Indian name of her new friend, but having heard Deerslayer give her this familiar appellation, she used it without any of the ceremony of civilized life.

"*You* good," whispered the young Indian; "you good, I know; it's so long since Hist have a friend—a sister—anybody to speak her heart to! You Hist friend; don't I say trut'?"

"I never had a friend," answered Hetty, returning the warm embrace with unfeigned earnestness; "I've a sister, but no friend. Judith loves me, and I love Judith; but that's natural, and as we are taught in the Bible; but I *should* like to have a *friend!* I'll be your friend with all my heart; for I like your voice, and your smile, and your way of thinking in everything except about the scalps—"

"No t'ink more of him—no say more of scalp," interrupted Hist, soothingly. "You paleface, I redskin; we bring up different fashion. Deerslayer and Chingachgook great friend, and no the same color; Hist and—what your name, pretty paleface?"

"I am called Hetty, though when they spell the name in the Bible, they always spell it Esther," and after this exchange of confidences, at the suggestion of Hist, the girls arose and openly approached the camp.

"May be Chingachgook get off Hurry and fader, as well as Hist, if let him have his way," whispered Wah-ta!-Wah to her companion, in a confiding, flattering way, just as they got near enough to the encampment to hear the voices of several of their own sex, who were apparently occupied in the usual toils of women of their class. "Tink of dat, Hetty, and put two, twenty finger on mouth. No get friends free without Serpent to do it."

A better expedient could not have been adopted to secure the silence and discretion of Hetty than that which was now presented to her mind. As the liberation of her father and the young frontiers-man was the great object of her adventure, she felt the connection between it and the services of the Delaware, and with an innocent laugh she nodded her head, and in the same suppressed manner promised a due attention to the wishes of her friend. Thus assured, Hist tarried no longer, but immediately and openly led the way into the encampment of her captors.

As the two girls came near the encampment, Hetty uttered a slight exclamation on catching sight of her father. He was seated on the ground with his back to a tree, and Hurry stood near him, indolently whittling a twig. Apparently they were as much at liberty as any of the others in or about the camp; and one unaccustomed to Indian usages would have mistaken them for visitors instead of supposing them to be captives. Hist led her new friend quite near them, and then modestly withdrew, that her own presence might be no restraint on her feelings. But Hetty merely approached and stood at her father's side without speaking, resembling a silent statue of filial affection. The old man expressed neither alarm nor surprise at her sudden appearance. In these particulars he had caught the stoicism of the Indians, well knowing that there was no more certain mode of securing their respect than by imitating their self-command. Nor did the savages themselves betray the least sign of surprise at this sudden appearance of a stranger among them. Still, a few warriors collected, and it was evident by the manner in which they glanced at Hetty as they conversed together that she was the subject of their discourse, and probable that the reasons of her unlooked-for appearance were matters of discussion. The force in the ark, the presence of Chingachgook excepted, was well known by them; no tribe or body of troops was believed to be near, and vigilant eyes were posted round the entire lake, watching, day and night, the slightest movement of those whom it would not be exaggeration now to term the besieged.

Hutter was inwardly much moved by the conduct of Hetty, though he affected so much indifference of manner. He recollected her gentle appeal to him before he left the ark, and misfortune rendered that of weight which might have been forgotten amid the triumph of success. Then he knew the simple, single-hearted fidelity of his child, and understood why she had come, and the total disregard of self that reigned in all her acts.

"This is not well, Hetty," he said, deprecating the consequences to the girl herself more than any other evil. "These are fierce Iroquois, and are as little apt to forget an injury as a favor."

"Tell me, father," returned the girl, looking furtively about her, as if fearful of being overheard, "did God let you do the cruel errand on which you came? I want much to know this, that I may speak to the Indians plainly if He did not."

"You should not have come hither, Hetty; these brutes will not understand your nature or your intentions."

"How was it, father? neither you nor Hurry seems to have anything that looks like scalps."

"If that will set your mind at peace, child, I can answer you, no. I had caught the young creatur' who came here with you, but her screeches soon brought down upon me a troop of the wild-cats that was too much for any single Christian to withstand. If that will do you any good we are as innocent of having taken a scalp this time as I make no doubt we shall also be innocent of receiving the bounty."

"Thank you for that, father! Now I can speak boldly to the Iroquois, and with an easy conscience. I hope Hurry, too, has not been able to harm any of the Indians?"

"Why, as to that matter, Hetty," returned the individual in question, "you've put it pretty much in the natyve character of the religious truth. Hurry has not been *able*, and that is the long and short of it. I've seen many squalls, old fellow, both on land and on the water, but never did I feel one as lively and as snappish as that which come down upon us night afore last, in the shape of an Indian hurrah-boys! Why, Hetty, you're no great matter at a reason or an idee that lies a little deeper than common, but you're human and have some human notions—now I'll just ask you to look at these circumstances. Here was old Tom, your father, and myself bent on a legal operation, as is to be seen in the words of the law and the proclamation, thinking no harm, when we were set upon by critturs that were more like a pack of hungry wolves than mortal savages even, and there they had us tethered like two sheep in less time than it has taken me to tell you the story."

"You are free, now, Hurry," returned Hetty, glancing timidly at the fine, unfettered limbs of the young giant. "You have no cords or withes to pain your arms or legs now."

"Not I, Hetty. My limbs have a free look, but that's pretty much the amount of it, since I can't use them in the way I should like. Even these trees have eyes; ay, and tongues, too; for, was the old man here or I to start one single rod beyond our limits, like as not four or five rifle bullets would be traveling arter us, carrying so many invitations to curb our impatience."

"It's so best, Hurry," she said. "It is best father and you should be quiet and peaceable till I have spoken to the Iroquois, when all will be well and happy. I don't wish either of you to follow, but leave me to myself. As soon as all is settled, and you are at liberty to go back to the castle, I will come and let you know it."

Hetty spoke with so much simple earnestness, seemed so confident of success, and wore so high an air of moral feeling and truth, that both the listeners felt more disposed to attach an importance to her mediation than might otherwise have happened. When she manifested an intention to quit them, therefore, they offered no obstacle, though they saw she was about to join the group of chiefs who were consulting apart, seemingly on the manner and motive of her own sudden appearance.

So, with Hist as companion and interpreter, the simple-minded Hetty, bent on doing good, went among the Indians with her Bible, and talked her simple religion, and spoke the Golden Rule, to these redmen of the forest.

The Indians could not see why they should use the Golden Rule toward their white prisoners, who certainly had not used it toward the Indian. But they did not interfere with Hetty or Hist, and when the Indian girl, leaving Hetty in the camp, went to talk to Tom Hutter and Hurry of buying their freedom, the Indians listened to Hetty's reading from the Bible, and finally, putting her on a raft, towed her to a point opposite the castle, and then had an Indian boy row her across.

When she was across, and Deerslayer had heard her story, the hunter was not ready to believe all she told him of the peaceable disposition of the Iroquois. He questioned the Indian boy, and learned that it was the intention of his tribe to take their prisoners with them back to their home lodges for torture or sacrifice.

Now, Deerslayer, who, with Judith, had been hunting through an old sea-chest of Tom Hutter's, proposed to the Indian boy that he go back to camp and offer as ransom for the two white prisoners two fine ivory elephants, belonging to a splendid set of chessmen, which the searchers had discovered in the old trunk.

The Indian boy was sent back to the Iroquois camp with the proposition of ransom, but when Chingachgook heard from Hetty that his dear Hist was in the Iroquois camp, he was ready to act as messenger for the ransom himself.

"I will go to the Iroquois camp," said the Delaware, gravely. "No one knows Chingachgook but Hist! and a treaty for lives and scalps should be made by a chief! Give me the strange beasts, and let me take a canoe."

Deerslayer dropped his head, and played with the end of a fish pole in the water, as he sat dangling his legs over the edge of the platform, like a man who was lost in thought by the sudden occurrence of a novel idea. Instead of directly answering the proposal of his friend, he began to soliloquize; a circumstance, however, that in no manner rendered his words more true, as he was remarkable for saying what he thought, whether the remarks were addressed to himself or to any one else.

"Yes, yes," he said, "this must be what they call love! I've heard say that it sometimes upsets reason altogether, leaving a young man as helpless as to calculation and caution as a brute beast. To think that the Sarpent should be so lost to reason, and cunning, and wisdom! We must sartainly manage to get Hist off, and have 'em married as soon as we get back to the tribe, or this war will be of no more use to the chief than a hunt a little oncommon and extr'ornary. Yes—yes—he'll never be the man he was till this matter is off his mind and he comes to his senses, like all the rest of mankind. Sarpent, you can't be in airnest, and therefore I shall say but little to your offer. But you're a chief, and will soon be sent out on the war path at the head of parties, and I'll just ask if you'd think of putting your forces into the inimy's hands, afore the battle is fou't? Now sit down by me here, and let us calculate our movements a little, for we shall soon either have a truce and a peace, or we shall come to an actyve and bloody war. You see the vagabonds can make logs sarve their turn, as well as the best raftsmen on the rivers: and it would be no great expl'ite for them to invade us in a body. I've been thinking of the wisdom of putting all old Tom's stores into the ark, of barring and locking up the castle, and of taking to the ark altogether. That is movable, and by keeping the sail up, and shifting places, we might worry through a great many nights, without them Canada wolves finding a way into our sheepfold."

Chingachgook listened to this plan with approbation. Did the negotiation for ransom fail there was now little hope that the night would pass without an assault; and the enemy had sagacity enough to understand that, in carrying the castle, they would probably become masters of all it contained, the offered ransom included, and still retain the advantages they had hitherto gained. Some precaution of the sort appeared to be absolutely necessary; for now the numbers of the Iroquois were known, a night attack could scarcely be successfully met. It would be impossible to prevent the enemy from getting possession of the canoes and the ark, and the latter itself would be a hold in which the assailants would be as effectually protected against bullets as were those in the building. For a few minutes both the men thought of sinking the ark in the shallow water, of bringing the canoes into the house, and of depending altogether on the castle for protection. But reflection satisfied them that, in the end, this expedient would fail. It was so easy to collect logs on the shore, and to construct a raft of almost any size, that it was certain the Iroquois, now they had turned their attention to such means, would resort to them seriously, so long as there was the certainty of success by perseverance. After deliberating maturely, and placing all the considerations fairly before them, the two young beginners in the art of forest warfare settled down into the opinion that the ark offered the only available means of security. This decision was no sooner come to than it was communicated to Judith. The girl had no serious objection to make, and all four set about the measures necessary to carrying the plan into execution.

The reader will readily understand that Floating Tom's worldly goods were of no great amount. A couple of beds, some wearing apparel, the arms and ammunition, a few cooking utensils, with the mysterious but half-examined chest, formed the principal items. These were all soon removed, the ark having been hauled on the eastern side of the building, so that the transfer could be made without being seen from the shore. It was thought unnecessary to disturb the heavier and coarser articles of furniture, as they were not required in the ark, and were of but little value in themselves. As great caution was necessary in removing the different objects, most of which were passed out of a window with a view to conceal what was going on, it required two or three hours before all could be effected. By the expiration of that time a raft made its appearance, moving from the shore. Deerslayer immediately had recourse to the glass, by the aid of which he perceived that two warriors were on it, though they appeared to be unarmed. The progress of the raft was slow, a circumstance that formed one of the great advantages that would be possessed by the scow in any future collision between them; the movements of the latter being comparatively swift and light. As there was time to make the dispositions for the reception of the two dangerous visitors, everything was prepared for them long before they had got near enough to be hailed. The Serpent and the girls retired into the building, where the former stood near the door, well provided with rifles, while Judith watched the proceedings without through a loop. As for Deerslayer, he had brought a stool to the edge of the platform, at the point toward which the raft was advancing, and taken his seat, with his rifle leaning carelessly between his legs.

When the heavy-moving craft was within fifty feet of him, Deerslayer hailed the Hurons, directing them to cease rowing, it not being his intention to permit them to land. Compliance, of course, was necessary, and the two grim-looking warriors instantly quitted their seats, though the raft continued slowly to approach, until it had driven in much nearer to the platform.

"Are ye chiefs?" demanded Deerslayer, with dignity. "Are ye chiefs? —or have the Mingos sent me warriors without names on such an ar'nd? If so, the sooner ye go back, the sooner the one will be likely to come that a warrior can talk with."

"Hugh!" exclaimed the elder of the two on the raft, rolling his glowing eyes over the different objects that were visible in and about the castle, with a keenness that showed how little escaped him. "My brother is very proud, but Rivenoak" (we use the literal translation of the term, writing as we do in English) "is a name to make a Delaware turn pale."

"That's true, or it's a lie, Rivenoak, as it may be; but I am not likely to turn pale, seeing that I was born pale. What's your ar'nd, and why do you come among light bark canoes on logs that are not even dug out?"

"The Iroquois are not ducks, to walk on water! Let the palefaces give them a canoe, and they'll come in a canoe."

"That's more rational than likely to come to pass. We have but four canoes, and being four persons, that's only one for each of us. We thank you for the offer, hows'ever, though we ask leave not to accept it. You are welcome, Iroquois, on your logs!"

"Thanks—my young paleface warrior—he has got a name—how do the chiefs call him?"

Deerslayer hesitated a moment, and a gleam of pride and human weakness came over him. He smiled, muttered between his teeth, and then, looking up proudly, he said—

" Mingo, like all who are young and actyve, I've been known by different names at different times. One of your warriors, whose spirit started for the happy grounds of your people as lately as yesterday morning, thought I desarved to be known by the name of Hawkeye ; and this because my sight happened to be quicker than his own, when it got to be life or death atween us."

Chingachgook, who was attentively listening to all that passed, heard and understood this proof of passing weakness in his friend, and on a future occasion he questioned him more closely concerning the transaction on the point where Deerslayer had first taken human life. When he had got the whole truth, he did not fail to communicate it to the tribe, from which time the young hunter was universally known among the Delawares by an appellation so honorably earned. The two Iroquois spoke to each other in low terms, and both drew near the end of the raft that was closest to the platform.

" My brother, Hawkeye, has sent a message to the Hurons," resumed Rivenoak, " and it has made their hearts very glad. They hear he has images of beasts with two tails ! Will he show them to his friends ? "

"Inimies would be truer," returned Deerslayer ; "but sound is n't sense, and does little harm. Here is one of the images ; I toss it to you under faith of treaties. If it 's not returned, the rifle will settle the p'int atween us."

The Iroquois seemed to acquiesce in the conditions, and Deerslayer arose and prepared to toss one of the elephants to the raft, both parties using all the precaution that was necessary to prevent its loss. As practice renders men expert in such things, the little piece of ivory was soon successfully transferred from one hand to the other. For a few minutes the old warriors apparently lost the consciousness of their situation in the intense scrutiny they bestowed on material so fine, work so highly wrought, and an animal so extraordinary. The lip of the moose is, perhaps, the nearest approach to the trunk of the elephant that is to be found in the American forest ; but this resemblance was far from being sufficiently striking to bring the new creature within the range of their habits and ideas, and the more they studied the image the greater was their astonishment. Nor did these children of the forest mistake the structure on the back of the elephant for a part of the animal. They were familiar with horses and oxen, and had seen towers in the Canadas, and found nothing surprising in creatures of burden. Still, by a very natural association, they supposed the carving meant to represent that the animal they saw was of a strength sufficient to carry a fort on its back ; a circumstance that in no degree lessened their wonder.

" Has my paleface brother any more such beasts ? " at last the senior of the Iroquois asked, in a sort of petitioning manner.

"There's more where them came from, Mingo," was the answer; "one is enough, however, to buy off fifty scalps."

"Why should Rivenoak and his brother leave any cloud between them?" the Indian said. "They are both wise, both brave, and both generous; they ought to part friends. One beast shall be the price of one prisoner."

"And, Mingo," answered the Deerslayer, determined to clinch the bargain if possible by a little extra liberality, "you'll see that a paleface knows how to pay a full price when he trades with an open heart and an open hand. Keep the beast you have. Show it to your chiefs. When you bring us our fri'nds two more shall be added to it —and"—hesitating a moment in distrust of the expediency of so great a concession, then deciding in its favor—"and, if we see them afore the sun sets, we may find a fourth to make up an even number."

This settled the matter. Every gleam of discontent vanished from the dark countenance of the Iroquois, and he smiled as graciously, if not as sweetly, as Judith Hutter herself. The piece already in his possession was again examined, and an ejaculation of pleasure showed how much he was pleased with this unexpected termination of the affair. In point of fact, both he and Deerslayer had momentarily forgotten what had become of the subject of their discussion in the

THE RELEASE OF HUTTER AND HURRY.

warmth of their feelings; but such had not been the case with Rivenoak's companion. This man retained the piece, and had fully made up his mind, were it claimed under such circumstances as to render its return necessary, to drop it in the lake, trusting to his being able to find it again at some future day. This desperate expedient, however, was no longer necessary; and, after repeating the terms of agreement, and professing to understand them, the two Indians finally took their departure, moving slowly toward the shore.

The bargain was carried out. Before night Hurry and Tom Hutter were returned to the castle, being brought, bound, across the lake upon the raft, guarded by two of the Mingos. The former prisoners were to climb from the raft to the castle, and the Iroquois were richer by four ivory chessmen. But when that piece of business was over, the Indians evidently thought their part of the bargain was complete, for that very evening Deerslayer found before the castle the Iroquois "declaration of war"—a sort of miniature fagot, composed of a dozen sticks bound tightly together with a deer skin thong. March seized it eagerly, and holding it close to a blazing knot of pine that lay on the hearth, and which gave out all the light there was in the room, ascertained that the ends of the several sticks had been dipped in blood.

But for all that Chingachgook the Serpent and his friend Deerslayer resolved to go upon the business that had brought them there,—the rescue of Hist, the Indian girl, from the Iroquois.

That night the two comrades set out upon their perilous venture. They succeeded, but as the Serpent leaped into the canoe with Hist in his arms, Deerslayer was not so fortunate. Laying his rifle in the bottom of the canoe, Deerslayer stooped to give the latter a vigorous shove from the shore, when a powerful Indian leaped through the bushes, alighting like a panther on his back. Everything was now suspended by a hair, a false step ruining all. With a generosity that would have rendered a Roman illustrious throughout all time, but which, in the career of one so simple and humble, would have been forever lost to the world but for this unpretending legend, Deerslayer threw all his force into a desperate effort, shoved the canoe off with a power that sent it a hundred feet from the shore as it might be in an instant, and fell forward into the lake himself, face downward; his assailant necessarily following him.

Although the water was deep within a few yards of the beach, it was not more than breast high at the spot where the two combatants fell. Still this was quite sufficient to destroy one who had sunk under the great disadvantages in which Deerslayer was placed. His hands were free, however, and the savage was compelled to relinquish his hug to keep his own face above the surface. For half a minute there was a desperate struggle, and then both stood erect, grasping each other's arms in order to prevent the use of the deadly knife in the darkness. What might have been the issue of this severe personal struggle can not be known, for half a dozen savages came leaping into the water to the aid of their friend, and Deerslayer yielded himself a prisoner with a dignity that was as remarkable as his self-devotion.

To quit the lake and lead their new captive to the fire occupied the Indians but another minute. So much engaged were they all with the struggle and its consequences that the canoe was unseen, though it still lay so near the shore as to render every syllable that was uttered perfectly intelligible to the Delaware and his betrothed, and the whole party left the spot. It was now too late to assail the other fugitives, for no sooner was his friend led into the bushes than the Delaware placed his paddle in the water, and the light canoe glided noiselessly away, holding its course toward the center of the lake, until safe from shot, after which it sought the ark.

When Deerslayer reached the fire he found himself surrounded by no less than eight grim savages, among whom was his old acquaintance Rivenoak. As soon as the latter caught a glimpse of the captive's countenance, he spoke apart to his companions, and a low but general exclamation of pleasure and surprise escaped them. There was no little admiration mingled in the ferocious looks that were thrown on the prisoner, an admiration that was as much excited by his present composure as by his past deeds.

The arms of Deerslayer were not pinioned, and he was left the free use of his hands, his knife having been first removed. The only precaution that was taken to secure his person was an untiring watchfulness, and a strong rope of bark that passed from ankle to ankle, not so much to prevent his walking as to place an obstacle in the way of his attempting to escape by any sudden leap. Even this extra provision against flight was not made until the captive had been brought to the light and his character ascertained. It was, in fact, a compliment to his prowess, and he felt proud of the distinction.

Then there followed the usual scene when Indians capture a brave prisoner. First, the squaws tried to anger him by insults, taunts, and gibes ; but Deerslayer did not notice them. Next, Rivenoak, the chief, tried by flattery and words of praise, and then by threats and promises of all the torture that Indian ingenuity could inflict, to prevail on the prisoner to betray his friends in the ark and become a brother to the Iroquois. But none of these things moved Deerslayer.

" Hawkeye is right," the Iroquois at length began ; "his sight is so strong that he can see truth in a dark night, and our eyes have been blinded. He is an

THE PERIL OF DEERSLAYER.

owl, darkness hiding nothing from him. He ought not to strike his friends. He is right."

"I am glad you think so, Mingo," returned the other, "for a traitor, in my judgment, is worse than a coward. I care as little for Tom Hutter as one paleface ought to care for another ; but I care too much for him to ambush him in the way you wished. In short, according to my idees, any sarcumventions, except open-war sarcumventions, are ag'in both law, and what we whites call 'gospel,' too."

"My paleface brother is right ; he is no Indian to forget his Manitou and his color. The Hurons know that they have a great warrior for their prisoner, and they will treat him as one. If he is to be tortured, his torments shall be such as no common man can bear ; if he is to be treated as a friend, it will be the friendship of chiefs."

As the Huron uttered this extraordinary assurance of consideration his eye furtively glanced at the countenance of his listener, in order to discover how he stood the compliment ; though his gravity and apparent sincerity would have prevented any man but one practised in artifices from detecting his motives. Deerslayer belonged to the class of the unsuspicious ; and acquainted with the Indian notions of what constituted respect, in matters connected with the treatment of captives, he felt his blood chill at the announcement, even while he maintained an aspect so steeled that his quick-sighted enemy could discover in it no signs of weakness.

"God has put me in your hands, Huron," the captive at length answered, "and I suppose you will act your will on me. I shall not boast of what I can do under torment, for I've never been tried, and no man can say till he has been ; but I'll do my indivours not to disgrace the people among whom I got my training. Hows'ever, I wish you now to bear witness, that I'm altogether of white blood, and, in a nat'ral way, of white gifts, too ; so, should I be overcome and forget myself, I hope you'll lay the fault where it properly belongs ; and in no manner put it on the Delawares, or their allies and friends the Mohicans. We're all created with more or less weakness, and I'm afeared it's a paleface's to give in under great bodily torment, when a redskin will sing his songs and boast of his deeds in the very teeth of his foes!"

"We shall see. Hawkeye has a good countenance, and he is tough—but why should he be tormented when the Hurons love him ? He is not born their enemy ; and the death of one warrior will not cast a cloud between them forever."

"So much the better, Huron ; so much the better. Still I don't wish to owe anything to a mistake about each other's meaning. It is so much the better that you bear no malice ; and yet it is ontrue that there is no inmity—

lawful inmity, I mean, atween us. So far as I have redskin feelin's at all, I've Delaware feelin's ; and I leave you to judge for yourself how far they are likely to be fri'ndly to the Mingos."

Finding that nothing could be done with Deerslayer, and resolved to attack the ark, recover Hist, and overcome Tom Hutter and Hurry, Rivenoak and his braves set out that night to carry out their plans.

HURRY STRUGGLES WITH THE INDIANS, BUT IS FINALLY CAPTURED.

In the surprise and fight that followed, Hurry, after a fierce struggle, was captured, and Tom Hutter was scalped and killed, but Chingachgook and Hist, with Judith and Hetty, escaped and drifted off in the ark.

Hurry, by shrewd management, flung himself into the lake, and, escaping from his captors, joined the girls on the ark.

They buried Tom Hutter in the lake, and then Hurry agreed to go to the nearest fort and seek assistance from the soldiers, leaving the Serpent and Hist to protect the girls in the ark.

So Hurry left them, and soon after Judith and Hetty entered a canoe, and paddling as near as possible to the spot where Hutter had found his watery grave, were earnestly discussing their future, when a canoe came paddling up the lake and steadily advanced toward the ark. One man was alone in the canoe. It was Deerslayer.

His approach was so calm and leisurely, however, as to fill the watchers with wonder, since a man who had effected his escape from enemies, by either artifice or violence, would not be apt to move with the steadiness and deliberation with which his paddle swept the water. By this time the day was fairly departing, and objects were already seen dimly under the shores.

"Welcome—welcome, Deerslayer!" exclaimed Judith, as the canoe approached ; "we have had a melancholy—a frightful day, but your return is, at least, one misfortune the less. Have the Hurons become more humane and let you go, or have you escaped from the wretches by your own courage and skill?"

"Neither, Judith—neither one nor t'other. The Mingos are Mingos still, and will live and die Mingos ; it is not likely their natur's will ever undergo much improvement. As for outwitting them, that might have been done, and it was done, too, atween the Sarpent yonder and me when we were on the trail of Hist "—here the hunter stopped to laugh in his own silent fashion—"but it's no easy matter to sarcumvent the sarcumvented."

"But if you have not escaped, Deerslayer, how came you here?" asked Judith.

"That's a natural question," replied Deerslayer, "and well put. The Mingos feel their loss here, in the late scrimmage, to their hearts' cores, and are ready to revenge it on any creatur' of English blood that may fall in their way. Nor, for that matter, do I much think they would stand at taking their satisfaction out of a Dutchman."

"They have killed father ; that ought to satisfy their wicked cravings for blood," observed Hetty, reproachfully.

"I know it, gal—I know the whole story—partly from what I've seen from the shore, since they brought me up from the point, and partly from their threats ag'in myself, and their other discourse. Well, life is unsartin at the best, and we all depend on the breath of our nostrils for it from day to day. If you've lost a stanch fri'nd, as I make no doubt you have, Providence will raise up new ones in his stead."

"We understand you, Deerslayer," returned Judith, hastily, "and take all that falls from your lips as it is meant, in kindness and friendship. Would to Heaven all men had tongues as true, and hearts as honest!"

"In that respect men *do* differ, of a sartainty, Judith. I've known them that was n't to be trusted any further than you can see them ; and others ag'in whose messages, sent with a small piece of wampum, perhaps, might just as much be depended on as if the whole business was finished afore your face. Yes, Judith, you never said truer words than when you said some men might be depended on, and some others might not."

"You are an unaccountable being, Deerslayer," returned the girl, not a little puzzled with the childish simplicity of character that the hunter so often betrayed—a simplicity so striking that it frequently appeared to place him nearly on a level with the fatuity of poor Hetty, though always relieved by the beautiful moral truth that shone through all that this unfortunate girl both said and did. "You are a most unaccountable man, and I often do not know how to understand you. But never mind, just now; you have forgotten to tell us by what means you are here."

"I!—oh! That's not very onaccountable, if I am myself, Judith. I'm out on furlough."

"Furlough! That word has a meaning among the soldiers that I understand; I can not tell what it signifies when used by a prisoner."

"It means just the same. You're right enough; the soldiers do use it, and just in the same way as I use it. A furlough is when a man has leave to quit a camp or a garrison for a sartain specified time; at the end of which he is to come back and shoulder his musket, or submit to his torments, just as he may happen to be a soldier or a captyve. Being the last, I must take the chances of a prisoner."

"Have the Hurons suffered you to quit them in this manner, without watch or guard?"

JUDITH AND HETTY PADDLE TO THE SPOT WHERE TOM HUTTER WAS BURIED.

"Sartain—I could n't have come in any other manner, unless, indeed, it had been by a bold rising or a sarcumvention."

"What pledge have they that you will ever return?"

"My word," answered the hunter, simply. "Yes, I own I gave 'em *that*, and big fools would they have been to let me come without it! Why, in that case, I should n't have been obliged to go back and ondergo any deviltries their fury may invent, but might have shouldered my rifle and made the best of my way to the Delaware villages. But they know'd this just as well as you and I do, and would no more let me come away without a promise to go back than they would let the wolves dig up the bones of their fathers!"

"Is it possible you mean to do this act of extraordinary self-destruction and recklessness?"

"What's that?"

"I ask if it can be possible that you expect to be able to put yourself again in the power of such ruthless enemies, by keeping your word?"

Deerslayer looked at his fair questioner for a moment with stern displeasure. Then the expression of his honest and guileless face suddenly changed, lighting as by a quick illumination of thought; after which he laughed in his ordinary manner.

"I did n't understand you at first, Judith; no, I did n't. You believe that Chingachgook and Hurry won't suffer it; but you do n't know mankind thoroughly yet, I see. Do n't be under any oneasiness, therefore, gal; I shall be allowed to go back according to the furlough; and if difficulties was made, I've not been brought up and edicated, as one may say, in the woods, without knowing how to look 'em down."

Judith made no answer for some little time. Argument, she felt, would be useless; nor was she, at that moment, disposed to lessen the dignity and high principle that were so striking in the intentions of the hunter by any attempt to turn him from his purpose. That something might yet occur to supersede the necessity for this self-immolation, she tried to hope; and then she proceeded to ascertain the facts in order that her own conduct might be regulated by her knowledge of circumstances.

"When is your furlough out, Deerslayer?" she asked, after both canoes were heading toward the ark, and moving with scarcely a perceptible effort of the paddles through the water.

"To-morrow noon; not a minute afore; and you may depend on it, Judith, I sha'n't quit what I call Christian company, to go and give myself up to them vagabonds an instant sooner than is downright necessary. They begin to fear a visit from the garrisons, and wouldn't lengthen the time a moment; and it's pretty well understood atween us that, should I fail in my ar'nd, the torments are to take place when the sun begins to fall, that they may strike upon their home trail as soon as it is dark."

This was said solemnly, as if the thought of what was believed to be in reserve duly weighed on the prisoner's mind, and yet so simply, and without a parade of suffering, as rather to repel than to invite any open manifestations of sympathy.

"Are they bent on revenging their losses?" Judith asked, faintly, her own high spirit yielding to the influence of the other's quiet but dignified integrity of purpose.

"Downright, if I can judge of Indian inclinations by the symptoms. They think, hows'ever, I do n't suspect their designs, I do believe ; but one that has lived so long among men of redskin gifts is no more likely to be misled in Injin's feelin's than a true hunter is like to lose his trail, or a stanch hound his scent. My own judgment is greatly ag'in my own escape, for I see the women are a good deal enraged on behalf of Hist, though I say it, perhaps, that should n't say it—seein' that I had a considerable hand myself in getting the gal off. Then there was a cruel murder in their camp last night, and that shot might just as well have been fired into my breast. Hows'ever, come what will, the Serpent and his wife will be safe, and that is some happiness, in any case."

"Oh! Deerslayer, they will think better of this, since they have given you until to-morrow noon to make up your mind!"

"I judge not, Judith; yes, I judge not. An Injin is an Injin, gal, and it's pretty much hopeless to think of swarving him when he's got the scent and follows it with his nose in the air."

That night in the ark Deerslayer told his friends why he had been sent back on parole.

It seemed the Iroquois supposed that Chingachgook was the only defender left on the ark. So they sent by Deerslayer a belt of wampum to the Serpent, offering him his life and freedom if he would send Hist back to their camp and go, himself, back to his own tribe.

When he had delivered this message, Deerslayer smiled at the Serpent. "Come, Chingachgook," he said, "let us hear *your* mind on this matter—are you inclined to strike across the hills toward your village, to give up Hist to a Huron, and to tell the chiefs at home that if they're act*y*ve and successful they may possibly get *on* the end of the Iroquois' trail some two or three days after the inimy has got *off* of it?"

The young chief arose, that his answer might be given with due distinctness and dignity. He stretched an arm before him, with a calm energy that aided in giving emphasis to his expressions.

"Wampum should be sent for wampum," he said; "a message must be answered by a message. Hear what the Great Serpent of the Delawares has to say to the pretended wolves from the great lakes, that are howling through our woods. They are no wolves; they are dogs that have come to get their tails and ears cropped by the hands of the Delawares. They are good at stealing young women: bad at keeping them. Chingachgook takes his own where he finds it; he asks leave of no cur from the Canadas. Tell the Huron dogs to howl louder, if they wish a Delaware to find them in the woods, where they burrow like foxes instead of hunting like warriors. When they had a Delaware maiden in their camp, there was a reason for hunting them up; now they will be forgotten, unless they make a noise. Chingachgook do n't like the trouble of going to his villages for more warriors; he can strike their runaway trail: unless they hide it underground he will follow it to Canada alone. He will keep Wah-ta !-Wah with him to cook his game; they two will be Delawares enough to scare all the Hurons back to their own country."

"That's a grand dispatch, as the officers call them things!" cried Deerslayer; "'twill set all the Huron blood in motion, most particularly that part where he tells 'em Hist, too, will keep on their heels, till they're fairly driven out of the country. Ah's me! big words ar'n't always big deeds, notwithstanding. The Lord send that we be able to be only one half as good as we promise to be. And now, Judith, it's your turn to speak, for them miscreants will expect an answer from you. The next message is to you. They say the Muskrat, as they call your father, has dove to the bottom of the lake; that he will never come up again, and that his young will soon be in want of wigwams, if not of food. The Huron huts, they think, are better than the huts of York; they wish you to come and try them. Your color is white, they own, but they think young women who 've lived so long in the woods, would lose their way in the clearin's. A great warrior among them has lately lost his wife, and he would be glad to put the Wild Rose (that's you, Judith) on her bench at his fireside. As for the Feeble-Mind, for so they call Hetty, she will always be honored and taken care of by red warriors. Your father's goods, they think, ought to go to enrich the tribe; but your own property, which is to include everything of a female natur', will go, like that of all wives, into the wigwam of the husband."

"And do *you* bring such a message to *me?*" exclaimed Judith, though the tone in which the words were uttered had more in it of sorrow than of anger. "Am I a girl to be an Indian's slave?"

"If you wish my honest thoughts on this p'int, Judith, I shall answer that I do n't think you'll willingly ever become any man's slave, redskin or white. You're not to think hard, hows'ever, of my bringing the message, as near as I could, in the very words in which it was given to me. Them was the conditions on which I got my furlough, and a bargain is a bargain, though it is made with a vagabond."

"Tell me, first—tell *us*, first, Deerslayer," said Judith, repeating the words merely to change the emphasis, "what effect will our answers have on *your* fate? If you are to be the sacrifice of our spirit, it would have been better had we all been more wary as to the language we use. What, then, are likely to be the consequences to yourself?"

"Lord, Judith, you might as well ask me which way the wind will blow next week, or what will be the age of the next deer that will be shot! I can only say that their faces look a little dark upon me; but it does n't thunder every time a black cloud rises, nor does every puff of wind blow up rain. That's a question, therefore, much more easily put than answered."

"But you can not mean to give yourself up again to those brutal savages, Deerslayer!" she said. "Why! 't would be the act of a madman."

"There's them that thinks it madness to keep their words, and there's them that do n't," said Deerslayer. "I'm one of the last. No redskin breathing shall have it in his power to say that a Mingo minds his word more than a man of white blood and white gifts, in anything that consarns me. I'm out on a furlough, and if I've strength and reason, I'll go in on a furlough afore noon to-morrow!"

And so it turned out. By Deerslayer's own advice the answers he took back to the Iroquois were both haughty and contemptuous.

Before he left Deerslayer talked long and earnestly with Judith, advising her what to do and how to act in the event of an Indian attack, and to try to hold out until relief came from the fort, to which Hurry had gone.

He went through her father's effects with her and discovered that neither Judith nor Hetty was the daughter of Tom Hutter, but that their father was an officer of the British army from whom Tom had taken them in childhood. Then, with words of farewell, he left them.

"If I have overdone the advice, Judith," he said, "I crave your pardon. Fri'ndship's an awful thing! Sometimes it chides us for not having done enough; and then ag'in it speaks in strong words for havin' done too much. Hows'ever, I acknowledge I've overdone the matter, and as I've a ra'al and strong regard for you, I rej'ice to say it, inasmuch as it proves how much better you are than my own vanity and consaits had made you out to be."

"Say no more, Deerslayer," cried Judith; "it pains me to hear you find fault with yourself. We will not talk any longer of these things, for I do not feel myself brave enough for the undertaking, and I should not like the Delawares, or Hist, or even Hetty, to notice my weakness. Farewell, Deerslayer, may God bless and protect you as your honest heart deserves blessing and protection, and as I must think He will."

The next instant she darted into the hut and was seen no more; though she spoke to Hist from a window to inform her that their friend expected her appearance.

The farewells were said to Hetty and to Hist. Then he held out his hand to the Serpent.

"There's my hand, Delaware," he said; "you know it's that of a fri'nd, and will shake it as such, though it never has done you one-half the good its owner wishes it had."

The Indian took the offered hand and returned its pressure warmly. Then falling back on his acquired stoicism of manner, which so many mistake for constitutional indifference, he drew up in reserve, and prepared to part from his friend with dignity. Deerslayer, however, was more natural. But he determined to depart now, and that without any further manifestations of feeling either from himself or from others.

"God bless you! Sarpent—God bless you!" cried the hunter, as the canoe left the side of the platform. "Your Manitou and my God only know when and where we shall meet ag'in; I shall count it a great blessing, and a full reward for any little good I may have done on 'arth, if we shall be permitted to know each other, and to consort together, hereafter, as we have so long done in these pleasant woods afore us."

Chingachgook waved his hand. Drawing the light blanket he wore over his head, as a Roman would conceal his grief in his robes, he slowly withdrew into the ark in order to indulge his sorrow and his musings alone. Deerslayer was gone. It was nearly noon when Deerslayer returned to the camp of the Iroquois.

The Hurons had been divided in their opinions concerning the probability of their captive's return. Most among them, indeed, had not expected it possible for a paleface to come back voluntarily, and meet the known penalties of an Indian torture; but a few of the seniors expected better things from one who had already shown himself so singularly cool, brave, and upright. The party had come to its decision, however, less in the expectation of finding the pledge redeemed than in the hope of disgracing the Delawares by casting into their teeth the delinquency of one bred in their villages. They would have greatly preferred that Chingachgook should be their prisoner and prove the traitor; but the paleface scion of the hated stock was no bad substitute, for their purposes, failing in their designs against the ancient stem. With a view to render the triumph as signal as possible, in the event of the hour's passing without the reappearance of the hunter, all the warriors and scouts of the party had been called in ; and the whole band, men, women, and children, were now assembled at this single point, to be a witness of the expected scene.

Rivenoak and another great warrior of the tribe called the Panther sat side by side, awaiting the approach of their prisoner, as Deerslayer put his moccasined foot on the strand ; nor did either move or utter a syllable until the young man had advanced into the center of the area, and proclaimed his presence with his voice. This was done firmly, though in the simple manner that marked the character of the individual.

"Here I am, Mingos," he said, in the dialect of the Delawares, a language that most present understood ; "here I am, and there is the sun. One is not more true to the laws of natur' than the other has proved true to his word. I am your prisoner ; do with me what you please. My business with man and 'arth is settled ; nothing remains now but to meet the white man's God, accordin' to a white man's duties and gifts."

A murmur of approbation escaped even the women at this address, and for an instant there was a strong and pretty general desire to adopt into the tribe one who owned so brave a spirit. Still there were dissenters from this wish, among the principal of whom might be classed the Panther and his sister, le Sumach, so called from the number of her children, who was the widow of the Wolf, now known to have fallen by the hand of the captive. Native ferocity held one in subjection, while the corroding passion of revenge prevented the other from admitting any gentler feeling at the moment. Not so with Rivenoak. This chief arose, stretched his arm before him, in a gesture of courtesy, and paid his compliments with an ease and dignity that a prince might have envied. As, in that band, his wisdom and eloquence were confessedly without rivals, he knew that on himself would properly fall the duty of first replying to the speech of the paleface.

"Paleface, you are honest," said the Huron orator. "My people are happy in having captured a man and not a skulking fox. We now know you ; we shall treat you like a brave. If you have slain one of our warriors, and helped to kill others, you have a life of your own ready to give away in return. Some of my young men thought that the blood of a paleface was too thin— that it would refuse to run under the Huron knife. You will show them it is not so ; your heart is stout as well as your body. It is a pleasure to make such a prisoner ; should my warriors say that the death of the Wolf ought not to be forgotten, and that he can not travel toward the land of spirits alone, that his enemy must be sent to overtake him, they will remember that he fell by the hand of a brave, and send you after him with such signs of friendship as shall not make him ashamed to keep your company. I have spoken ; you know what I have said."

"True enough, Mingo, all true as the gospel," returned the simple-minded hunter; "you *have* spoken, and I *do* know not only what you have *said*, but, what is still more important, what you *mean*. I dare to say your warrior, the Wolf, was a stout-hearted brave, and worthy of your fri'ndship and respect, but I do not feel unworthy to keep his company, without any passport from your hands. Nevertheless, here I am, ready to receive judgment from your council, if, indeed, the matter was not detarmined among you afore I got back."

"Killer of the deer," continued Rivenoak, "my aged men have listened to wise words; they are ready to speak. You are a man whose fathers came from beyond the rising sun; we are children of the setting sun; we turn our faces toward the Great Sweet Lakes when we look toward our villages. It may be a wise country and full of riches toward the morning, but it is very unpleasant toward the evening. We love most to look in that direction. When we gaze at the east we feel afraid, canoe after canoe bringing more and more of your people in the track of the sun, as if their land was so full as to run over. The red men are few already; they have need of help. One of our best lodges has lately been emptied by the death of its master; it will be a long time before his son can grow big enough to sit in his place. There is his widow! she will want venison to feed her and her children, for her sons are yet like the young of the robin before they quit the nests. By your hand has this great calamity befallen her. She has two duties; one to the Wolf, and one to his children. Scalp for scalp, life for life, blood for blood, is one law; to feed her young another. We know you, Killer of the Deer. You are honest; when you say a thing it is so. You have but one tongue, and that is not forked like a snake's. Your head is never hid in the grass; all can see it. What you say that will you do. You are just. When you have done wrong it is your wish to do right again as soon as you can. Here is the Sumach: she is alone in her wigwam, with children crying around her for food; yonder is a rifle; it is loaded and ready to be fired. Take the gun; go forth and shoot a deer; bring the venison and lay it before the widow of the Wolf; feed her children; call yourself her husband. After which your heart will no longer be Delaware but Huron; Sumach's ears will not hear the cries of her children; my people will count the proper number of warriors."

"I feared this, Rivenoak," answered Deerslayer, when the other had ceased speaking; "yes, I did dread that it would come to this. However, the truth is soon told, and that will put an end to all expectations on this head. Mingo, I'm white, and Christian-born; 'twould ill become me to take a wife, under redskin forms, from among heathen. That which I would n't do in peaceable times, and under a bright sun, still less would I do behind clouds, in order to save my life. I may never marry: most likely Providence, in putting me up here in the woods, has intended I should live single, and without a lodge of my own: but should such a thing come to pass, none but a woman of my own color and gifts shall darken the door of my wigwam. As for feeding the young of your dead warrior, I would do that cheerfully, could it be done without discredit; but it can not, seeing that I can never live in a Huron village. Your own young men must find the Sumach in venison, and the next time she marries, let her take a husband whose legs are not long enough to overrun territory that do n't belong to him. We fou't a fair battle, and he fell; in this there is nothin' but what a brave expects, and should be ready to meet. As for getting a Mingo heart, as well might you expect to see gray hairs on a boy, or the blackberry growing on the pine. No, no, Huron; my gifts are white, so far as wives are consarned; it is Delaware in all things touchin' Injins."

These words were scarcely out of the mouth of Deerslayer before a common murmur betrayed the dissatisfaction with which they had been heard. The aged women, in particular, were loud in their expressions of disgust; and the gentle Sumach herself, a woman quite old enough to be our hero's mother, was not the least pacific in her denunciations. But all the other manifestations of disappointment and discontent were thrown into the background by the fierce resentment of the Panther. This grim chief had thought it a degradation to permit his sister to become the wife of a paleface of the Yengeese, at all, and had only given a reluctant consent to the arrangement—one by no means unusual among the Indians, however—at the earnest solicitations of the bereaved widow; and it goaded him to the quick to find his condescension slighted, the honor he had with so much regret been persuaded to accord, contemned. The animal from which he got his name does not glare on his intended prey with more frightful ferocity than his eyes gleamed on the captive; nor was his arm backward in seconding the fierce resentment that almost consumed his breast.

"Dog of the palefaces!" he exclaimed, in Iroquois, "go yell among the curs of your own evil hunting-grounds!"

The denunciation was accompanied by an appropriate action. Even while speaking, his arm was lifted and the tomahawk hurled. Luckily the loud tones of the speaker had drawn the eye of Deerslayer toward him, else would that moment have probably closed his career. So great was the dexterity with which this dangerous weapon was thrown, and so deadly the intent, that it would have riven the skull of the prisoner, had he not stretched forth an arm and caught the handle in one of its turns, with a readiness quite as remarkable as the skill with which the missile had been hurled. The projectile force was so great, notwithstanding, that when Deerslayer's arm was arrested his hand was raised above and behind his own head, and in the very attitude necessary to return the attack. It is not certain whether the circumstance of finding himself unexpectedly in this menacing posture and armed, tempted the young man to retaliate, or whether sudden resentment overcame his forbearance and prudence. His eye kindled, however, and a small red spot appeared on each cheek, while he cast all his energy into the effort of his arm and threw back the weapon at his assailant. The unexpectedness of this blow contributed to its success, the Panther neither raising an arm nor bending his head to avoid it. The keen little ax struck the victim in a perpendicular line with the nose, directly between the eyes, literally braining him on the spot. Sallying forward, as the serpent darts at its enemy even while receiving its own death-wound, this man of powerful frame fell his length into the open area formed by the circle, quivering in death. A common rush to his relief left the captive, for a single instant, quite without the crowd, and, willing to make one desperate effort for life, he bounded off with the activity of a deer. There was but a breathless instant, when the whole band, old and young, women and children, abandoning the lifeless body of the Panther where it lay, raised the yell of alarm, and followed in pursuit.

Sudden as had been the event which induced Deerslayer to make this desperate trial of speed, his mind was not wholly unprepared for the fearful emergency. In the course of the past hour he had pondered well on the chances of such an experiment, and had shrewdly calculated all the details of success and failure. At the first leap, therefore, his body was completely under the direction of an intelligence that turned all its efforts to the best account, and prevented everything like hesitation or indecision at the important instant of the start. To this alone was he indebted for the first great advantage—that of getting through the line of sentinels unharmed. The manner in which this was done, though sufficiently simple, merits a description.

Although the shores of the point were not fringed with bushes, as was the case with most of the others on the lake, it was owing altogether to the circumstance that the spot had been so much used by hunters and fishermen. This fringe commenced on what might be termed the mainland, and was as dense as usual, extending in long lines both north and south. In the latter direction, then, Deerslayer held his way; and, as the sentinels were a little without the commencement of this thicket before the alarm was clearly communicated to them, the fugitive had gained its cover. To run among the bushes, however, was out of the question, and Deerslayer held his way for some forty or fifty yards, in the water which was barely knee deep, offering as great an obstacle to the speed of his pursuers as it did to his own. As soon as a favorable spot presented, he darted through the line of bushes, and issued into the open woods.

Several rifles were discharged at Deerslayer while in the water, and more followed as he came out into the comparative exposure of the clear forest. But the direction of his line of flight,—which partially crossed that of the fire,—the haste with which the weapons had been aimed, and the general confusion that prevailed in the camp, prevented any harm from being done. Bullets whistled past him, and many cut twigs from the branches at his side, but not one touched even his dress. The delay caused by these fruitless attempts was of great service to the fugitive, who had gained more than a hundred yards on even the leading men of the Hurons, ere something like concert and order had entered into the chase. To think of following with rifle in hand was out of the question; and after emptying their pieces in vague hopes of wounding their captive, the best runners of the Indians threw them aside, calling out to the women and boys to recover and load them again, as soon as possible.

Deerslayer knew too well the desperate nature of the struggle in which he was engaged, to lose one of the precious moments. He also knew that his only hope was to run in a straight line, for as soon as he began to turn, or double, the greater number of his pursuers would put escape out of the question. He held his way, therefore, in a diagonal direction up the acclivity, which was neither very high nor very steep, in this part of the mountain, but which was sufficiently toilsome, for one contending for life, to render it painfully oppressive.

Deerslayer had a desperate project in view. Abandoning all thoughts of escape by the woods, and artfully concealing himself until his pursuers had passed, he turned and made the best of his way toward the canoe. He knew where it lay; could it be reached, he had only to run the gantlet of a few rifles, and success would be certain. None of the warriors had kept their weapons, which would have retarded their speed, and the risk would come either from the uncertain hands of the women or from those of some well-grown boy; though most of the latter were already out in hot pursuit. Everything seemed propitious to the execution of this plan, and the course being a continued descent, the young man went over the ground at a rate that promised a speedy termination to his toil.

As Deerslayer approached the point, several women and children were passed, but, though the former endeavored to cast dried branches between his legs, the terror inspired by his bold retaliation on the redoubted Panther was so great that none dared come near enough seriously to molest him. He went by all triumphantly, and reached the fringe of bushes. Plunging through these, our hero found himself once more in the lake and within fifty feet of the canoe. Here he ceased to run, for he well understood that his breath was now all-important to him. He even stooped, as he advanced, and cooled his parched mouth, by scooping up water in his hand to drink. Still the moments pressed, and he soon stood at the side of the canoe. The first glance told him that the paddles had been removed! This was a sore disappointment after all his efforts, and, for a single moment, he thought of turning and of facing his foes by walking with dignity into the center of the camp again. But an infernal yell, such as the American savage alone can raise, proclaimed the quick approach of the nearest of his pursuers, and the instinct of life triumphed. Preparing himself duly, and giving a right direction to its bows, he ran off into the water, bearing the canoe before him, threw all his strength and skill into a last effort, and cast himself forward so as to fall into the bottom of the light craft, without materially impeding its way. Here he remained on his back, both to regain his breath and to cover his person from the deadly rifle. The lightness, which was such an advantage in paddling the canoe, now operated unfavorably. The material was so like a feather that the boat had no momentum ; else would the impulse in that smooth and placid sheet have impelled it to a distance from the shore that would have rendered paddling with the hands safe. Could such a point once be reached, Deerslayer thought he might get far enough out to attract the attention of Chingachgook and Judith, who would not fail to come to his relief with other canoes,—a circumstance that promised everything. As the young man lay in the bottom of the canoe he watched its movements by studying the tops of the trees on the mountain-side, and judged of his distance by the time and the motion. Voices on the shore were now numerous, and he heard something said about manning the raft, which fortunately for the fugitive lay at a considerable distance on the other side of the point.

Perhaps the situation of Deerslayer had not been more critical that day than it was at this minute. It certainly had not been one half as tantalizing. He lay perfectly quiet for two or three minutes, trusting to the single sense of hearing, confident that the noise in the lake would reach his ears did any one venture to approach by swimming. Once or twice he fancied that the element was stirred by the cautious movement of an arm, and then he perceived it was the wash of the water on the pebbles of the strand ; for, in mimicry of the ocean, it is seldom that those little lakes are so totally tranquil as not to possess a slight heaving and setting on their shores. Suddenly all the voices ceased, and a death-like silence pervaded the spot—a quietness as profound as if all lay in the repose of an inanimate life. By this time the canoe had drifted so far as to render nothing visible to Deerslayer, as he lay on his back, except the blue void of space, and a few of those brighter rays that proceed from the effulgence of the sun, marking its proximity. It was not possible to endure this uncertainty long. The young man well knew that the profound stillness foreboded evil, the savages never being so silent as when about to strike a blow,—resembling the stealthy foot of a panther ere he takes his leap. He took out a knife, and was about to cut a hole through the bark in order to get a view of the shore, when he paused from a dread of being seen in the operation, which would direct the enemy where to aim their bullets. At this instant a rifle *was* fired, and the ball pierced both sides of the canoe, within 18 inches of the spot where his head lay. This was close, but our hero was not appalled. He lay still half a minute longer, and then he saw the summit of an oak coming slowly within his narrow horizon.

Unable to account for this change, Deerslayer could restrain his impatience no longer. Hitching his body along, with the utmost caution, he got his eye at the bullet-hole, and fortunately commanded a very tolerable view of the point. The canoe, by one of those imperceptible impulses that so often decide the fate of men, as well as the course of things, had inclined southerly, and was slowly drifting down the lake. It was lucky that Deerslayer had given it a shove sufficiently vigorous to send it past the end of the point ere it took this inclination, or it must have gone ashore again. As it was, it drifted so near it as to bring the tops of two or three trees within the range of the young man's view, as has been mentioned, and, indeed, to come in quite as close proximity with the extremity of the point as was at all safe. The distance could not much have exceeded a hundred feet, though fortunately a light current of air from the southwest began to set it slowly off shore.

Deerslayer now felt the urgent necessity of resorting to some expedient to get further from his foes, and, if possible, to apprise his friends of his situation. The distance rendered the last difficult, while the proximity to the point rendered the first indispensable. As was usual in such craft, a large, round, smooth stone was in each end of the canoe, for the double purpose of seats and ballast; one of these was within reach of his feet. The stone he contrived to get so far between his legs as to reach it with his hands, and then he managed to roll it to the side of its fellow in the bows, where the two served to keep the trim of the light boat, while he worked his own body as far aft as possible. Before quitting the shore, and as soon as he perceived that the paddles were gone, Deerslayer had thrown a bit of dead branch into the canoe, and this was within reach of his arm. Removing the cap he wore, he put it on the end of his stick, and just let it appear over the edge of the canoe, as far as possible from his own person. This *ruse* was scarcely adopted before the young man had proof of how much he had underrated the intelligence of his enemies. In contempt of an artifice so shallow and commonplace, a bullet was fired directly through another part of the canoe, which actually razed his skin. He dropped the cap, and instantly raised it immediately over his head as a safeguard. It would seem that this second artifice was unseen, or what was more probable, the Hurons, feeling certain of recovering their captive, wished to take him alive.

Deerslayer lay passive a few minutes longer, his eye at the bullet-hole, however, and much did he rejoice at seeing that he was drifting gradually further and further from the shore. When he looked upward, the tree-tops had disappeared, but he soon found that the canoe was slowly turning, so as to prevent his getting a view of anything at his peep-hole but of the two extremities of the lake. He now bethought him of the stick, which was crooked, and offered some facilities for rowing, without the necessity of rising. The experiment succeeded, on trial, better even than he had hoped, though his great embarrassment was to keep the canoe straight. That his present manœuver was seen soon became apparent by the clamor on the shore, and a bullet entering the stern of the canoe, traversed its length, whistling between the arms of our hero, and passed out at the head. This satisfied the fugitive that he was getting away with tolerable speed, and induced him to increase his efforts. He was making a stronger push than common, when another messenger from the point broke the stick out-board, and at once deprived him of his oar. As the sound of voices seemed to grow more and more distant, however, Deerslayer determined to leave all to the drift, until he believed himself beyond the reach of bullets. This was nervous work, but it was the wisest of all the expedients that offered ; and the young man was encouraged to persevere in it by the circumstance that he felt his face fanned by the air, a proof that there was a little more wind.

By this time, Deerslayer had been twenty minutes in the canoe, and he began to grow a little impatient for some signs of relief from his friends. The position of the boat still prevented his seeing in any direction, unless it were up or down the lake ; and, though he knew that his line of sight must pass within a hundred yards of the castle, it, in fact, passed that distance to the westward of the buildings. The profound stillness troubled him also, for he knew not whether to ascribe it to the increasing space between him and the Indians, or to some new artifice. At length, wearied with fruitless watchfulness, the young man turned himself on his back, closed his eyes, and awaited the result in determined acquiescence. If the savages could so completely control their thirst for revenge, he was resolved to be as calm as themselves, and to trust his fate to the interposition of the currents and air.

Some additional ten minutes may have passed in this quiescent manner on both sides, when Deerslayer thought he heard a slight noise, like a low rubbing against the bottom of his canoe. He opened his eyes of course, in expectation of seeing the face or arm of an Indian rising from the water, and found that a canopy of leaves was impending directly over his head. Starting to his feet, the first object that met his eye was Rivenoak, who had so far aided the slow progress of the boat as to draw it on the point, the grating on the strand being the sound that had first given our hero the alarm. The change in the drift of the canoe had been altogether owing to the baffling nature of the light currents of air, aided by some eddies in the water.

"Come," said the Huron, with a quiet gesture of authority to order his prisoner to land; "my young friend has sailed about till he is tired; he will forget how to run again, unless he uses his legs."

"You've the best of it, Huron," returned Deerslayer, stepping steadily from the canoe, and passively following his leader to the open area of the point; "Providence has helped you in an unexpected manner. I'm your prisoner ag'in, and I hope you'll allow that I'm as good at breaking jail as I am at keeping furloughs."

"My young friend is a moose!" exclaimed the Huron. "His legs are very long; they have given my young men trouble. But he is not a fish; he can not find his way in the lake. We did not shoot him; fish are taken in nets, and not killed by bullets. When he turns moose again he will be treated like a moose."

"Ay, have your talk, Rivenoak; make the most of your advantage. 'Tis your right, I suppose, and I know it is your gift. On that p'int there'll be no words atween us; for all men must and ought to follow their gifts. Hows'ever, when your women begin to ta'nt and abuse me, as I suppose will soon happen, let 'em remember that if a paleface struggles for life so long as it's lawful and manful, he knows how to loosen his hold on it, decently, when he feels that the time has come. I'm your captyve; work your will on me."

When the whole band was arrayed once more around the captive, a grave silence, so much the more threatening from its profound quiet, pervaded the place. Deerslayer perceived that the women and boys had been preparing splinters of the fat pine roots, which he well knew were to be stuck into his flesh and set in flames, while two or three of the young men held the thongs of bark with which he was to be bound. The smoke of a distant fire announced that the burning brands were in preparation, and several of the elder warriors passed their fingers over the edges of their tomahawks, as if to prove their keenness and temper. Even the knives seemed loosened in their sheaths, impatient for the bloody and merciless work to begin.

"Killer of the Deer," recommenced Rivenoak, certainly without any signs of sympathy or pity in his manner, though with calmness and dignity; "Killer of the Deer, it is time that my people knew their minds. The sun is no longer over our heads; tired of waiting on the Hurons, he has begun to fall near the pines on this side of the valley. He is traveling fast toward the country of our French fathers; it is to warn his children that their lodges are empty, and that they ought to be at home. The roaming wolf has his den, and he goes to it when he wishes to see his young. The Iroquois are not poorer than the wolves. They have villages, and wigwams, and fields of corn; the good spirits will be tired of watching them alone. My people must go back and see to their own business. There will be joy in the lodges when they hear our whoop from the forest. It will be a sorrowful whoop; when it is understood, grief will come after it. There will be one scalp-whoop, but there will be only one. We have the fur of the Muskrat; his body is among the fishes. Deerslayer must say whether another scalp shall be on our pole. Two lodges are empty; a scalp, living or dead, is wanted at each door."

"Then take 'em dead, Huron," firmly, but altogether without dramatic boasting, returned the captive. "My hour is come, I do suppose; and what must be, must. If you are bent on the tortur', I'll do my indivours to bear up ag'in it, though no man can say how far his natur' will stand pain until he's been tried."

"The paleface cur will begin to put his tail between his legs," cried a young and garrulous savage, who bore the appropriate title of the Crow—a sobriquet he had gained from the French by his facility in making unseasonable noises, and from an undue tendency to hear his own voice. "He is no warrior; he has killed the Wolf when looking behind him not to see the flash of his own rifle. He grunts like a hog already; when the Huron women begin to torment him, he will cry like the young of the catamount. He is a Delaware woman, dressed in the skin of the English."

"Have your say, young man, have your say," returned Deerslayer, unmoved; "you know no better, and I can overlook it. Talking may aggravate women, but can hardly make knives sharper, fire hotter, or rifles more sartain."

Rivenoak saw that his warriors were anxious to begin the torture, and, accordingly, gave the signal to proceed.

No sooner did the young men understand that they were at liberty to commence than some of the boldest and most forward among them sprang into the arena, tomahawk in hand. Here they prepared to throw that dangerous weapon, the object being to strike the tree as near as possible to the victim's head without absolutely hitting him. This was so hazardous an experiment that none but those who were known to be exceedingly expert with the weapon were allowed to enter the lists at all, lest an early death might interfere with the expected entertainment. In the truest hands it was seldom that the captive escaped injury in these trials; and it often happened that death followed, even when the blow was not premeditated. In the particular case of our hero, Rivenoak and the older warriors were apprehensive that the example of the Panther's fate might prove a motive with some fiery spirit suddenly to sacrifice his conqueror, when the temptation of effecting it in precisely the same manner, and possibly with the identical weapon with which the warrior had fallen, offered. This circumstance of itself rendered the ordeal of the tomahawk doubly critical for the Deerslayer.

It would seem, however, that all who now entered what we shall call the lists, were more disposed to exhibit their own dexterity than to resent the deaths of their comrades. Each prepared himself for the trial with the feelings of rivalry rather than the desire of vengeance; and for the first few minutes the prisoner had little more connection with the result than grew out of the interest that necessarily attached itself to a living target. The young men were eager, instead of being fierce, and Rivenoak thought he still saw signs of being able to save the life of the captive when the vanity of the young men had been gratified; always admitting that it was not sacrificed to the delicate experiments that were about to be made.

The first youth who presented himself for the trial was called the Raven, having as yet had no opportunity of obtaining a more warlike sobriquet. He was remarkable for high pretensions rather than for skill or exploits, and those who knew his character thought the captive in imminent danger when he took his stand and poised the tomahawk. Nevertheless, the young man was good-natured, and no thought was uppermost in his mind other than the desire to make a better cast than any of his fellows. Deerslayer got an inkling of this warrior's want of reputation by the injunctions that he had received from the seniors; who, indeed, would have objected to his appearing in the arena at all but for an influence derived from his father, an aged warrior of great merit, who was then in the lodges of the tribe. Still, our hero maintained an appearance of self-possession. He had made up his mind that his hour was come, and it would have been a mercy instead of a calamity to fall by the unsteadiness of the first hand that was raised against him. After a suitable number of flourishes and gesticulations that promised much more than he could perform, the Raven let the tomahawk quit his hand. The weapon whirled through the air with the usual evolutions, cut a chip from the sapling to which the prisoner was bound, within a few inches of his cheek, and stuck in a large oak that grew several yards behind him. This was decidedly a bad effort, and a common sneer proclaimed as much, to the great mortification of the young man. On the other hand, there was a general but suppressed murmur of admiration at the steadiness with which the captive stood the trial. The head was the only part he could move, and this had been purposely left free that the tormentors might have the amusement, and the tormentor endure the shame of dodging, and otherwise attempting to avoid the blows. Deerslayer disappointed these hopes by a command of nerve that rendered his whole body as immovable as the tree to which he was bound. Nor did he even adopt the natural and usual expedient of shutting his eyes; the firmest and oldest warrior of the redmen never having more disdainfully denied himself this advantage under similar circumstances.

The Raven had no sooner made his unsuccessful and puerile effort than he was succeeded by the Moose, a middle-aged warrior who was particularly skilful in the use of the tomahawk, and from whose attempt the spectators confidently looked for gratification. This man had none of the good-nature of the Raven, but would gladly have sacrificed the captive to his hatred of the palefaces generally, were it not for the greater interest he felt in his own success as one particularly skilful in the use of this weapon. He took his stand quietly, but with an air of confidence, poised his little ax but a single instant, advanced a foot with a quick motion, and threw. Deerslayer saw the keen instrument whirling toward him, and believed all was over; still, he was not touched. The tomahawk had actually bound the head of the captive to the tree by carrying before it some of his hair; having buried itself deep beneath the soft bark. A general yell expressed the delight of the spectators, and the Moose felt his heart soften a little toward the prisoner, whose steadiness of nerve alone enabled him to give this evidence of his consummate skill.

The Moose was succeeded by the Bounding Boy, who came leaping into the circle like a hound or a goat at play. The Bounding Boy skipped about in front of the captive, menacing him with his tomahawk, now on one side and now on the other, and then again in front, in the vain hope of being able to extort some sign of fear by this parade of danger. At length Deerslayer's patience became exhausted by all this mummery, and he spoke for the first time since the trial had actually commenced.

"Throw away, Huron!" he cried, "or your tomahawk will forget its ar'nd. Why do you keep loping about like a fa'an that's showing its dam how well it can skip, when you're a warrior grown yourself, and a warrior grown defies you and all your silly antics? Throw, or the Huron gals will laugh in your face."

Although not intended to produce such an effect, the last words aroused the "bounding" warrior to fury. The same nervous excitability which rendered him so active in his person made it difficult to repress his feelings, and the words were scarcely past the lips of the speaker when the tomahawk left the hand of the Indian. Nor was it cast without good-will and a fierce determination to slay. Had the intention been less deadly the danger might have been greater. The aim was uncertain, and the weapon glanced near the cheek of the captive, slightly cutting the shoulder in its evolutions. This was the first instance in which any other object than that of terrifying the prisoner and of displaying skill had been manifest; and the Bounding Boy was immediately led from the arena, and was warmly rebuked for his intemperate haste, which had come so near defeating all the hopes of the band.

To this irritable person succeeded several other young warriors, who not only hurled the tomahawk, but who cast the knife—a far more dangerous experiment—with reckless indifference; yet they always manifested a skill that prevented any injury to the captive. Several times Deerslayer was grazed, but in no instance did he receive what might be termed a wound. The unflinching firmness with which he faced his assailants, more especially in the sort of rally with which this trial terminated, excited a profound respect in the spectators; and when the chiefs announced that the prisoner had well withstood the trials of the knife and the tomahawk, there was not a single individual in the band who really felt any hostility toward him with the exception of Sumach and the Bounding Boy. These two discontented spirits got together, it is true, feeding each other's ire; but as yet their malignant feelings were confined very much to themselves, though there existed the danger that the others ere long could not fail to be excited by their own efforts into that demoniacal state which usually accompanied all similar scenes among the redmen.

Rivenoak now told his people that the paleface had proved himself to be a man. He might live with the Delawares, but he had not been made woman with that tribe. He wished to know whether it was the desire of the Hurons to proceed any further. Even the gentlest of the females, however, had received too much satisfaction in the late trials to forego their expectations of a gratifying exhibition; and there was but one voice in the request to proceed. The politic chief, who had some such desire to receive so celebrated a hunter into his tribe as a European minister has to devise a new and available means of taxation, sought every plausible means of arresting the trial in season; for he well knew, if permitted to go far enough to arouse the more ferocious passions of the tormentors, it would be as easy to dam the waters of the great lakes of his own region as to attempt to arrest them in their bloody career. He therefore called four or five of the best marksmen to him and bid them put the captive to the proof of the rifle, while, at the same time, he cautioned them touching the necessity of their maintaining their own credit by the closest attention to the manner of exhibiting their skill.

When Deerslayer saw the chosen warriors step into the circle with their arms prepared for service, he felt some such relief as the miserable sufferer who has long endured the agonies of disease feels at the certain approach of death. Any trifling variance in the aim of this formidable weapon would prove fatal; since, the head being the target, or rather the point it was desired to graze without injury, an inch or two difference in the line of projection must at once determine the question of life or death.

In the torture by the rifle there was none of the latitude permitted that appeared in the case of even Gesler's apple, a hair's-breadth being in fact the utmost limits that an expert marksman would allow himself on an occasion like this. Victims were frequently shot through the head by too eager or unskilful hands; and it often occurred that, exasperated by the fortitude and taunts of the prisoner, death was dealt intentionally in a moment of ungovernable irritation. All this Deerslayer well knew, for it was in relating the traditions of such scenes, as well as of the battles and victories of their people, that the old men beguiled the long winter evenings in their cabins. He now fully expected the end of his career, and experienced a sort of melancholy pleasure in the idea that he was to fall by a weapon as much beloved as the rifle. He had spent an hour, the day before in trying, with Chingachgook, the famous rifle which Tom Hutter had owned, proving his skill and the accuracy of the weapon by bringing down an eagle on the wing ; and now, as the preparations for the torture proceeded, the thought of his own marksmanship returned to his mind.

DEERSLAYER SHOOTS AN EAGLE ON THE WING.

The warriors took their places and prepared to exhibit their skill, as there was a double object in view—that of putting the constancy of the captive to the proof, and that of showing how steady were the hands of the marksmen under circumstances of excitement. The distance was small, and, in one sense, safe. But in diminishing the distance taken by the tormentors, the trial to the nerves of the captive was essentially increased. The face of Deerslayer, indeed, was just removed sufficiently from the ends of the guns to escape the effects of the flash, and his steady eye was enabled to look directly into their muzzles, as it might be, in anticipation of the fatal messenger that was to issue from each. The cunning Hurons well knew this fact; and scarce one leveled his piece without first causing it to point as near as possible at the forehead of the prisoner, in the hope that his fortitude would fail him, and that the band would enjoy the triumph of seeing a victim quail under their ingenious cruelty. Nevertheless, each of the competitors was still careful not to injure; the disgrace of striking prematurely being second only to that of failing altogether in attaining the object. Shot after shot was made, all the bullets coming in close proximity to the Deerslayer's head without touching it. Still no one could detect even the twitching of a muscle on the part of the captive, or the slightest winking of an eye. So exact was Deerslayer's estimation of the line of fire that his pride of feeling finally got the better of his resignation, and, when five or six had discharged their bullets into the tree, he could not refrain from expressing his contempt at their want of hand and eye.

"You may call this shooting, Mingos," he exclaimed, "but we've squaws among the Delawares, and I have known Dutch gals on the Mohawk, that could outdo your greatest indivours. Ondo these arms of mine, put a rifle into my hands, and I'll pin the thinnest war-lock in your party to any tree you can show me; and this at a hundred yards: ay, or at two hundred if the object can be seen, nineteen shots in twenty; or, for that matter, twenty in twenty, if the piece is creditable and trusty!"

A low, menacing murmur followed this cool taunt; the ire of the warriors kindled at listening to such a reproach from one who so far disdained their efforts as to refuse even to wink when a rifle was discharged as near his face as could be done without burning it. Rivenoak perceived that the moment was critical, and, still retaining his hope of adopting so noted a hunter into his tribe, the politic old chief interposed in time, probably to prevent an immediate resort to that portion of the torture which must necessarily have produced death through some extreme bodily suffering, if in no other manner. Moving into the center of the irritated group he addressed them with his usual wily logic and plausible manner, at once suppressing the fierce movement that had commenced.

"I see how it is," he said. "We have been like the palefaces when they fasten their doors at night out of fear of the redman. They use so many bars that the fire comes and burns them before they can get out. We have bound the Deerslayer too tight; the thongs keep his limbs from shaking, and his eyes from shutting. Loosen him; let us see what his own body is really made of."

But even as they loosed the bands that bound their captive, there came an extraordinary interruption.

A young Indian came bounding through the Huron ranks, leaping into the very center of the circle, in a way to denote the utmost confidence, or a temerity bordering on foolhardiness. Five or six sentinels were still watching the lake at different and distant points ; and it was the first impression of Rivenoak that one of these had come in with tidings of import. Still, the movements of the stranger were so rapid, and his war-dress, which scarcely left him more drapery than an antique statue, had so little distinguishing about it, that, at the first moment, it was impossible to ascertain whether he were friend or foe. Three leaps carried this warrior to the side of Deerslayer, whose withes were cut in the twinkling of an eye, with a quickness and precision that left the prisoner perfect master of his limbs. Not till this was effected did the stranger bestow a glance on any other object ; then he turned and showed the astonished Hurons the noble brow, fine person, and eagle eye of a young warrior, in the paint and panoply of a Delaware. He held a rifle in each hand, the butts of both resting on the earth, while from one dangled its proper pouch and horn. This was Killdeer, Deerslayer's own gun, which, even as he looked boldly and in defiance on the crowd around him, he suffered to fall back into the hands of its proper owner. The presence of two armed men, though it was in their midst, startled the Hurons. Their rifles were scattered about against the different trees, and their only weapons were their knives and tomahawks. Still, they had too much self-possession to betray fear. It was little likely that so small a force would assail so strong a band ; and each man expected some extraordinary proposition to succeed so decisive a step. The stranger did not seem disposed to disappoint them ; he prepared to speak.

"Hurons," he said, "this earth is very big. The great lakes are big, too; there is room beyond them for the Iroquois ; there is room for the Delawares on this side. I am Chingachgook, the son of Uncas; the kinsman of Tamenund; that paleface is my friend. My heart was heavy when I missed him ; I followed him to your camp to see that no harm happened to him. All the Delaware girls are waiting for Hist ; they wonder that she stays away so long. Come, let us say farewell, and go on our path."

"Hurons, this is your mortal enemy, the Great Serpent of them you hate !" cried Briarthorn, the chief who had claimed Hist as his captive and bride. "If he escape blood will be in your moccasin prints from this to the Canadas. *I* am *all* Huron."

As the last words were uttered, the traitor cast his knife at the naked breast of the Delaware. A quick movement of the arm turned aside the blow, the dangerous weapon burying its point in a pine. At the next instant a similar weapon glanced from the hand of the Serpent and quivered in the recreant's heart. A minute had scarcely elapsed from the moment in which Chingachgook bounded into the circle and that in which Briarthorn fell, like a log, dead in his tracks. The rapidity of events prevented the Hurons from acting; but this catastrophe permitted no further delay. A common exclamation followed, and the whole party was in motion. At this instant a sound unusual to the woods was heard, and every Huron, male and female, paused to listen, with ears erect and faces filled with expectation. The sound was regular and heavy, as if the earth were struck with beetles. Objects became visible among the trees of the background, and a body of troops was seen advancing with measured tread. They came upon the charge, the scarlet of the king's livery shining among the bright green foliage of the forest.

The scene that followed is not easily described. It was one in which wild confusion, despair, and frenzied efforts were so blended as to destroy the unity and distinctness of the action. A general yell burst from the inclosed Hurons; it was succeeded by the hearty cheers of England. Still not a musket or rifle was fired, though that steady, measured tramp continued, and the bayonet was seen gleaming in advance of a line that counted nearly sixty men. The Hurons were taken at a fearful disadvantage. On three sides was the water, while their formidable and trained foes cut them off from flight on the fourth. Each warrior rushed for his arms, and then all on the point, man, woman, and child, eagerly sought the covers. In this scene of confusion and dismay, however, nothing could surpass the discretion and coolness of Deerslayer. He threw himself on a flank of the retiring Hurons, who were inclining off toward the southern margin of the point in the hope of escaping through the water. Deerslayer watched his opportunity, and finding two of his recent tormentors in a range, his rifle first broke the silence of the terrific scene. The bullet brought down both at one discharge. This drew a general fire from the Hurons, and the rifle and war-cry of the Serpent were heard in the clamor. Still the trained men returned no answering volley, the whoop and piece of Hurry alone being heard on their side, if we except the short, prompt word of authority, and that heavy, measured, and menacing tread. Presently, however, the shrieks, groans, and denunciations that usually accompany the use of the bayonet, followed. That terrible and deadly weapon was glutted in vengeance. The scene that succeeded was one of those of which so many have occurred in our own times, in which neither age nor sex forms an exemption to the lot of a savage warfare.

So was Deerslayer rescued and succor came to the girls in the ark. Soon after Hetty sickened and died; Judith left the lake and the woods, and went to England to seek a home among her own people.

As for Deerslayer, he for a time was irresolute as to his course; but in the end he determined to join the Serpent and Hist and return to the land of the Delawares. That night the three "camped" on the head-waters of their own river, and the succeeding evening they entered the village of the tribe— Chingachgook and his betrothed in triumph, their companion honored and admired.

The war that then had its rise was stirring and bloody. The Delaware chief rose among his people, until his name was never mentioned without eulogiums, while another Uncas, the last of his race, was added to the long line of warriors who bore that distinguished appellation. As for the Deerslayer, under the name of Hawkeye he made his fame spread far and near, until the crack of his rifle became as terrible to the ears of the Mingos as the thunders of the Manitou. His services were soon required by the officers of the crown, and he especially attached himself in the field to one in particular, with whose after-life he had a close and important connection. You who would like to know more about this scout and hunter should read the story of "The Last of the Mohicans."

THE LAST OF THE MOHICANS
A TALE OF INDIAN ADVENTURE.

BY JAMES FENIMORE COOPER.

WAY off in the woods, in the heart of the New York forests, there rode one beautiful summer day, many years ago, a party of four people—men and women.

They were looking about them in anxiety and trouble, and well they might, for these four travelers and their Indian guide were lost in the woods.

Two of the party were sisters. Their names were Cora and Alice Munro. Their father was a colonel in the British army, who lived with his soldiers in a fort near Lake George, in New York. They were in care of a fine young soldier, who was their father's chief officer. His name was Duncan Heyward. With them was a half-foolish—what boys call "luney"—singing master, who did not know a gun from a fishing pole, and had joined the young officer through fear of trouble. For it was in troublesome times that these people were traveling through the woods. The English people who lived in New York, and the French people who lived in Canada, were at war, and the Indians were helping one side or the other. The Indians, you know, used to fight in the woods, behind trees and among the bushes, where no one could see them; so whoever traveled in the great dark woods that then covered the land was in constant danger from hostile Indians.

There was an Indian with this party, but he was standing beside a tree, silent and sulky. He said he had lost the path to the Fort.

Just as they had come along the deer path they were traveling, out into an open space in the woods, they saw a hunter and two Indians.

The hunter was a white man. He was such a sure shot with his trusty rifle that men called him "Hawkeye." His real name was Natty Bumpo. His

CORA, A PRISONER TO THE HURONS.

rifle, of which he was very proud, he called "Killdeer," because it was so sure; but the Indians, who knew him and were afraid of him, called him, because of this terrible gun, "The Long Carbine"—the carbine is a kind of gun, you know.

"What, you are lost?" he said, in answer to Duncan's explanation. "Lost in the woods with an Indian for a guide? Whoever heard of such a thing?"

He took a look at the Indian guide. The white man and the red man stood face to face, but neither spoke. Then the hunter went back to Duncan.

"He's a Mingo," he said, "and I would n't trust him. He'll get you into trouble. You'd better let me shoot him."

"No, no," answered Duncan; "that would not be right. I'll talk with him."

So he went forward to talk with the guide, while Hawkeye joined his two Indian companions.

They were splendid looking redmen—a father and his son. The father's name was Chingachgook; the son's name was Uncas. They belonged to a tribe called Mohicans. The Indian guide whom Hawkeye suspected belonged to a tribe called Hurons, and was known as the "Sly Fox."

While Hawkeye talked with Uncas and his father, Duncan told the Fox that he had found some one who could show them the way to the Fort.

THE PARTY EMBARK IN HAWKEYE'S CANOE.

"A white man? Then I will go away," said the Fox.

But Duncan did not wish him to, for if this Indian were a bad one, as Hawkeye said, he could at once bring other Indians upon the party and kill them. So Duncan tried to keep him, and when the Indian would not promise to go quietly with him, he tried to seize him. But the Fox, with a sudden move, pulled away from him, and darted into the forest.

Quick as he ran away, the two Indians, Uncas and his father, darted after him, and a ball from Hawkeye's rifle followed him. The Fox was too swift for them, however, though by the blood on the sumach leaves Hawkeye knew that he had hit him.

Hawkeye told Duncan that as long as the Fox was at liberty they were in danger, and they must get away as fast as they could.

Duncan then asked the hunter to help him, and the sisters who were in his care, so that they could get to the Fort, and, after talking to the two Mohicans, Hawkeye said he would do so, but first they must get to a safe hiding-place out of the way of Sly Fox and his band; for the hunter was sure that the Fox had meant to lead the party into danger.

So, telling them to be very quiet, Hawkeye led the travelers to his secret hiding-place. He took them to the river bank, where he tied the horses to the trees, drew a canoe of bark from a place of concealment, and then paddled them to a cavern behind a great fall of water into which he guided the canoe very skilfully. There, he told them, they would be safe and sound.

But when the morning came and the hunter made ready to go on the journey, alas! the Fox and his savages had tracked them to their hiding-place by means of the horses and tried to get at them in their cave.

But the hunter and his Indian friends, the Mohicans, fought long and bravely against the Huron foemen, and kept them away from the river and the rocky cavern, killing many and wounding many. One of the Hurons had climbed to the top of a tree which overlooked their hiding-place, and brought them into great danger by firing at them from this point of vantage. The defenders, however, fired at every exposed portion of his body, and finally he fell from his perch, but clung by one hand to the limb of the tree. A shot from Hawkeye made the body fall into the water. It was his last shot: their powder had given out, and they could no longer hold the savages off.

They would not desert the two girls, and prepared to stay and die for them under the Huron attack. But Cora, the elder of the sisters, said it was not right to do this, and they must save their own lives, even if she and her sister were captured by the Indians.

Duncan, of course, would not leave the sisters, and the poor music teacher had been hurt by an Indian bullet. So, at last, Hawkeye and the two Indians, one by one, left them.

But as the hunter dropped into the water to swim to the further shore he said to Cora, "Trust to me. If the Indians take you off, break off a piece of twig now and then as you go. Someone will follow you."

So they left them, and soon after the Huron Fox and his band, with yells of joy, broke into the cavern and carried the four travelers away captive.

The Hurons were very angry to know that their especial enemies, Hawkeye, Uncas, and his father, had escaped them, for they greatly wished to capture these three.

They prepared, however, to carry their other captives away; but Duncan tried hard to get the Fox to set them free and conduct them to Cora's father at the Fort. He offered the Huron great rewards if he would do this.

The Fox, however, would promise nothing, and the Indians led their

A SHOT FROM HAWKEYE MADE THE BODY FALL.

captives away. At last they rested on a small hill, and there the Fox told Duncan he must talk alone with "the dark hair." This was Cora, the elder sister. She listened to the Fox. He told her how the white men had ill-treated him, how even her own father, who commanded at the Fort, had done so, and that now he would have his revenge. But he promised, after Cora had pleaded with him, to send her sister Alice and Duncan without harm to her father if she would do one thing.

"And what is that?" asked Cora.

"Let the daughter of the English chief follow me to the tribe of the Hurons and live in my wigwam forever," said the Fox.

"Be the cruel Huron's wife? Never." So Cora thought; and when she knew that the revengeful Fox wished to do this only to make her father suffer and be sad, she called him a monster and defied him.

The Fox left her without a word. But he joined his companions at once, and made a speech that so stirred them up against their captives that they seized them and prepared the fire to burn and torture them.

The Fox tried to work on Cora's feelings by telling her how her sister would suffer. But when Cora told Alice and Duncan what the bad Huron demanded as the price of their safety, they both were angry and said they had rather die all together.

"Then die!" shouted the Fox, and flung his tomahawk at Alice, just missing her fair head. This made Duncan so angry that with a mighty strain he snapped his bonds, and threw himself upon another Indian, who had his tomahawk up, ready to kill. But as they fell together to the ground, the Indian on top, and Duncan certain that he was about to be slain, bang! came the crack of a rifle, and the Indian fell dead by his side.

Duncan sprang to his feet. The Hurons knew not what to make of this sudden attack. Then there came a shout from the thicket, and the Hurons broke out into a howl.

"The Long Carbine!" they cried.

Sure enough, it was Hawkeye.

In an instant he and his two friends, Chingachgook and Uncas, were among the captives, cutting them loose.

But the Fox acted quickly. He gave a loud war-whoop and rushed straight at Chingachgook. Then Hawkeye and his friends began a fierce fight.

"Kill the Mingos!" he cried, and, raising Killdeer as a club, he struck right and left among the Hurons.

As they fought, a big Huron, springing at Cora, seized her by her long hair, bent her head, and flourished his dreadful scalping knife, but with a bound the young Mohican, Uncas, sprang against him, and buried his knife in the Huron's heart.

At the same time Chingachgook, who was fighting with the Fox, bore him to the ground in triumph.

"Well done! Victory for the Mohican," cried Hawkeye.

But just as he was on the point of finishing the Fox by a blow of his rifle, the sly Fox rolled from under him, and, tumbling over the cliff, sprang to his feet and ran like the wind.

"He's a lying varlet," said Hawkeye, "but 'tis like him."

But the sisters thankfully exclaimed, "We are saved; we are saved."

Then Hawkeye told them how he and his Mohican friends, after swimming away from the cave, had furnished themselves with more powder for their guns, and had then quietly followed the Hurons until, at just the right moment, they were able to rush in and set them free.

So they went on cautiously through the forest. There was danger all about them. Once they just escaped another band of Indians; once they almost ran into the arms of their French enemies; and at last, when they reached Fort Edward, which Cora's father commanded, they found the Fort all surrounded by an army of French and Indians.

For, while they were struggling to find their way to their father, Colonel Munro, in the Fort, the Frenchmen and their Indian allies had marched against the Fort, led on by a famous French general named Montcalm, and encamped about it. Their cannons were aimed upon it, their soldiers were all about it, and there was no way to help the Fort or the soldiers within it.

All this the sisters and their friends saw, as, on a hill above the lake, they looked down upon the Fort and the camps of the enemy.

"And still we must get in," said Duncan. "It is better to be there than here, in danger of the savage Indians."

"But how?" asked Hawkeye.

"Let us ask Montcalm," said Cora. "He will not keep a child from its father."

"You could not get to him alone, with all these Indians around," said the hunter. "But see! there is our chance. A fog is shutting down; with that covering us we may follow the lead of the Mohicans; they can smell the way to the fort."

Very quietly the party followed the Mohicans, but they soon almost ran upon a French picket. As they turned away a cannon ball came booming from the Fort and landed near them. This showed Uncas which way the Fort must be, and they moved along the furrow which the ball had plowed up.

Right in the thick fog they came upon another French sentry.

"Who goes there?" he cried in French.

Duncan answered, also in French, and bade his party push right on. But the Frenchman suspected something was wrong and told his men to fire.

Bang! bang! spoke fifty muskets; but in the fog no aim could be taken, and none of the fugitives were struck.

"Fire!" cried Hawkeye; "they will think we are from the Fort."

Duncan and the Indians did so; but again in the fog they lost their way to the Fort. Again Uncas found the furrow of the cannon-ball and gave the direction.

But now the whole French army was aroused, and musket shots rang out all about them.

There came a roar from the Fort. Munro's cannons were booming out. "Turn back!" cried the scout. "The fort is the other way. We were following the furrow to the woods."

They turned and ran toward the Fort, the French pursuing them. The fog covered everything.

"Stand firm, my men," cried a voice above them. "Wait till you see the enemy; then, when I tell you, fire low."

But Alice had recognized the voice. It was her father's.

"Father! father!" she cried out of the mist. "Do not shoot. It is I— Alice. It is your daughters. Oh, spare us! save us!"

"My child, my daughter," came the voice above them, now full of tenderness and anxiety. "Quick, boys! throw open the sally-port. To the field, to the field, all! Pull not a trigger or you'll kill my girls. Charge bayonets! Drive off those dogs of Frenchmen."

The rusty hinges creaked; the great gate swung open; a long, dark-red line of English soldiers poured out of the Fort. It was Duncan's own regiment of Royal Americans, and, flying to their head, he led them in a gallant charge that sent the Frenchmen flying to their tents.

Duncan had now the satisfaction of restoring the girls to their gray-haired father, the commander of the Fort, who folded his daughter in his arms, and while tears of joy and contentment poured down his cheeks, cried:

"O Lord, I thank thee! Now let danger come as it will."

The danger came soon enough. Although safe in the Fort, still the siege roared all about it, and help did not come.

Colonel Munro now sent Hawkeye with a message to the general of the British army not far away, begging him to send help at once, or they could not save the Fort from the French. But Hawkeye was captured by French soldiers, the letter he was bringing back in reply was taken from him, and he was sent back into the Fort, and the Colonel saw there was no way but to ask the French to take the Fort and let the English soldiers go in peace.

Montcalm, the French commander, promised Munro that if he gave up the Fort his men should keep their guns and their flag, and march out of the Fort free men.

There was nothing else to be done but accept these generous terms. No help would come to them from the British army. So Colonel Munro thanked General Montcalm for his kindness.

The next day Munro and his garrison sadly gave up the Fort they had defended so bravely. The Frenchmen marched in; the Englishmen marched out, and with them went Cora and Alice, with the women and children, the sick and the wounded.

But while the column was moving from the Fort and toward the forest, a stealthy Indian went gliding about among the red allies of the Frenchmen. It was the Sly Fox, the Huron.

Suddenly he gave the fatal and fearful warwhoop, and at the signal the swarming Indians with one leap were upon the fugitives. The terrible tomahawk fell in its deadly work, and two thousand howling savages pursued their horrid work of murder, while no Frenchman stopped them. The word of Montcalm was broken.

Colonel Munro rushed to the French camp to tell Montcalm what he thought of him, and bid him stop the murder.

DUNCAN RESTORES THE GIRLS TO THEIR GRAY-HAIRED FATHER.

But as he went, the wicked Fox sprang among the fugitives, and, seizing the fainting Alice, ran to the forest, followed by Cora, who told him to give up her sister. So he took both the girls away captive. But the simple-minded music teacher followed on, resolved to help the poor girls if he could.

The Indian put the sisters on one of their own ponies, while he, upon the other, led their pony along by the bridle-rein, the singer, still following on behind, mounted upon a stray horse which had got away in the tumult.

So, although the two girls were saved from the dreadful murder of the English prisoners by the Indians, over one thousand in all being slain, they were in the power of this cruel and revengeful Huron chieftain, the Fox, who would keep them captive to carry out some dark plan of his own.

A day or two after the capture of the Fort and the murder of its brave defenders, five men came from the forest and searched the ground all around the ruined Fort.

They were Hawkeye, and his two Indian friends, the Mohicans, Colonel Munro, the father of the captured girls, and their friend, young Duncan Heyward. In the retreat from the Fort and the terrible time that followed, both the soldiers had been with their men, and had left the two girls in care of the poor singing teacher.

After the dreadful day was over they were afraid that the girls had been killed, and were now hunting among the victims, fearing that they might find them, and yet anxious to know what had happened to them.

The scout, Hawkeye, and his Indian companion, were helping them, but they could find no trace of the two girls.

At last, when they were about to give up their search, Uncas, the young Mohican, caught sight of something which attracted his attention, and a moment later was seen taking from a bush and triumphantly waving the green riding-veil of Cora. It was a trace, and when her father begged him to follow it up, the young Mohican said, "Uncas will try," and darted away on the trail.

Searching carefully, he came upon the print of an Indian's moccasin on the soft edge of a pond. He studied it carefully. Then he rose to his feet.

"Well, Uncas, what does it tell you?" asked Hawkeye.

"The Sly Fox," replied Uncas.

His father, Chingachgook, also examined the footprint. He, too, declared it to be made by the moccasin of the Huron.

Then they knew that the two girls were captives, and in the power of the Huron Fox.

They passed the night within the ruined Fort, and after Hawkeye and the Mohicans had held a long discussion as to the way to track the lost girls and their captor, they fell asleep, while the scout and the Indians watched in turn, for fear of surprise by hostile Frenchmen or prowling Indians.

Early in the morning they started along the path which Hawkeye had decided upon. They paddled along the shores and the islands of beautiful Lake George in a canoe, watching carefully. Suddenly they came upon a Huron camp-fire and two canoes. Another and then another canoe appeared.

The trackers would not give up and go back. They decided to push on and run the "gantlet," as the Indians call it.

They paddled, and turned, and dodged, and twisted, not firing a shot while they were out of the reach of the Hurons, although Hawkeye's trusty rifle, Killdeer, could have reached the enemy.

At last a Huron bullet struck the paddle in the hands of Chingachgook and sent it spinning, but Uncas swiftly turned the canoe so that his father could get back his lost paddle, and then they kept on.

The pursuing Hurons now knew whom they were chasing. "The Big Serpent!" "The Long Carbine!" "The Bounding Elk!" they shouted, giving the names by which they knew Chingachgook, Hawkeye, and Uncas.

For reply Hawkeye simply shook Killdeer at his pursuers in mockery, and the canoe darted on amid another shower of Huron bullets.

UNCAS WAVING IN TRIUMPH THE GREEN RIDING-VEIL OF CORA.

Nearer and nearer came the Hurons; a bullet struck the paddle in the hands of Hawkeye.

"That will do," said the scout. "Now we'll answer. Major Heyward, if you will take the paddle, I will let Killdeer take part in this conversation."

With that he passed his paddle to Duncan, and with quick aim knocked over the Huron who was in the bow of the leading canoe. The Hurons stopped a moment, and the Mohicans spun ahead.

They left their pursuers far behind, and, getting into the widest part of the lake, paddled almost to its northern end in safety.

There they came upon another Indian camp, but, running ashore in time, they lifted their canoe out of the water and carried it over the ground until they were out of harm's way.

Hawkeye had lost the trail, but Uncas soon found it again. The captives had been carried north.

With eyes on the ground and the bushes, they studied out the trail in a way that is most wonderful, and which boys and girls would find impossible. But that is one of the things that life in the woods teaches; scouts, and trappers, and Indians can read the leaves and twigs and grass as you would the pages of a book.

So, step by step, they followed the trail that Uncas had found, until at last Hawkeye stopped and began to look around.

"I scent the Hurons," he said. "They are near here somewhere."

Dividing the party, he sent them in different directions to discover the Indian encampment.

As Duncan followed on the path that Hawkeye had given him, suddenly he came upon a curious figure. It was stained and befeathered like an Indian, and yet did n't seem to be one. Duncan was still wondering whether to signal his companions, when Hawkeye stepped beside him. As soon as he saw the figure he aimed his rifle; then he put it down.

"It is not a Huron, nor any of the Canada tribes," he said, "but he is dressed as if he had been plundering a white man—the rascal."

Then he drew toward the strange figure, either to kill or capture it. He lifted his hand as if to strike. Then Duncan, who was anxiously watching the hunter, saw him shake with silent laughter.

The strange Indian was the poor, half-foolish singing-master.

He told them that the girls were well, though they were no longer together; they were kept safely, but securely, by their Indian captors—Cora in the lodge of a tribe in the mountains, and Alice in the village of the Hurons, about two miles away.

"Ah," said Heyward, "how lonely my poor Alice must be, separated from her dear sister."

"She is," said the singing-master, "but I have tried to cheer her up with song."

"Song! Why, can the poor girl sing here, a captive among these blood-thirsty savages?" asked Heyward.

The singing-master, whose name, it should be said, was David Gamut, told the young man that of course Alice was sad, and that she cried more than she smiled; but he said that she sometimes would sing hymns with him, and even the Indians were surprised at the beauty of their songs.

"But do they let you go about like this?" asked Hayward.

"They do," David replied. "I suppose my music does them so much good that they love to hear my voice, and let me come and go as I please."

Hawkeye smiled, and looking at Heyward nodded toward David and tapped his own forehead with his fingers.

By this he meant that David Gamut was not just right in his head, and that the Indians, who never harm a crazy man or one who is half-witted, did not stop David in his coming and going.

"He's a non-compuser, you know," he said to Heyward (that was his word for one not in his right mind, or, as it is in Latin, *non compos mentis*), "and the Injuns never harm a non-compuser. But, friend, when you can come and go as you please, why did you not get back to the Fort and tell us where the young ladies where "

David shook his head. "That would be deserting them in captivity and sorrow," he replied. "I could never do that."

When the white men heard of this friendly desire to help and defend the girls, they were greatly pleased, and even the two Indians, Uncas and his father, showed what they thought of his bravery by their "Ugh!" of satisfaction.

Then Heyward and Hawkeye got David to tell them the whole story of his and the sisters' captivity, and what the Fox had done to throw pursuers off the track and get his captives to a place of safety. As has been related, he separated the sisters, and David told them of the tribe with whom Cora had been placed. He did not think they were Hurons, but he knew that they were somewhat friendly with the Fox's tribe, which had encamped so near them.

The two Mohicans and Hawkeye listened carefully to David's story.

"Did you notice what kind of knives these people had?" asked Hawkeye. David had not.

"Had they had their corn-feast? What is their totem?" asked the scout.

"We've had plenty of feasts of corn," said David, "and it is good. I do n't know what their totem is. Music? Of that they have none; they are idol worshippers."

"No, no, friend," said the scout. "Even the Mingo adores the one true God. They lie who say the Injuns are idol worshippers—much as I hate them, I will say this, they worship no idols."

"You may be right," said David. "But I have seen strange images painted about, which they seem to take pride in—one especially, a foul and horrid beast."

"A serpent?" asked Hawkeye, quickly.

"No; but another low and creeping thing," David answered; "a tortoise."

"Ugh!" broke out both the Mohicans, while Hawkeye nodded thoughtfully.

Then the two Indians talked together earnestly in their own language, and Chingachgook, opening his mantle, showed, worked upon his breast in blue, the figure of a tortoise.

At last Hawkeye spoke. He told Colonel Munro and Heyward that the totem of the Indians was the mark of certain families of redskins, and that those with the same mark were brothers, pledged to help each other, even though they belonged to different tribes. The sagamore, Chingachgook, he told them, was of the Delaware blood, though of the Mohican tribe, and was the great chief of the Tortoise family, or totem.

"Those with whom the lady, Cora, is placed, are some of those of the Tortoise clan," he added. "Perhaps we may work upon them and set the girl free; perhaps not. But we can try, though the way is a hard and dangerous one. For, you see, there has been a long quarrel between even these brothers of the Tortoise clan, and the tomahawks of the Delaware are against those of the Mohican."

They talked long of what they might do to rescue the sisters. Heyward even declared himself ready to rush into the Indian camp and carry Alice away by force. But Hawkeye showed him how foolish and impossible this was, and said that it was much the best way to have David go back as if nothing had happened, though he could let the girls know that help was near. Then, when the rescuers made a signal like the cry of the bird called the whip-poor-will, David was to come into the woods.

But here Heyward broke in. He, too, would go with David, he declared. "Fix me up to look like a fool or a mad fellow, and I will go. I will do everything I can to save my dear Alice."

Hawkeye tried to stop him, but it was no use. The young man was determined to go.

"Fix me up," he said; "disguise me, paint me, make me anything you choose, but go I will. David says the Indians are of different tribes; you say they may be of different clans. Cora is with the new people. Alice is with the Hurons. You may work as you please to release Cora; I will go myself into the Huron camp and rescue Alice, or die."

When Hawkeye saw how brave and determined young Heyward was, he did not try to hold him back any longer, but, instead, did what he could to help him.

"The sagamore," he said, pointing to Chingachgook, "has as many paints as a picture-man. He can use them, too. Sit down on this log. He can make a fool or a crazy fellow of you so well that you will not know yourself."

So Heyward sat down, and Chingachgook set to work to disguise him by painting. This he did so well that when he was through Heyward's face looked like that of some simple traveling juggler rather than that of a soldier of the king. His uniform he had already exchanged for a suit of buckskin.

When all was ready, Heyward bade Colonel Munro an affectionate good-by, and promised to rescue his dear youngest daughter or die in the attempt.

Hawkeye then led Heyward aside and told him how to act. He said that he should leave Colonel Munro and Chingachgook together while he and Uncas tried to get at Cora among the Hurons.

"And now," he said, taking the young soldier by the hand, "good-by and God bless you. You have pluck and spirit, a stout heart and a true one. Be careful. You will need to be as sharp as a needle if you are to get the best of a Mingo. If you fail, be sure the Mingos will pay for their victory dearly. Heaven bless and help you. You are good and true, but to get the better of a Mingo you may have to do things that a white man and a soldier would not think of doing."

Then Heyward and David left him, and the scout, looking after the brave young man in open admiration, slowly shook his head, and then, turning, disappeared with his companions in the forest.

After walking about half an hour, David and Heyward came suddenly upon a lot of Indian boys who were having great fun in their way—playing warrior, and medicine-man, and sacrifice, and yelling and whooping to their hearts' content. When the boys saw the newcomers they disappeared with a yell, but their cry brought some of the older Indians from their lodges, and Duncan Heyward had to put on the air of his make-believe character.

He followed David into the lodge. It was the council-house of the tribe, and was built of bark and branches. Within were many old men and warriors, and a flaring torch cast its red glare upon the faces and figures of this savage throng, who sat about silently as David and Heyward entered and seated themselves upon the pile of brush that each man brought for himself from a great pile in the lodge. They sat long in silence; but at last one of the older warriors spoke, and to him Heyward explained that he was a doctor—what the Indians call a medicine-man—sent by the French governor to his red brothers, the Hurons of the Great Lakes, far to the westward of that place, to see if any were sick and needed healing.

"But why are you painted?" the chief asked. "We have heard that our white brothers boast that their faces are pale."

This was a sharp question, but Heyward was quick with an answer.

"When an Indian chief comes among his white fathers," the young man replied, with steady and quiet voice, "he lays aside his buffalo robe to wear the shirt that is given him. My red brothers have given me paint and I wear it."

This was a ready and sensible answer, and the Indians gave the gesture and grunt of pleasure. Heyward thought his way would now be easy, when suddenly a long, high, shrill war-whoop startled all the lodge and sent all the warriors flocking through the door. Outside the encampment was alive, men, women, and children, old as well as young, making a great hullabaloo, as if welcoming with pleasure some unexpected event. Heyward went out with David to see what it was all about.

It was the return of a war party, and with them came a prisoner. At once all the Indians, men, women, and children, formed in a double line and stood facing each other, with clubs, and knives, and tomahawks, ready to strike. Heyward knew what this meant. The prisoner must run the gantlet; up and down between those dreadful lines he must run, and if he did so and came out alive he was a prisoner of honor, set aside to die like a hero.

Large piles of brush scattered about the clearing were now set afire, and their blaze lit up the scene.

Heyward now saw the prisoner, although the light was not certain enough to tell his features.

The signal yell was given, and the prisoner, who was, Heyward saw, a young, lithe, splendidly built brave, started on his fearful race. Up and down he ran, leaping, dodging, turning, and doing all so skilfully that neither knife nor club could touch him. Now he would leap high in air; now he would break through the throng, when his pursuers would rush after to turn or stop him.

In one of these breaks he ran straight toward young Heyward, the red crowd hard at his heels. A tall and powerful Huron was nearest him, and had his tomahawk high in air ready for the death blow. But as he passed, Heyward, the young soldier, suddenly put out his foot and tripped up the Huron, who fell heavily to the ground, while Heyward merely stepped back into the shadow, and the brave young runner, gaining a small, painted post that stood before the door of the great lodge, leaned quietly and calmly against it. That post was "goal,"—the safety post,—and, once gained, the captive's death-race was over.

The young Indian stood there calmly and quietly, as if he had no thought or care for his captors.

The squaws and boys gathered about him and began to taunt and plague him with insulting words, trying to make him angry. But he never said a word.

And as he stood there, unconcerned and haughty, caring nothing for the words and laughter and insults of his tormentors, leaning carelessly and quietly against the safety post, his face was suddenly turned toward a strong and blazing light, and then Heyward recognized the captive. It was Uncas, the Mohican.

As he looked upon the young Indian in surprise and amazement, wondering how he came to be a prisoner in the power of the Hurons, a warrior came forward, and, driving back the yelling women and children, took Uncas by the arm and led him into the council-lodge.

There all the chiefs and warriors followed ; Heyward entered also, and no one stopped him.

In the midst of his captors Uncas still stood calm and collected. Even his Huron foemen admired his courage.

" Delaware," said one of the principal chiefs, addressing Uncas, " though of a nation of women, you have shown yourself a man. I would give you food, but he who eats with a Huron is his friend. You are our foe. Rest here in peace until the morning. Then you die."

" Seven nights and as many days have I fasted on the trail of the Huron," said Uncas. " I can travel the path of death without waiting to eat."

" Two of my young men are in pursuit of your companion," said the chief; "when they return, then will our wise men say to you, live or die."

" Your young men will never get back," said Uncas. " Twice has your prisoner heard a gun that he knows. A Huron has no ears to hear that sound."

Heyward knew who Uncas meant—he had heard the gun of Hawkeye.

" If your tribe are so skilful, why are you, one of the bravest, here?"

" I was trapped by a flying coward, not taken like a man, in open fight," said Uncas. " Even the cunning beaver may be caught, if he falls into the snare."

The torches died out ; the throng of warriors departed ; but Heyward was able to get near Uncas, and to hear him say :

" The Hurons are dogs. The Gray Head" (by which he meant Colonel Munro) "and the sagamore are safe. Go! We are strangers. I have said enough."

Heyward would have heard more, but Uncas quietly forced him out of danger, and he slowly left the lodge and mingled with the dusky forms without. But still, as the lights would flicker up, he could see within the lodge the upright figure of the Mohican, Uncas.

Heyward wandered among the lodges, trying to find some sign or trace of the lost Alice, while, at the same time, he worried about the fate of Uncas.

Straying from hut to hut, only to meet with fresh disappointments, he walked around the whole Indian village, and so came back again to the council-lodge, where the warriors were again assembled, smoking the pipe of council.

Hoping to find David, the singing-master, Heyward entered the council-lodge; but the "non-compuser," as Hawkeye called the poor David, was not there. Uncas still stood under guard, like some firm statue rather than a living man.

As Heyward sat silent in the lodge one of the chiefs addressed him:

"Our French father has sent you to heal the sick," he said. "I thank him. An evil spirit of illness lives in the wife of one of my young men. Can my brother, the cunning medicine-man, frighten this evil one away?"

The young soldier had not expected to be thus put to the test, and yet he must not refuse, for that would be dangerous. So he replied carefully, and as if his medicine was a mystery:

"There are different kinds of evil spirits," he said. "Some will fly before the power of medicine; others are too strong."

"But my brother is a great medicine," said the cunning Indian. "He will try, will he not?"

And Heyward answered simply, "He will try."

The chief smoked on in silence for some time longer. Then he drew his robe about him and motioned to Heyward to follow him to the lodge of the sick woman.

But, as he did so, the doorway of the lodge was darkened by the form of a tall and powerful warrior. He entered, and, as he seated himself upon the same brush heap with Heyward, the young soldier felt his heart drop with horror. The new-comer was his bitter enemy, the Sly Fox.

Pipes were relighted, and for ten minutes no word was spoken. All smoked in silence.

Then one of the chiefs told of the capture of the Mohican, or the Delaware, as the Hurons called him, and pointed at the silent Uncas.

The Fox looked at the young Mohican. As their eyes met, the form of Uncas dilated; his nostrils opened like those of a tiger at bay; but still he stood unmoved. But, upon the face of the Fox, came a look of fierce joy; he gave a great breath of satisfaction, and with that came the words:

"The Elk; it is the Bounding Elk."

As the Hurons recognized the name of their bitterest enemy, and knew that Uncas was in their power, they started to their feet, and repeated his name in surprise; outside, the women and children, hearing the name, echoed it with a shrill howl of joy.

Uncas enjoyed his victory, but made no sign beyond the quiet smile of scorn. But the Fox had seen that smile, and, raising his arm, shook it at the captive until its silver ornaments rattled in his excitement.

"Mohican, you die!" he cried.

"The healing waters will never bring your dead Hurons to life," answered Uncas, contemptuously. "Your men are squaws; your women owls. Go! Call together the Huron dogs, that they may look upon a warrior. Away! I smell the blood of a coward."

This made the Fox very, very angry. At once he began a long and heated speech to the Huron warriors, telling them how much the Hurons had suffered from this young warrior who was now their captive, and from his father and his companion, the white man, Hawkeye.

Enraged and worked to the pitch of frenzy by this speech, the Hurons shouted for revenge, and one warrior, springing to his feet, whirled his tomahawk about his head, and, with a yell of hate, flung it straight at Uncas. The Fox tried to stop it, but too late. It flashed through the air, and, cutting the war-plume from the scalp-lock of the young Mohican, passed through the wall of the lodge and fell outside.

Heyward sprang to his feet as if he would save his friend; but when he saw that the blow had failed, his terror changed to admiration, for Uncas did not flinch. Still looking his enemy in the eye, he made no motion beyond one of pity and contempt for so unskilful an aim.

The Fox saw that he was safe. "He must not die thus," said the Huron; "the sun must shine on his shame. Go! Take him where there is silence. Let us see if a Delaware can sleep at night, and in the morning die."

The warriors on guard led their prisoner away, but as he passed from the lodge the eye of Uncas caught that of Heyward, and in it the young soldier read, "Hope."

The Fox, too, left the lodge. The other warriors fell to smoking once more, and after a half-hour or so the chief, who had asked for Heyward's help, arose, and, beckoning to the supposed physician, passed out into the evening, followed by Heyward.

They turned aside from the Indian encampment and walked toward the mountain. A winding path led through the low brushwood, while the bonfires, made by the Indian boys at play, lighted up the scene in fitful flashes.

One of these streams of light fell across their path, and, lighting up the whole face of the mountain, disclosed a dark and mysterious-looking object in the path before them.

As they paused, it arose. The large, black ball began to sway to and fro before them, and at length Heyward discovered, from its actions and its growls, that it was a bear; but not a bear bent on their destruction. It appeared more like a tamed animal—the pet or companion of some Indian conjuror or medicine-man, as was often the case.

The Huron saw this, and proceeded; but Heyward was not used to such monsters, and he passed the beast in some uncertainty. When, however, they had pushed past the bear, the monster rose, and swung along in the path behind them.

Heyward was uneasy at this, but just then his Indian conductor pushed aside a door of bark, and the young soldier, following, entered a cavern in the bosom of the mountain.

The bear was right on their heels, and came into the cavern behind them. They were now in a straight and long gallery in a chasm of the rocks, where retreat would bring them right against the big bear. It was not a pleasant situation, but Heyward made the best of it, and kept as closely as possible to his conductor. The bear growled at his heels, and once or twice pressed against him, as if to push him out of the den.

Soon a glimmer of light appeared before them, and they entered a large cavity in the rock, which had been divided by stone, sticks, and bark into numerous rooms.

Into one of these the Huron led young Heyward, and there he found the sick woman, surrounded by squaws, and in the center of them his friend David.

He saw at once that the woman was too sick to live. But while he wondered what he could do to carry out his make-believe part of a doctor, David was before him. The half-witted singing-master, believing that music could cure everything, began singing a hymn. The Indians, who never interfere with the actions of a crazy man, did not stop him, and Heyward was glad of the chance to think out what he should do.

But as the last sound of the song died away, the young soldier was surprised at hearing the strains repeated, he almost thought sung, behind him. Turning, he saw crouched near him in a corner of the cabin, and swinging restlessly from side to side, the shaggy monster of the bear that had followed him into the cave.

At the sound, David stopped in surprise. He looked at the bear; he looked at Heyward; and then, saying, "She expects you and is near you," he rushed from the cavern.

After David had gone, Heyward sat surprised and puzzled, while the bear still moved restlessly to and fro.

But the Huron chief, who had brought the young soldier to the sick-room, sent the squaws out of the apartment, and, pointing at the sick girl, said, "Now let my brother show his power."

Heyward was puzzled, and yet knew that he must do something without delay if he was to play the doctor as he had intended. Just what he would have done, he could not say; but the bear, as if to interrupt him, kept growling and moving more savagely than ever.

The Huron chief looked at the beast.

"The cunning spirits are jealous," he said. "I go, brother; deal justly by this sick one. Peace," he added, beckoning to the restless bear; "I go."

He left the cavern, and Heyward was alone in that wild and desolate place with a dying woman and a dangerous bear. But when the Indian was far away and all was still, suddenly the bear's actions changed. Instead of growling angrily and moving restlessly about, his whole shaggy body shook violently, as if some odd thoughts were disturbing him. He stood erect; the huge claws pawed clumsily about his head; then the huge head itself fell back, and out of the skin appeared the honest, sturdy, silently laughing countenance of Hawkeye, the scout.

Heyward was speechless with surprise.

"Hist!" said the scout. "Be quiet. Any sound will bring the varlets back."

"What does this mean?" whispered the soldier.

"Where is Uncas?" asked Hawkeye.

"A captive," Heyward answered. "He dies in the morning."

"I feared so," the scout said sadly. "We fell in with the war party and he was taken. He was too hot on the trail and fell into the trap. I followed after, and had a scrimmage or two with the Hurons, until I came almost into their camp. Then, what should I do but happen upon one of their medicine-men, dressing up in this bearskin to go through some of his mummeries. I straightened him out with a rap on the head, left him with a gag in his mouth, and, crawling into the skin, played the bear so as to get in near to Uncas and to you. Where is the lady?"

"I do not know," answered Heyward, disconsolately. "I have searched every lodge, but have found no trace of her."

"You heard what the singing man said," remarked Hawkeye. "'She expects you, and is nigh you,' he said."

"Yes; but I thought he meant this sick woman, whom I can do nothing for," Heyward answered.

"No, no; the simpleton meant more, I know," said Hawkeye. "See, here are walls. Walls are for a bear to climb. There may be honey hid in those rocks."

So, laughing at his own joke, the scout, still in the bearskin, climbed to the top of the rocky wall; but no sooner was he up than he slipped down again.

"She is here," he whispered. "By that door you will find her. I would have spoken to her, but I was afraid a monster like me would disturb her. But, indeed, Major, you are not much better looking in all that paint."

Heyward, who had sprung toward the spot pointed out by Hawkeye, stopped suddenly. He had forgotten his own disguise.

"Do I look so very badly?" he said.

"Well," said the scout, "I have seen you when you looked better. A squaw might not object, but a young white woman would rather see a white man. Here, go to this spring. You can wash off your face, and when you come back we can paint you over again. A conjurer like you has to change his colorings, you know."

Heyward speedily cleared the paint from his face and hurried along the passage shown him by Hawkeye. The scout, left alone, searched about to see what provisions the Hurons had that he could draw upon, if needed; for this cavern was one of their storehouses.

Heyward followed the passage and finally found Alice in an apartment full of the things which the Indians had brought from the captured Fort. She was hoping to see him, for David had told her he was near.

Alice was overjoyed to see Duncan Heyward once more. She felt sure that he would soon, somehow, get her out of that terrible place. They talked long and earnestly together, but just as Heyward was telling Alice how much he thought of her and what he would do for her, he felt a tap on his shoulder, and, looking up, saw the mocking face of the Fox looking down at them.

He laughed wickedly as Heyward looked about for some weapon to attack him and found none.

"The palefaces trap the cunning beavers," said the Huron, "but the redskin knows how to take the paleface."

"Huron, do your worst!" cried Heyward, never thinking what that worst might mean—a death at the stake for both the captives. "I despise you."

"Will the white man say that at the stake?" the Fox said.

"Here, to your face, or before all your tribe," cried the soldier.

"The Sly Fox is a great chief," returned the Indian. "He will go and bring his young men, to let them see whether a paleface can laugh at torture."

He turned to go, when right in his path rose the figure of a great bear. Hawkeye was on his trail.

As the bear, standing upon its legs, beat the air with its paws, the Huron motioned it aside impatiently.

"Fool!" he said, "go play with children and squaws. Leave men to their wisdom."

But, as he tried to pass the bear, the beast thrust out its paws and caught the Indian in a grasp stronger than any "bear's hug"' could be.

HAWKEYE AND THE BEAR TAKE THE FOX PRISONER.

Heyward let go of Alice, whom he had caught to save her from the wrath of the Indian, and watched the struggle breathlessly. But when he saw the Huron's arms pinned to his side by the strength of the powerful muscles of the scout, he caught up a buckskin thong and wound it all about the legs, arms, and feet of the Fox, until their enemy was securely bound in twenty folds of the thong. Then Hawkeye released his hold on the Indian and Heyward threw him to the ground. Then the scout put a gag in the Indian's mouth, so that he could not call for help, and then told Heyward to take Alice quickly and follow him out into the woods.

But Alice had fainted.

"Wrap her up in these Indian clothes," said Hawkeye. "Cover all her form. Now, take her in your arms and follow me. I'll do the rest."

Heyward did as he was told, and, with Alice in his arms, passed out of the apartment. They looked in at the sick Indian woman. She still lay in the same quiet condition. As they came near the door of the cavern they heard voices outside. It was the friends of the sick woman waiting until the medicine-man should tell them to come in.

"You talk, Major," said the scout. "Tell 'em we have shut up the evil spirit in the cave, and are taking the sick woman to the woods for strengthening herbs and roots. Be shrewd and cunning."

Then the scout became the bear once more, and they came into the air.

Heyward told the father and husband of the sick woman what the scout had suggested, and when the father said he would go into the cavern and fight the evil spirit, Heyward said:

"What! Is my brother mad? Is he cruel? He will meet the disease, and it will enter him; or he will drive out the disease, and it will chase his daughter into the woods. No! Wait here, and if the evil spirit appears, beat him down with clubs."

They heeded his words, and, gathered at the entrance to the cavern, stood there with knives, and tomahawks, and clubs, all ready to strike down the evil one if he should come out.

Then Hawkeye and Heyward, carrying the silent Alice, passed into the woods.

When Alice had recovered, and the three had walked far from the Indian village, Hawkeye told them what to do.

"We can not escape this way," he said. "The Hurons will be on our trail before we have gone a dozen miles. Your only hope is the village of the other people, where this lady's sister is held. If they are true Delawares, you will be safe from the Hurons. Follow this brook, and climb the hill, and you will see their camp-fires. Go, now, and Heaven be with you!"

"But you?" cried Heyward. "What shall you do?"

"Uncas is with the Hurons," the scout replied. "The last of the high blood of the Mohicans is in their power. I must go to him. If he dies, I will die in his defense."

They begged him not to, but it was useless; he was determined.

"I taught the boy how to use the rifle," he said. "I have fought by his side in many a bloody scrimmage, and so long as I could hear the crack of his piece in one ear and that of his father, the sagamore, in the other, I knew no enemy was on my back. Winters and summers, nights and days, have we roved the wilderness together, eating of the same dish, one sleeping while the other watched, and I tell you Uncas shall not be carried to torture without my being at hand; before the last of the Mohicans shall perish for want of a friend, good faith shall depart from the earth and Killdeer become harmless and silent."

Then he turned and walked back toward the Huron lodges, while Heyward and Alice, after mournfully watching his departure, went forward on their way to the village of the Delawares.

Slowly and thoughtfully Hawkeye walked back to the Huron encampment. Wrapped in the bearskin, he approached a hut rather in front of the others. A light shone through the crevices, and Hawkeye, looking in, saw that it was the hut of David Gamut, the singing-master.

David had not yet recovered from the surprise of hearing a bear sing. He was even now thinking the whole thing over, when suddenly that same bear appeared at the door of his hut.

"What are you, dark and mysterious monster?" he exclaimed.

"A man like yourself," replied Hawkeye.

"Can this be?" said David, in surprise. "I have found many marvelous things in my travels, but never anything like this."

"Now do you know me?" demanded Hawkeye, thrusting his head out of the bearskin. "Where is Uncas?"

"A captive, and doomed to death," replied David, sadly.

"Can you lead me to him?" asked Hawkeye.

"I can; but what good will it do you or him?" inquired David.

But Hawkeye told him to go ahead; and, covering his head again with the bearskin, followed David from his hut.

As they walked, Hawkeye learned from David that, because of his supposed foolishness, the singing-master was allowed to visit Uncas whenever he desired. He had also talked and sung with one of the Mohican's guards, and, as an Indian likes such attention, the Huron guard let the crazy singing-master do about as he pleased. When Hawkeye had found all this out, he carefully laid his plans so as to use David to help out the scheme he had thought out for the help of Uncas.

As the two approached the lodge in which Uncas, the Mohican, was kept prisoner, Hawkeye did not try to hide from the Indians. He knew that they supposed the figure in the bearskin to be one of their wise conjurors or medicine-men, and that they thought he and the foolish singing-master were to take part in some mysterious actions with the captive.

But the Huron guards did not leave the lodge door, and David, carrying out Hawkeye's instructions, asked the Hurons if they would like to see their captive whine, and weep, and plead for mercy, like a coward.

The Hurons, of course, said they would like to see this mighty enemy of their tribe humbled and weak, and they asked David if he could make him thus.

David told them to step aside, and they would go into the lodge and blow upon the dog of a Delaware (for so he called Uncas to them) and weaken him.

The Indians drew aside from the lodge door, and David and Hawkeye entered.

In a distant corner of the silent and gloomy room they saw Uncas, lying down and bound hand and foot. Hawkeye told David to stay by the door and keep out the curious Hurons, while he, wrapped in the bearskin, approached the Mohican.

The young Indian did not even look up at the disguised scout. He supposed that the Hurons had sent the animal in to annoy or frighten him, and he would not betray the least sign or movement of interest.

Then the supposed bear began to growl and dance, and as he did so Uncas saw that there was something not just right in the actions of the brute. But he looked all the more contemptuously and scornfully upon the false bear, and, leaning against the wall, shut his eyes as if he wished not to see so disagreeable and foolish a sight.

At that instant there came from David the signal arranged by Hawkeye —the low hissing of a snake.

Uncas rose to his feet as soon as he heard the sound. He bent his head and looked cautiously around until once more he gazed upon the shaggy hide of the bear. As he did so, out of the bear's mouth came the same hissing sound as of the snake.

Then Uncas said low but deeply:

"Hawkeye!"

As he spoke David came toward him.

"Cut his bands," said Hawkeye.

THE LAST OF THE MOHICANS.

The singing-master did as he was told, and Uncas, relieved of his bonds, stood erect and free. At the same moment Hawkeye dropped from him the bearskin.

Uncas at once saw what his friend had done to help and save him, but he said nothing.

Then Hawkeye, drawing a large knife from his belt, handed it to Uncas.

"The red Hurons are outside," he said. "Let us stand ready," and he, too, drew a long and glittering knife.

"We will go," said Uncas.

"But where?" asked Hawkeye.

"To the Tortoises," replied Uncas; "they are the children of my grandfather."

"Yes; the same blood runs in your veins," said Hawkeye, "but time and distance may have changed its color: and what shall we do with the Mingos at the door? They count six, and this singer is good for nothing."

"The Hurons are boasters, and run like snails," said Uncas; "the Delaware can run like deer. We can pass them."

"You may, lad," replied Hawkeye, "but the gift of a white man lies more in his arms than his legs. I can strike down a Mingo as well as any man, but when it comes to a race they would prove to much for me."

As he spoke these words, Uncas, who had gone near to the door to lead the way out, turned back, and sat himself once more in the lodge. But Hawkeye continued, "But, there is no reason, Uncas, why you should stay. Take the leap past the Mingos. I will go into the skin again and try my cunning."

The young Mohican made no reply, but quietly folded his arms and leaned back against the wall.

"Come, why do you wait?" said Hawkeye. "I have time enough, but you have not."

"Uncas will stay," said the Mohican.

"For what?"

"To fight with his father's brother," said Uncas, "and die with the friend of the Delawares."

Hawkeye grasped his friend's hand.

"I thought so," he said; "it would have been more like a Mingo than a Mohican had you left me. But I gave you the chance. Well, what can't be done by courage must be done by wit. Put on the skin, Uncas; you can play the bear as well as I."

Uncas silently slipped into the skin, while Hawkeye, turning to the singing-master, said:

"Now, friend David, you won't mind an exchange of garments. Take my hunting-cap and shirt; give me your blanket and hat. Let me have your book and spectacles, too. If ever we meet again, you shall have them back."

The singing-master made the exchange without objection, and Hawkeye appeared in David's clothes and glasses.

"When the Hurons find you here in place of Uncas," said Hawkeye, "though they will at first be angry, they will remember that you are a non-compuser, and will not harm you. But if you wish to take the chances with us, do so. Which will you do—make the rush, or stay quietly here?"

"I will stay," replied David. "The young Delaware has battled bravely for me. This and more will I brave for him."

"Spoken like a man, and a brave one, friend David," said Hawkeye. "Lie still, keep silent; but when you must speak, break out at once in singing. That will tell the Indians what and who you are. Farewell, and God bless you. You are a good and brave man," and shaking the singing-master warmly by the hand, he left the lodge with Uncas dressed as the bear.

Hawkeye drew himself up to look like the singing-master, and, keeping time with his hand, began to sing one of David's hymns. As he drew near the Indians he sang louder and more vigorously, but the Hurons stopped him.

"Is the Delaware dog afraid?" asked an Indian. "Will the Hurons hear his groans and whines?"

The bear growled so savagely that the Indian dropped his hold on the scout and eyed the brute, uncertain whether it were bear or man. Hawkeye burst out into a new and louder song, and the Indians, remembering that the singer was a crazy man, drew back and let both him and his companion pass.

Slowly and calmly Uncas and Hawkeye passed through the encampment. They saw the Indians cautiously approach the hut where the supposed Uncas lay; but no one entered yet, for fear of the spell put on the captive, and at last, through the darkness, the two got clear of the village.

Then they began to run toward the forest. As they did so, they heard a long, loud cry from the lodge in which Uncas had been confined.

Uncas dropped his bearskin.

Another chorus of cries came to their ears.

Hawkeye rushed on, and presently drew from the bushes two rifles, with powder- and shot-bags.

"Here is your weapon, Uncas," he said, "and here is Killdeer. Now let them follow, if they dare."

And throwing their rifles to a low trail, like hunters ready for a shot, they dashed forward, and were soon deep in the darkness of the forest.

As for David, when the Hurons discovered that it was he, instead of Uncas, in the lodge, he expected, from their cry of surprise and rage, that they would surely kill him. But, remembering Hawkeye's advice, he broke out into song, and, as fitting his own death, chose a funeral hymn.

The Indians, hearing this, remembered that poor David was not all right in his head, and, leaving him alone, they rushed into the air to arouse the village and track the fugitives.

At once, two hundred warriors were afoot and ready for the chase. But a leader was needed, and all called for the Fox. Where was he?

Messengers were sent to bring him, but none could find him. The whole encampment was aroused, and in the search they came upon the poor conjurer whom Hawkeye had knocked over and deprived of his bearskin.

He now told his story, whereupon the father of the sick woman whom Heyward had been sent to cure became suspicious. Rushing to the cavern in which he had been told the evil spirit was kept, he found his daughter still and cold. She was dead.

But whom had the conjurer carried out? Before he and his companions could decide, one of them saw a dark-looking object come rolling out of another apartment nearby.

Thinking of the evil spirit, and not knowing what to do, they stood waiting and watching, until the rolling object came into the light and lifted itself up. Then they broke out in amazement. It was the Fox, bound and gagged.

At once ready knives cut his bonds and released him. The Fox arose to his feet, shook himself like a lion cut loose, grasped his knife, and looked about for some one to wreak his vengeance on.

"Let the Delaware die," he said, at length.

But when he knew that Uncas had escaped he was more angry than ever.

"An evil spirit has been among us," said one of the Hurons, "and the Delaware has blinded our eyes."

"An evil spirit?" cried the Fox. "Yes, evil. It is he who has taken so many Huron scalps. It is he who bound the arms of the Fox."

"Who is it?" asked several voices.

"It is the dog who carries the heart and cunning of a Huron under a pale skin—the Long Carbine!"

At the sound of the feared and hated Indian name of Hawkeye, the scout, every warrior sprang to his feet, and when it was understood that this daring foeman had been not only in their encampment but within their grasp, all the Hurons were frantic with rage.

But, with the usual restraint of the redman, they speedily became quiet again, and returned with the Fox to the council-lodge.

Here he told the assembled warriors how they had been insulted and disgraced by these "dogs of palefaces."

At once all were bent on revenge ; a long consultation followed ; and then the Fox, in a long and carefully worded speech, so worked upon the feelings, the desires, and the hatred of his warriors, that, when he had concluded, they gave the whole affair into his charge, and promised to do as he told them and follow wherever he led them.

So, before daylight, next morning, the Huron Fox and twenty picked warriors, armed with rifles but without their hideous war-paint, left the encampment, and in Indian file—that is, one by one—walked along the trail that led to the village of the Tortoises, where Cora had been sent, and where Heyward and Alice had fled for refuge. These Tortoises were a half-tribe of the Delawares, which, in years before, had separated from the body of the nation, and, migrating far to the North, had lived in enmity with their former brethren, and generally in sympathy with the Hurons. They were, however, rather passive in the present contest, and were treated by the Hurons with great consideration in the hope of winning their active help.

There was excitement in the lodges of the Delawares, for among them had come both guests and captives. These were housed in a large lodge in the center of the village, and already the chiefs were in consultation as to how they should be treated.

Among the Indians there was a great respect for hospitality. A guest in a camp or village was sacred. He could not be harmed even by an enemy, nor be troubled in any way. If an Indian said " You are welcome," the person so welcomed became a guest whose safety was the Indian's care, and whom he would let no one molest or take away.

Hawkeye knew this, and when he sent Heyward and Alice there, when he went there himself, although they presented themselves as prisoners, they also claimed the rights of hospitality, because they had gone into the Delaware village of their own accord and not as captured prisoners. So they felt safe.

As for Cora, she had been taken as a prisoner to the Delawares by the Huron Fox. They had promised to keep her safe, but she must be given up to the Fox whenever he came or sent for her.

The Huron knew this, but his revenge was not satisfied with one victim ; he desired to strike all who were against him, and it was with some plan of this sort in his mind that he sought the Delaware village.

He reached it during the consultation of the chiefs. He entered it without war-paint, as a friend asking hospitality ; and, though the Delawares feared and disliked him, they could not act against one who had accepted the hospitality of their tribe.

The Delawares welcomed the Huron with courtesy, and, after a breakfast had been offered him, the Fox asked the Delawares if his prisoner, Cora, had given them any trouble.

"She is welcome," they replied.

"If she gives any trouble to my brothers," said the Fox, "let her be sent to my squaws. The path between the Huron and the Delaware is open."

But the only reply was, "She is welcome."

"Do my young men leave the Delawares room on the mountains for their hunts?" he at length continued.

"The Lenape" (for thus the Delawares called themselves) "are rulers of their own hills," returned the other, a little haughtily.

"It is well. Justice is the master of the redskins! Why should they brighten their tomahawks and sharpen their knives against each other? Are not the palefaces thicker than the swallows in the season of flowers?"

"Good!" exclaimed two or three of his auditors at the same time.

The Fox waited a little, to permit his words to soften the feelings of the Delawares, before he added:

"Have there not been strange moccasins in the woods? Have not my brothers scented the feet of white men?"

"Let my Canada father come," returned the other, evasively; "his children are ready to see him."

"When the great Canada chief comes, it is to smoke with the Indians in their wigwams. The Hurons say, too, he is welcome. But the English have long arms, and legs that never tire! My young men dreamed they had seen the trail of the English nigh the village of the Delawares!"

"They will not find the Lenape asleep."

"It is well. The warrior whose eye is open can see his enemy," said the Fox, once more shifting his ground when he found himself unable to penetrate the caution of his companion. "I have brought gifts to my brother. His nation would not go on the war-path, because they did not think it well: but their friends have remembered where they live."

When he had thus announced his liberal intention, the crafty chief arose and gravely spread his presents before the dazzled eyes of his hosts. They consisted principally of trinkets of little value, plundered from the slaughtered females of the captured Fort. In the division of the baubles the cunning Huron discovered no less art than in their selection. While he bestowed those of greater value on the two most distinguished warriors, he gave to those of less note compliments as well as presents, and so won all to him.

The Delawares became less cautious and cold, after the gifts and words of the Fox had flattered them, and their chief said to their visitor:

"My brother is a wise chief. He is welcome."

"The Hurons love their friends, the Delawares," said the Sly Fox, "and why should they not? The redskins should be friends, and use their eyes, together, to watch the white men. Has not my brother scented spies in the woods?"

The Delaware chief, whose Indian name meant "The Hard Heart," forgot the sternness that gave him the name. He grew friendly.

"There have been strange moccasins about my camp," he said. "They have been tracked into my lodges."

"Did not my brother beat out the dogs?" asked the Fox, who now knew that those he sought were there.

"It would not do," answered Hard Heart. "The stranger is always welcome to the Delaware."

"Yes, the stranger is," said the Fox, "but not the spy."

"Are the women of the English sent out as spies?" asked the Delaware.

"Did not the Huron say he took women in the battle at the Fort?"

"He did," replied the Fox, "and he told no lie. The English have sent out their scouts. They have been in my wigwams, but they found there no one to say welcome. Then they fled to the Delawares—'For,' say they, 'the Delawares are our friends; their minds are turned from their French father.'"

The Delawares felt this word. For in the war between France and England they had taken no side, although their villages were, some of them, in the French country of Canada. But they would not admit that they had deserted the French.

"Let my father look in my face," said Hard Heart; "he will see no change. It is true, my young men did not go out on the war-path; they had dreams for not doing so. But they love and venerate the great French chief."

"Will he think so when he hears that his greatest enemy is fed in the camp of his children? when he is told a bloody Englishman smokes at your fire? that the paleface who has slain so many of his friends goes in and out among the Delawares? Go! My great French father is not a fool!"

"Where is the Englishman that the Delawares fear?" returned the other. "Who has slain my young men? Who is the mortal enemy of my Great Father?"

"The Long Carbine!"

The Delaware warriors started at the well-known name of Hawkeye, the scout, betraying by their amazement that they now learned for the first time that one so dangerous to the Indian allies of France was within their power.

"What does my brother mean?" demanded Hard Heart, in a tone that, by its wonder, far exceeded the usual apathy of his race.

"A Huron never lies," returned the Fox coldly, leaning his head against the side of the lodge and drawing his slight robe across his tawny breast. "Let the Delawares count their prisoners; they will find one whose skin is neither red nor pale."

A long and musing pause succeeded. The chief consulted apart with his companions, and messengers were dispatched to collect certain others of the most distinguished men of the tribe.

As warrior after warrior dropped in, they were each made acquainted in turn with the important intelligence that the Fox had just communicated. The air of surprise, and the usual low, deep, guttural exclamation, were common to them all. The news spread from mouth to mouth, until the whole encampment became powerfully agitated. The women suspended their labors to catch such syllables as unguardedly fell from the lips of the consulting warriors. The boys deserted their sports, and, walking fearlessly among their fathers, looked up in curious admiration as they heard the brief exclamations of wonder they so freely expressed at the temerity of their hated foe. In short, every occupation was abandoned for the time, and all other pursuits seemed given up, in order that the tribe might freely indulge, after their own peculiar manner, in an open expression of feeling.

When the excitement had a little abated, the old men disposed themselves seriously to consider what the tribe ought to do in a case of so much delicacy and embarrassment. During all these movements, and in the midst of the general commotion, the Fox had not only kept his seat, but the very attitude he had first taken against the side of the lodge, where he remained without moving, and as if he did not care what the result might be. But he did.

The council of the Delawares was short. It was followed by a general assemblage of the whole tribe. The warriors began to collect in front of the encampment, and there the Fox went also, to see what would be done.

In a half-hour all the tribe, including even the women and children, were in the place of meeting. The morning sun, just climbing above the mountain tops, lighted up the scene. Fully a thousand Indians of the Delaware nation were now in assembly.

But so important a gathering only the oldest and most experienced chieftain could conduct. No one moved. All seemed to be waiting for one particular person to preside, and the looks of the whole throng seemed fixed upon a particular lodge, that was protected from the weather more carefully than any other.

Suddenly the door of this lodge parted, and every man, woman, and child rose from the ground and stood waiting.

Three old men came from the lodge; but one was very, very old. His form seemed bent with the weight of a hundred years and more. His dark, wrinkled countenance was in singular contrast with the long, white locks which floated on his shoulders, long, thick, and massive, as if it had been generations since his hair had been cut.

The dress of this patriarch—for such, considering his vast age, in conjunction with his relationship and influence with his people, he might very properly be called—was rich and imposing, though strictly after the simple fashions of the tribe. His robe was of the finest skins, which had been deprived of their fur in order to admit of a figured representation of various deeds in arms done in former years. His bosom was loaded with medals, some in massive silver, and one or two even in gold, gifts of various Christian rulers during the long period of his life. He also wore armlets, and bands above the ankles, of the latter precious metal. His head, on the whole of which the hair had been permitted to grow, the pursuits of war having so long been given up, was encircled by a sort of plated crown, which, in its turn, bore lesser and more glittering ornaments, that sparkled amid the glossy hues of three drooping ostrich feathers, dyed a deep black, in touching contrast to the color of his snow-white locks. His tomahawk was nearly hid in silver, and the handle of his knife shone like a horn of solid gold. So soon as the first hum of emotion and pleasure which the sudden appearance of this venerated individual created had a little subsided, the name of "Tamenund" was whispered from mouth to mouth. The Huron, Fox, had often heard the fame of this wise and just Delaware—a reputation that even proceeded so far as to bestow on him the rare gift of holding secret communion with the Great Spirit, and which has since transmitted his name, with some slight alteration, to the white usurpers of his ancient territory, under the name of "Tammany," the saint and sachem of the New York Indians.

The Huron chief, therefore, stepped eagerly out a little from the throng, to a spot whence he might catch a nearer glimpse of the features of the man whose decision was likely to produce so deep an influence on his own fortunes.

The old man's eyes were closed as he passed the Huron, and, leaning upon his two aged assistants, he walked slowly to the chief seat of council, and seated himself, like a father, in the center of his nation.

Then several of the younger warriors, at the command of a chief, left the crowd and went to the lodge in which the white prisoner-guests were kept.

In a few moments they returned, and with them came the prisoners who were the cause of all this stir and consultation of a nation—the sisters, Cora and Alice, Heyward, the soldier, and Hawkeye, the scout.

Cora stood foremost among the prisoners, entwining her arms in those of Alice in the tenderness of sisterly love. Notwithstanding the fearful and menacing array of savages on every side of her, no apprehension on her own account could prevent the noble-minded maiden from keeping her eyes fastened on the pale and anxious features of the trembling Alice. Close at their side stood Heyward, with an interest in both at this moment of intense uncertainty. Hawkeye had placed himself a little in the rear, with a deference to the superior rank of his companions that no similarity in the state of their present fortunes could induce him to forget. Uncas was not there.

When perfect silence was again restored, and after the usual long, impressive pause, one of the two aged chiefs who sat at the side of the patriarch arose, and demanded aloud, in very intelligible English, "Which of my prisoners is the Long Carbine?"

Neither Duncan nor the scout answered. The former, however, glanced his eyes around the dark and silent assembly, and recoiled a pace when they fell on the malignant visage of Huron Fox. He saw at once that this wily savage had some secret agency in their being thus summoned before the nation, and he determined to do all that he could to keep the Indian from carrying out his plans. He saw that Hawkeye's danger was great, and he made up his mind to aid him if he could. Before he could speak, however, the question was repeated, "Which is the Long Carbine?"

"Give us arms and try us," said Heyward. "We will soon show you to whom the name belongs."

"Are you the man?" exclaimed the Delaware, looking at the young soldier curiously. "What brought you to the camp of the Delawares?"

"My necessities," answered Heyward. "I came for food, shelter, and friends."

"It can not be," the old chief replied. "The woods are full of game; the head of a warrior needs no other shelter than a sky without clouds; and the Delawares are the enemies, and not the friends, of the English. Go! The mouth has spoken, the heart has said nothing."

Then Hawkeye spoke. He told them that he had not answered to the name of the Long Carbine because Killdeer was not a carbine, but a grooved rifle, and, besides, he did not allow any Mingo to give him a name when he had one of his own. "My father," he said, "named me Nathaniel; my friends, the Delawares, called me Hawkeye; and those are the names I answer to."

The eyes of all present, which had hitherto been gravely scanning the person of Duncan Heyward, were now turned, on the instant, toward the tall form of this new pretender to the distinguished name. It was in no degree remarkable that there should be found two who were willing to claim so great an honor, for impostors, though rare, were not unknown among the natives; but it was altogether material to the just and severe intentions of the Delawares that there should be no mistake in the matter. Some of their old men consulted together in private, and then, as it would seem, they determined to interrogate their visitor on the subject.

"My brother has said that a snake crept into the camp," said the chief to the Fox; "which is he?"

The Huron pointed to the scout.

"Will a wise Delaware believe the barking of a wolf?" exclaimed Heyward, still more confirmed in the evil intentions of his ancient enemy. "A dog never lies; but when was a wolf known to speak the truth?"

The eyes of the Fox flashed fire; but suddenly recollecting the necessity of maintaining his presence of mind, he turned away in silent disdain, well assured that the sagacity of the Indians would not fail to extract the real merits of the point in controversy. He was not deceived; for, after another short consultation, the wary Delaware turned to him again, and expressed the determination of the chiefs, though in the most considerate language.

"My brother has been called a liar," he said, "and his friends are angry. They will show that he has spoken the truth. Give my prisoners guns, and let them prove which is the man."

Guns were handed to the two friendly opponents, and while Heyward smiled to think of himself trying to stand a shooting match with Hawkeye, he determined to keep up the deception until he knew what the Fox meant to do.

So he fired at the little earthen vessel which had been set as a mark for them, and came so near that even Hawkeye nodded his head, as if to say that the soldier had done better than he expected.

Then one of the young Indians touched the scout's arm. "Can the paleface beat that?" he asked.

"Yes, Huron!" exclaimed the scout, raising his short rifle in his right hand, and shaking it at the Fox with as much ease as if it were a reed; "yes, Huron, I could strike you now, and no power on earth could prevent the deed. The soaring hawk is not more certain of the dove than I am this moment of you, did I choose to send a bullet to your heart. Why should I not? Why? Because it is not right or manly, and I might draw down the evil on tender and innocent heads. If you know such a being as God, thank him, therefore, in your inward soul—for you have reason!"

The flushed countenance, angry eyes, and swelling figure of the scout, produced a sensation of secret awe in all that heard him. The Delawares held their breath in expectation; but the Fox himself, even while he distrusted the forbearance of his enemy, remained immovable and calm, where he stood wedged in by the crowd, as one who grew to the spot.

"Beat it!" repeated the young Delaware at the elbow of the scout.

"Beat what, fool?—what?" exclaimed Hawkeye, still flourishing the weapon angrily above his head, though his eye no longer sought the person of the Fox.

"If the white man is the warrior he pretends," said the aged chief, "let him strike nigher to the mark."

The scout laughed aloud,—a noise that produced the startling effect of an unnatural sound on Heyward,—then, dropping the piece heavily into his extended left hand, it was discharged, apparently by the shock, driving the fragments of the vessel into the air, and scattering them on every side. Almost at the same instant the rattling sound of the rifle was heard, as he suffered it to fall contemptuously to the earth.

The first impression of so strange a scene was engrossing admiration. Then a low, but increasing, murmur ran through the multitude, and finally swelled into sounds that denoted a lively opposition in the sentiments of the spectators.

Some said it was a good shot; others said it was only by accident that it had struck the mark.

And Heyward said, still hoping to shield Hawkeye by his method of denying to the scout the name and fame he had secured:

"That was only chance."

"Chance!" cried Hawkeye, now greatly worked up, and determined to show that he was the rightful owner of the name of the Long Carbine, and not understanding Heyward's plan to save him by insisting that he himself was the man. "Chance! Does yonder lying Huron think it chance, too? Give him a gun, and place us face to face, without cover or dodge, and let us settle the question as to who can shoot the best."

"Of course, he is a liar," Heyward returned, coolly. "You know he said that you are the Long Carbine."

Hawkeye was now roused to a stubborn determination to prove his right to the name. He seized the rifle, and even the Fox could not longer doubt the result.

"Now let it be proved, in the face of all the Delawares, which is the better man. Do you see that gourd hanging against yonder tree, Major? If you are a marksman, let me see you break the shell."

Heyward saw the gourd a hundred yards away, and, taking aim very carefully, fired.

He was bound to make a good shot. Had his life depended on the result, he could not have been more careful in his aim.

He fired; and three or four young Indians, who sprang forward at the report, cried that the ball was in the tree a very little to one side of the gourd.

The warriors returned an expression of commendation, and then looked inquiringly at the soldier's rival.

"It may do for your regiment," said Hawkeye, laughing once more, in his own silent, heartfelt manner; "but had my gun often turned so much from the true line, many a marten, whose skin is now in a lady's muff, would still be in the woods; ay, and many a bloody Mingo, who has departed to his final account, would be playing his games to this very day between the provinces. I hope the squaw who owns the gourd has more of them in her wigwam, for this will never hold water again!"

The scout had shaken his priming and cocked his piece while speaking; and, as he ended, he threw back a foot and slowly raised the muzzle from the earth; the motion was steady, uniform, and in one direction. When on a perfect level, it remained for a single moment without tremor or variation, as though both man and rifle were carved in stone. During that stationary instant, it poured forth its contents in a bright, glancing sheet of flame. Again the young Indians bounded forward, but their hurried search and disappointed looks announced that no traces of the bullet were to be seen.

"Go!" said the old chief to the scout, in a tone of strong disgust. "Thou art a wolf in the skin of a dog. I will talk to the 'Long Rifle' of the English."

"Ah! had I that piece which furnished the name you use, I would obligate myself to cut the thong and drop the gourd without breaking it!" returned Hawkeye, perfectly undisturbed by the other's manner. "Fools! If you would find the bullet of a sharpshooter in these woods, you must look *in* the object, and not around it!"

The Indian youths instantly understood what he meant, for this time he spoke in the Delaware tongue, and, tearing the gourd from the tree, they held it on high with an exulting shout. There was a hole in the bottom, which had been cut by the bullet after passing through the usual opening in the centre of its upper side.

A great shout broke from all the Indians. There was no longer any doubt. They knew now who was the Long Carbine,—who the dreaded enemy of the Huron.

"Why did you wish to stop my ears?" the Delaware chief asked Heyward. "Are the Delawares fools, that they could not know the young panther from the cat? Speak, brother," he added, turning to the Fox; "the Delawares listen."

Then the Fox, standing in the center of the circle, and directly before the prisoners, began to speak.

He spoke of the difference between the red man and the white; of the greed, and tyranny, and rapacity of the white man; of the greatness of the Indians until the white man had come to their destruction; of the power of the Delawares in the old days; of their deeds, their glory, their happiness, their losses, their defeats, their misery; of his great reverence and love for them, even though he came of another tribe and nation. Then he stopped.

"I have done," he said. "My tongue is still, for my heart is glad. I listen."

Old Tamenund, or Tammany, the aged chief of all the Delawares, said:

"Who speaks of things gone? Why tell the Delawares of good that is past? Better thank the Great Spirit for what remains to us. What does the Huron want?"

"Justice," replied the Fox, standing before the chief. "His prisoners are with his brothers, and he comes for his own."

Tamenund turned his head toward one of his supporters, and listened to the short explanation the man gave. Then, facing the applicant, he regarded him a moment with a deep attention; after which he said, in a low and reluctant voice:

"Justice is the law of the Great Spirit. My children, give the stranger food. Then, Huron, take thine own and depart."

On the delivery of this solemn judgment, the patriarch seated himself, and closed his eyes again, as if better pleased with the images of his own ripened experience than with the visible objects of the world. Against such a decree there was no Delaware sufficiently hardy to murmur, much less oppose himself. The words were barely uttered when four or five of the younger warriors, stepping behind Heyward and the scout, passed thongs so dexterously and rapidly around their arms as to hold them both in instant bondage. The former was too much engrossed with the half-fainting Alice to be aware of their intentions before they were executed; and the latter, who considered even the hostile tribes of the Delawares a superior race of Indians, submitted without resistance. Perhaps, however, the manner of the scout would not have been so passive had he fully comprehended the language in which the preceding dialogue had been conducted.

The Fox cast a look of triumph around the whole assembly before he proceeded to the execution of his purpose. Perceiving that the men were unable to offer any resistance, he turned his looks on Cora. She met his gaze with an eye so calm and firm that his resolution wavered. Then, turning swiftly, he caught up Alice from the arms of the warrior against whom she leaned, and, beckoning Heyward to follow, he motioned for the encircling crowd to open. But Cora, instead of obeying the impulse he had expected, rushed to the feet of the patriarch, Tamenund, and, raising her voice, exclaimed aloud:

"Just and venerable Delaware, on thy wisdom and power we lean for mercy! Be deaf to yonder artful and remorseless monster, who poisons thy ears with falsehoods to feed his thirst for blood. Thou that hast lived long, and that hast seen the evil of the world, shouldst know how to temper its calamities to the miserable."

The old man opened his eyes slowly and looked at the queenly girl.

"Who art thou?" he said.

Cora told him that she was a woman of the hated English race, but begged for mercy, for release, for permission simply to depart, and not to be delivered to the cruel Huron Fox.

Then she said, "Is Tamenund a father?"

The old man looked out upon the people, who revered him as their chief ruler. Then he smiled benignantly.

"Of a nation," he answered.

"For myself," said Cora, "I ask nothing. Like thee and thine, venerable chief," she continued, pressing her hands on her heart, while her head drooped until her burning cheeks were nearly concealed in the maze of dark, glossy tresses that fell in disorder upon her shoulders, "the curse of my ancestors has fallen heavily on their child. But yonder is one who has never known the weight of Heaven's displeasure until now. She is the daughter of an old and failing man, whose days are near their close. She has many, very many, to love her and delight in her; and she is too good, much too precious, to become the victim of that villain."

"I know that the palefaces are a proud and hungry race. I know that they claim not only to have the earth, but that the meanest of their color is better than the sachems of the redman. The dogs and crows of their tribes," continued the earnest old chieftain, without heeding the wounded spirit of his listener, whose head was nearly crushed to the earth in shame, as he proceeded, "would bark and caw before they would take a woman to their wigwams whose blood was not of the color of snow. But let them not boast before the face of the Great Spirit too loud. They entered the land at the rising, and may yet go off at the setting sun. I have often seen the locusts strip the leaves from the trees, but the season of blossoms has always come again."

"It is so," said Cora, drawing a long breath, as if reviving from a trance, raising her face, and shaking back her shining veil, with a kindling eye that contradicted the death-like paleness of her countenance; "but why—it is not permitted us to inquire. There is yet one of thine own people who has not been brought before thee; before thou lettest the Huron depart in triumph, hear him speak."

Observing Tamenund to look about him doubtingly, one of his companions said:

"It is a snake—a redskin in the pay of the English. We keep him for the torture."

"Let him come in," the old chief commanded.

There was a pause; then the circle opened, and Uncas stood before him, his eye fixed on the patriarch.

"With what tongue does the prisoner speak?" he asked.

"Like his fathers," Uncas replied; "with the tongue of a Delaware."

At this sudden and unexpected answer, a low, fierce yell ran through the multitude that might not inaptly be compared to the growl of the lion, as his choler is first awakened—a fearful omen of the weight of his future anger. The effect was equally strong on the sage, though differently exhibited. He passed a hand before his eyes, as if to exclude the least evidence of so shameful a spectacle, while he repeated, in his low, guttural tones, the words he had just heard.

"A Delaware! I have lived to see the tribes of the Lenape driven from their council-fires, and scattered, like broken herds of deer, among the hills of the Iroquois! I have seen the hatchets of a strange people sweep woods from the valleys, that the winds of heaven had spared! The beasts that run on the mountains and the birds that fly above the trees have I seen living in the wigwams of men; but never before have I found a Delaware so base as to creep, like a poisonous serpent, into the camps of his nation."

"The singing birds have opened their bills," returned Uncas, in the softest notes of his own musical voice; "and Tamenund has heard their song."

The sage started, and bent his head aside, as if to catch the fleeting sounds of some passing melody.

"Does Tamenund dream?" he exclaimed. "What voice is at his ear? Have the winters gone backward? Will summer come again to the children of the Lenape?"

A solemn and respectful silence succeeded this incoherent burst from the lips of the Delaware prophet. His people readily construed his unintelligible language into one of those mysterious conferences he was believed to hold so frequently with a superior intelligence, and they awaited the issue of the revelation in awe. After a patient pause, however, one of the aged men spoke.

"The false Delaware trembles lest he should hear the words of Tamenund," he said. "He is a hound that howls when the English show him a trail."

"Delaware," said the aged chief and father of his tribe, "thou art not worthy of thy name. He who deserts his tribe is a traitor. He is yours, my children. Deal justly by him."

It was the sentence of Uncas. At once a cry of vengeance burst from all the nation, and a chief proclaimed, in a high voice, that the captive was condemned to endure the dreadful trial of torture by fire.

At once they prepared for the sacrifice. But the prisoners were deeply moved by the sad fate of their friend, Uncas. Heyward struggled madly with his captors; Hawkeye began to look around him, earnestly and hopefully, as if he expected aid of some sort for his friend, while Cora again threw herself at the feet of the patriarch, a suppliant for mercy.

Throughout the whole of these trying moments, Uncas had alone preserved his serenity. He looked on the preparations with a steady eye, and, when the tormentors came to seize him, he met them with a firm and upright attitude. One among them, if possible more fierce and savage than his fellows, seized the hunting-shirt of the young warrior, and, at a single effort, tore it from his body. Then, with a yell of frantic pleasure, he leaped toward his unresisting victim, and prepared to lead him to the stake. But, at that moment, when he appeared most a stranger to the feelings of humanity, the purpose of the savage was arrested as suddenly as if some unknown power had appeared in the behalf of Uncas. The eyeballs of the Delaware seemed to start from their sockets ; his mouth opened, and his whole form became frozen in an attitude of amazement. Raising his hand, with a slow and regulated motion, he pointed with a finger to the bosom of the captive. His companions crowded about him in wonder, and every eye was, like his own, fastened intently on the figure of a small tortoise beautifully tattooed on the breast of the prisoner, in a bright blue tint.

For a single instant Uncas enjoyed his triumph, calmly smiling on the scene. Then, motioning the crowd away, with a high and haughty sweep of his arm, he advanced in front of the nation with the air of a king, and spoke in a voice louder than the murmur of admiration that ran through the multitude:

"Men of the Lenni Lenape!" he said, "my race upholds the earth! Your feeble tribe stands on my shell! What fire that a Delaware can light would burn the child of my fathers?" he added, pointing proudly to the simple blazonry on his skin. "The blood that came from such a stock would smother your flames! My race is the grandfather of nations!"

"Who art thou?" demanded Tamenund, rising at the startling tones he heard, more than at any meaning conveyed by the language of the prisoner.

"Uncas, the son of Chingachgook," answered the captive, modestly turning from the nation, and bending his head in reverence to the other's character and years; "a son of the great chief, clan of the Turtle."

"The hour of Tamenund is nigh!" exclaimed the sage; "the day is come, at last, to the night! I thank the Great Spirit that one is here to fill my place at the council-fire. Uncas, the child of Uncas, is found! Let the eyes of a dying eagle gaze on the rising sun!"

The youth stepped lightly, but proudly, on the platform, where he became visible to the whole agitated and wondering multitude. Tamenund held him long at the length of his arm, and read every turn in the fine lineaments of his countenance, with the untiring gaze of one who recalled days of happiness.

"Is Tamenund a boy?" at length the bewildered prophet exclaimed. "Have I dreamed of so many snows—that my people were scattered like floating sands—of the white men, more plenty than the leaves on the trees? The arrow of Tamenund would not frighten the fawn; his arm is withered like the branch of a dead oak; the snail would be swifter in the race; yet is Uncas before him as they went to battle against the palefaces! Uncas, the panther of his tribe, the eldest son of the Lenape, the wisest sagamore of the Mohicans! Tell me, ye Delawares, has Tamenund been a sleeper for a hundred winters?"

The calm and deep silence which succeeded these words sufficiently announced the awful reverence with which his people received the communication of the patriarch. None dared to answer, though all listened in breathless expectation of what might follow. Uncas, however, looking in his face with the fondness and veneration of a favored child, presumed on his own high and acknowledged rank to reply:

"Four warriors of his race have lived, and died," he said, "since Uncas, the friend of Tamenund, led his people in battle. The blood of the Turtle has been in many chiefs, but all have gone except Chingachgook, and Uncas, his son."

"It is true," said the old man. "Our wise men have often said that two warriors of the unchanged race were in the hills of the English. Why have their seats at the council-fires of the Delawares been so long empty?"

"Once," said Uncas, "we were rulers and sagamores. But when the Delawares gave way before the white men, we, the Mohicans, said, 'We are children of the sea. Here will we stay until the Great Spirit says, Come!' Such, Delawares, is the belief of the children of the Turtle. We are the last of the Mohicans. But our eyes are on the rising, and not on the setting, sun. It is enough."

The Delawares listened with respect. Uncas watched them carefully. Then, when he saw that he was honored by them all, he thought of his white friends. Looking over the throng, he first saw Hawkeye, bound and a prisoner.

He stepped to the side of the scout, and, with a quick and angry stroke of his knife, cut him loose; then, taking him by the hand, he led him to the feet of Tamenund.

"Father," he said, "look at this paleface—a just man and the friend of the Delawares."

"What name is his?"

"We call him Hawkeye," Uncas replied, "for his sight never fails. The

Mingos—the Hurons—know him better by the death he gives their warriors. They call him the Long Carbine."

"The Long Carbine!" exclaimed Tamenund, regarding the scout sternly. "My son has not done well to call him friend."

"I call him so who so proves himself," returned the young chief, calmly. "If Uncas is welcome among the Delawares, then is Hawkeye with his friends."

"The paleface has struck down my young men," said the old chief. "For this is his name great."

Then Hawkeye spoke.

"That I have slain the Mingos," he said, "I am no man to deny, even at their own council-fires; but that, knowingly, my hand has ever harmed a Delaware, is not true, for I am friendly to them and all that belongs to their nation."

A low exclamation of applause passed among the warriors, who exchanged looks with each other like men that first began to perceive their error.

"Where is the Huron?" demanded Tamenund. "Has he stopped my ears?"

The Fox, whose feelings during that scene in which Uncas had triumphed may be much better imagined than described, answered to the call by stepping boldly in front of the patriarch.

"The just Tamenund," he said, "will not keep what a Huron has lent."

"Tell me, son of my brother," returned the sage, avoiding the dark countenance of the Fox, and turning gladly to the more ingenuous features of Uncas, "has the stranger a conqueror's right over you?"

"He has none. The panther may get into snares set by the women; but he is strong, and knows how to leap through them."

"The Long Carbine?"

"Laughs at the Mingos. Go, Huron, ask your squaws the color of a bear."

"The stranger and the white maiden that came into my camp together?"

"Should journey on an open path."

"And the woman that the Huron left with my warriors?" Uncas made no reply.

"And the woman that the Mingo has brought into my camp?" repeated Tamenund, gravely.

"She is mine," cried the Fox, shaking his hand in triumph at Uncas. "Mohican, you know that she is mine."

"My son is silent," said Tamenund, endeavoring to read the expression of the face that the youth turned from him in sorrow.

"It is so," was the low answer.

A short and impressive pause succeeded, during which it could be seen that the tribe, reluctantly, admitted the Fox's claim. Then Tamenund spoke:

"Huron, depart," he said.

"As he came, just Tamenund?" demanded the cruel Fox.

"Huron, would you take one against her wishes to your wigwam?" said the old chief. "An unwilling maiden makes an unhappy wigwam. Take you the wampum and our love."

"Nothing but what I brought will I take," declared the Fox.

"Then," said Tamenund, "depart with thine own. The Great Spirit forbids that a Delaware should be unjust."

The Fox strode to Cora's side and grasped her by the arm. The Delawares fell back in silence, and Cora prepared to submit to her fate.

But Duncan Heyward sprang to her side. "Huron, have mercy!" he said. "I will give you enough as ransom to make you richer than any of your people were ever yet known to be."

"I am a redskin; I want not the beads of the palefaces."

"Gold, silver, powder, lead—all that a warrior needs shall be in thy wigwam; all that becomes the greatest chief."

"No," cried the Fox, violently shaking the hand which grasped the unresisting arm of Cora; "I have my revenge!"

"Mighty ruler of Providence!" exclaimed Heyward, clasping his hands together in agony; "can this be suffered? To you, just Tamenund, I appeal for mercy."

"The words of the Delaware are said," returned the sage, closing his eyes and dropping back into his seat, alike wearied with his mental and his bodily exertions. "Men speak not twice."

"That a chief should not misspend his time in unsaying what has once been spoken, is wise and reasonable," said Hawkeye, motioning to Duncan to be silent; "but it is also prudent in every warrior to consider well before he strikes his tomahawk into the head of his prisoner. Huron, I love you not; nor can I say that any Mingo has ever received much favor at my hands. It is fair to conclude that, if this war does not soon end, many more of your warriors will meet me in the woods. Put it to your judgment, then, whether you would prefer taking such a prisoner as that into your encampment, or one like myself, who am a man that it would greatly rejoice your nation to see with naked hands."

"Will the 'Long Rifle' give his life for the woman?" demanded the Fox, hesitatingly; for he had already made a motion toward quitting the place with his victim.

"No, no; I said not so much as that," returned Hawkeye, drawing back with suitable discretion when he noted the eagerness with which the Fox listened to his proposal. "It would be an unequal exchange to give a warrior, in the prime of his age and usefulness, for the best woman on the frontiers. I might consent to go into winter quarters now—at least six weeks afore the leaves will turn—on condition you will release the maiden."

The Huron shook his head, and made an impatient sign for the crowd to open.

"Well, then," added the scout, with the musing air of a man who had not half made up his mind, "I will throw Killdeer into the bargain. Take the word of an experienced hunter, the piece has not its equal atween the provinces."

Still the Fox disdained to reply, continuing his efforts to disperse the crowd.

"Perhaps," added the scout, losing his dissembled coolness, exactly in proportion as the other manifested an indifference to the exchange, "if I should condition to teach your young men the real virtue of the we'pon, it would smooth the little difference in our judgments."

The Huron fiercely ordered the Delawares, who still lingered in a deep belt around him, in hopes he would listen to the amicable proposal, to open his path, threatening, by the glance of his eye, another appeal to the infallible justice of their "prophet."

"What is ordered must sooner or later arrive," continued Hawkeye, turning with a sad and humble look to Uncas. "The varlet knows his advantage, and will keep it. God bless you, boy; you have found friends among your natural kin, and I hope they will prove as true as some you have met who had no Indian cross. As for me, sooner or later I must die; it is therefore fortunate there are but few to make my death-howl. After all, it is likely the imps would have managed to master my scalp, so a day or two will make no great difference in the everlasting reckoning of time. God bless you," added the rugged woodsman, bending his head aside ; and then, instantly changing its direction again, with a wistful look toward the youth, "I loved both you and your father, Uncas, though our skins are not of the same color and our ways are different. Think of me when on a lucky trail, boy ; you'll find the rifle in the place we hid it. And hark you, Uncas, use it freely on the Mingos ; it may soften your grief at my loss and ease your own mind. Now, Huron, I accept your offer. Release the woman. I am your prisoner."

At this generous proposition a murmur of approval at the manliness of the sacrifice went through the throng. But the Fox paused only a moment. Then, looking at Cora, he said:

"The Fox has but one mind. Come," and he put his hand on the shoulder of the captive girl. "A Huron does not talk twice. We will go."

"Take off your hand," said Cora. "I will follow you, though it is to my death. Hawkeye, from my soul I thank you. Your generous offer is of no avail. But neither could I accept it. Serve me even more, I pray you, by saving my sister and returning her to my father. Would that I could hear but one last word from his dear lips. Duncan, good-by. Be faithful and kind to Alice."

Then she kissed her unconscious sister, a long, deep, loving kiss, and, turning proudly to her captor, said, "Now, sir, if it please you, I will follow. Go on."

"Go then, brute," cried Heyward, "Go, if you will. These Delawares have their laws, which forbid them to detain you. But—I am not held by their laws. Go, if you wish, and go at once."

The Huron listened to Heyward's threat to follow, at first with a fierce display of joy, and then with a look of cunning coldness.

"The woods are open," he was content with answering, "the 'Open Hand' can come."

"Hold," cried Hawkeye, seizing Duncan by the arm, and detaining him by violence; "you know not the craft of the imp. He would lead you to an ambushment, and your death——"

JUST THEN, DOWN FROM THE HEIGHT, STRAIGHT UPON THE HURON, LEAPED UNCAS.

"Huron," interrupted Uncas, who, submissive to the stern customs of his people, had been an attentive and grave listener to all that passed; "Huron, the justice of the Delawares comes from the Great Spirit. Look at the sun. He is now in the upper branches of the hemlock. Your path is short and open. When the sun is seen above the trees, there will be men on your trail."

"I hear a crow!" exclaimed the Fox, with a taunting laugh. "Go," he added, shaking his hand at the crowd, which had slowly opened to admit his passage—"where are the petticoats of the Delawares? Let them send their arrows and their guns to the Wyandots; they shall have venison to eat and corn to hoe. Dogs, rabbits, thieves—I spit on you!"

His parting gibes were listened to in a dead, boding silence, and, with these biting words in his mouth, the triumphant Huron passed unmolested into the forest, followed by his passive captive, and protected by the inviolable laws of Indian hospitality.

For a while all was still in the council of the Delawares. Then, as the Huron and his prisoner disappeared in the forest and the law of their hospitality had been fulfilled, the reaction came.

"Vengeance!" was the cry. "Death to the wicked Huron."

The village was in a great stir. The women and children, and the patriarch Tamenund, were sent away or conducted to their lodges, and then all the chiefs and braves of the Lenni Lenape, as the Delawares called their nation in its broadest and loftiest name, gathered for the war-dance and the war-trail.

Uncas, the Mohican, whom the mark of the Turtle and the favor of Tamenund had put into such a prominent position, led the war-dance, clothed only in his girdle and leggings, and with one-half of his face painted in deadly black. He chanted the war-song, he struck the war-post with his tomahawk, he raised his voice in the shout of his battle-cry. A hundred eager young warriors leaped from the ground at the cry, and, following their leader's action, encircled the war-post with their dance and song, and splintered it with their gleaming tomahawks.

Then, when the sun stood above the tops of the hemlocks, Uncas saw that the truce of hospitality promised to the Huron was over, and he told his warriors at once to prepare for the warpath.

Hawkeye had sent an Indian boy to the place where his guns had been hidden, and now held once again his beloved Killdeer. He had also returned to Uncas the Mohican's own rifle. Then Uncas told the Delawares of the strength in war of the scout and of the command that Duncan Heyward held in the army of the English. To Hawkeye was given the command of twenty active, skilful Delaware forest hunters. But Heyward declined a command, and said he preferred to act as a volunteer by the side of the scout. Uncas himself led upon the war-path two hundred warriors and their chiefs.

Just as they were ready to start, who should appear on the scene but David, the singing-master. He said that the Hurons were making so much noise and "ungodly revelry," as he called their war-songs and dances, that he had fled to the Delawares in search of peace.

He did not find it among them; but he did find his friends. He told them that the Hurons were now hidden in the forest in wait for the Delawares, and that the Fox, after placing Cora in the cave they knew of, was himself at the head of the Hurons, "raging," so David expressed it, "like a raging wolf."

Then Hawkeye determined to call to his assistance Chingachgook, the sagamore, and Colonel Munro, and with his twenty men to strike the right of the Hurons. At the same time Uncas, with his force, was to assail them in front, and, after driving them in, they would unite forces and attack the village, release Cora, and, by a swift and skilful dash, defeat the whole Huron force.

This was carried out as agreed. There was fierce and bitter forest fighting between the hostile tribes. Many Delawares fell; many Hurons were killed. But Hawkeye led his men resistlessly against the foe, and Uncas, with his warriors, pressed them so hard that at last the Hurons broke and ran, except one little knot of desperate fighting men, who, under the lead of the Fox, backed slowly, fighting, up the rocky hillside.

Step by step they were forced back, with Uncas in the lead of the pursuers, hunting the baffled Fox like a hound upon the stag.

One by one the companions of the Huron were killed; he stood alone against the vengeance of Uncas and the pursuit of Hawkeye, Heyward, and David. For the poor singing-master was as determined to assist and save Cora as were the Indian, and the scout, and the soldier.

Suddenly the Fox disappeared into the mouth of the cave in which Heyward had once discovered Alice, and from which he had saved her.

Not stopping to consider, the pursuers leaped in after the retreating Hurons. Far ahead in the gloomy passages they could get, now and then, glimpses of the fleeing Hurons. But when, on a path that seemed leading up the mountain, they caught the flutter of a white dress, Heyward gave a shout.

"Cora! It is Cora!" he cried.

"Cora! Cora!" echoed Uncas, and bounded forward like a deer.

"Courage, courage," cried the scout in his cheeriest voice. "We are coming."

But the Hurons knew the passages better than did their pursuers, and were out of the cave before them, although with Cora to carry they could not make the speed in flight that would save them.

Brought to bay, with the Delaware and the white men almost upon him, the Fox turned, and, waiting but a brief moment, lifted his knife as if to kill the girl. Just then, down the height, straight upon the Huron, leaped Uncas, and, as he did so, another Huron, who had fled with the Fox, buried his knife in Cora's heart.

The Fox sprang upon Uncas as he fell, and plunged his weapon in his back, but the Mohican leaped to his feet and struck down the murderer of Cora with the last of his failing strength. Then he swayed and fell, while the Fox, driving his knife once more into the bosom of Uncas, himself fell dead over the precipice, shot down by the avenging rifle of Hawkeye, the friend of Uncas.

The battle was over. The Delawares were victors, but at what a cost: Uncas had fallen, Cora was dead, and the cruel Fox, instead of being a prisoner in their hands for punishment, had fallen in the fight.

Cora, wrapped in Indian robes, was buried in the forest, while her aged father stood beside her bowed in grief.

But Uncas was arrayed for the grave in full Indian fashion, and in the most gorgeous ornaments that the wealth of the tribe could furnish.

At last, the long funeral rites were over.

Colonel Munro, with his remaining daughter, Alice, and Heyward and David accompanying them, turned from Cora's grave toward the post of the English army; and so all the white men except Hawkeye passed from the eyes of the Delawares and were lost in the depths of the forest.

Deserted by all of his color, Hawkeye returned to the spot where his own sympathies led him with a force that no ideal bond of union could bestow. He was just in time to catch a parting look of the features of Uncas, whom the Delawares were already inclosing in his last vestments of skins. They paused to permit the longing and lingering gaze of the sturdy woodsman, and, when it was ended, the body was enveloped, never to be unclosed again. Then the whole nation was collected about the temporary grave of the chief—temporary, because it was proper that, at some future day, his bones should rest among those of his own people.

The Indian service was over. Then Chingachgook, the sagamore, the father of Uncas, stood before them.

"Why do my brothers mourn?" he said, regarding the dark race of dejected warriors by whom he was environed; "why do my daughters weep? That a young man has gone to the happy hunting-grounds? That a chief has filled his time with honor? He was good; he was dutiful; he was brave. Who can deny it? The Great Spirit had need of such a warrior, and he has called him away. As for me, the son and the father of Uncas, I am a blazed pine in a clearing of the palefaces. My race has gone from the shores of the salt lake and the hills of the Delawares. But who can say that the serpent of his tribe has forgotten his wisdom? I am alone—"

"No, no!" cried Hawkeye, who had been gazing with a yearning look at the rigid features of his friend, with something like his own self-command, but whose philosophy could endure no longer. "No, sagamore, not alone. The gifts of our colors may be different, but God has so placed us as to journey in the same path. I have no kin, and, I may also say, like you, no people. He was your son, and a redskin by nature; and it may be that your blood was nearer—but, if ever I forget the lad who has so often fou't at my side in the war, and slept at my side in peace, may He who made us all, whatever may be our color or our gifts, forget me! The boy has left us for a time; but, sagamore, you are not alone."

Chingachgook grasped the hand that, in the warmth of feeling, the scout had stretched across the fresh earth, and in that attitude of friendship these two sturdy and intrepid woodsmen bowed their heads together, while scalding tears fell to their feet, watering the grave of Uncas like drops of falling rain.

In the midst of the awful stillness with which such a burst of feeling, coming, as it did, from the two most renowned warriors of that region, was received, Tamenund lifted his voice to disperse the multitude.

"It is enough," he said. "Go, children of the Lenape; the anger of the Great Spirit is not done. Why should Tamenund stay? The palefaces are masters of the earth; the time of the redmen has not come again. My day has been too long. In the morning I saw the children of the Great Turtle, strong and happy. The night has come; yet have I lived to see the close of a mighty race,—Uncas, the last of the Mohicans."

PATHFINDER SHOOTS AT THE TARGET.

THE PATHFINDER

A TALE OF THE THOUSAND ISLANDS.

BY JAMES FENIMORE COOPER.

MANY years ago, a girl named Mabel Dunham was traveling to join her father. He was a soldier in a fort on Lake Ontario, one of the great fresh-water lakes that lie between New York and Canada.

Mabel's mother was dead, and her father had sent for her at the East to join him at the Fort. At the time of this story, almost all the great New York State, except along the Hudson River, was a wilderness—beautiful lakes, broad rivers, splendid mountains, but only inhabited by a few settlers, by soldiers, hunters, and Indians. The French, who lived in Canada, were all the time trying to get control of all the land on both sides of the great lakes, and were stirring up the Indians to be on their side, and against the English soldiers and settlers in New York.

So a journey from New York City to the Fort on Lake Ontario was through great forests and among savage Indians. It was full of danger and adventure, and only a brave girl could enjoy it. But Mabel Dunham was a soldier's daughter, and as brave as she was pretty. She was traveling in the care of her uncle, a regular old sea-water sailor. His name was Cap, and he did not think much of dry land, or woods, or rivers, while, as for the fresh-water lakes he had heard about, he called them "wash-tubs," and said no one could ever be in danger on them. To him there was nothing like the ocean, and all his talk was sea-talk.

They had been guided through the forests by an Indian. He was of the Tuscarora tribe, and his name was Arrowhead; his wife, whose name was June, was with him.

As Mabel, and Cap, and Arrowhead, and June were going through the for-

THE PATHFINDER.

est, they met at last, at a point agreed upon, the guides who were to take them the rest of the way.

The chief of these was a hunter and scout whose name was Natty Bumpo, but whom the soldiers called Pathfinder, because he never lost his way, and always knew just where the path he was traveling led to. So this made him a splendid guide.

THE THREE WHITE MEN SHOOTING THE RAPIDS.

With him was a Mohican Indian, his companion and friend on many a hunt, named Chingachgook, and a young man who was the captain of a very smart brig, or cutter, called the "Scud," one of the swiftest sailing vessels on Lake Ontario. The sailor's name was Jasper Western, and he was just as good in a canoe on the river as in his cutter on the lake.

They had many perilous adventures in the woods and on the river before they reached the Fort on the lake. At one time the three white men were nearly wrecked while shooting the rapids in the Oswego River. Arrowhead and his wife deserted them, and the hostile Indians called the Iroquois very nearly captured them. Indeed, Chingachgook was overcome by them after a terrible combat in the river, where he and Jasper were endeavoring to secure their canoe, but Pathfinder was a great guide, and brought them safely out of every danger, while Jasper looked carefully after Mabel, and at last they reached the Fort on the lake in safety, and Mabel was in the arms of the father whom she had not seen for years.

Sergeant Dunham, Mabel's father, was a grim and crusty old soldier. He had a good, kind heart, and loved his daughter dearly. But he had always been a soldier, and his ways were those of a man accustomed to obeying and being obeyed.

Mabel was such a pretty girl that all the soldiers in the Fort fell in love with her. But none of them loved her so dearly as did the sailor, Jasper Western, who, in their long and perilous journey to the lake, had seen what a good, brave, gentle girl she was. But he was a little afraid of Sergeant Dunham, and, as he was a modest, quiet, young fellow, he did not dare to tell Mabel's father that he loved the sergeant's daughter.

Sergeant Dunham, it seems, thought a great deal of Pathfinder, and believed he was just the one to make a kind husband and a good protector for Mabel. So he did not pay much attention to young Jasper Western, but he did talk to Pathfinder and tell him that he was just the man he desired as the husband of his daughter. But Mabel knew nothing about this.

Cap and Pathfinder were good friends, but could never agree, because one loved the ocean and the other the woods, and each claimed his choice the best. Now, Cap would not believe that Jasper, who was only a fresh-water sailor, was much of a sailor anyway, and he did not hesitate to tell him so.

They were soon to have a chance to prove whether this was so or not, for Major Duncan, the commander of the fort, decided to send some of his soldiers to take the place of others in a smaller fort on the St. Lawrence—the great river that leads from Lake Ontario to the Atlantic Ocean. Sergeant Dunham was to lead with the party, and as it was to be a stay of a month or more, he determined to take Mabel with him.

They were to sail to the St. Lawrence on Jasper Western's cutter, the "Scud." Pathfinder and Cap were to be of the party, and Lieutenant Muir, one of Major Duncan's assistants, went, too—not in command, but as a volunteer. Lieutenant Muir was a widower, who was also in love with Mabel, but the girl would not listen to his suit. He thought, however, that this trip would give him the chance to plead his cause.

So here they were all to be together on the little brig,—Mabel Dunham, and the three men, each of whom either wished to be or was selected to be her husband—Lieutenant Muir, Pathfinder, and Jasper Western. But Mabel liked Jasper best.

The embarkation of so small a party was a matter of no great delay or embarrassment. The whole force confided to the care of Sergeant Dunham consisted of but ten privates and two non-commissioned officers, though Mr.

Muir was to accompany the expedition as a volunteer, and some duty connected with his own department, as had been arranged between him and his commander, was the avowed object. To these must be added the Pathfinder and Cap, with Jasper and his subordinates, one of whom was a boy. The males of the entire party, consequently, consisted of less than twenty men and a lad of fourteen. Mabel and the wife of a common soldier were the only females.

COMBAT BETWEEN CHINGACHGOOK AND THE IROQUOIS.

Sergeant D u n h a m carried off his command in a large bateau, and then returned for his final orders, and to see that his brother-in-law and daughter were properly attended to. Having pointed out to Cap the boat that he and Mabel were to use, he ascended the hill to seek his last interview with Major Duncan.

It was nearly dark when Mabel found herself in the boat that was to carry her off to the cutter. So very smooth was the surface of the lake that it was not found necessary to bring the bateau into the river to receive its freight, but the beach outside being totally without surf, and the water as tranquil as that of a pond, everybody embarked there. As Cap had said, there was no heaving and settling, no working of vast lungs, nor any respiration as of an ocean ; for, on Ontario, unlike the Atlantic, gales were not agitating the element at one point while calms prevailed at another.

This the distances did not permit; and it is the usual remark of mariners that the sea gets up faster and goes down sooner on all the great lakes of the west than on the different seas of their acquaintance. When the boat left the land, therefore, Mabel would not have known that she was afloat on so broad a sheet of water by any movement that is usual to such circumstances. The oars had barely time to give a dozen strokes when the boat lay at the cutter's side.

Jasper was in readiness to receive his passengers, and, as the deck of the "Scud" was but two or three feet above the water, no difficulty was experienced in getting on board her. As soon as this was effected, the young man pointed out to Mabel and her companion the accommodations prepared for their reception, and they took possession of them. The little vessel contained four apartments below, all between-decks having been expressly constructed with a view to the transportation of officers and men, with their wives and families. First in rank was what was called the after-cabin, a small apartment that contained four berths, and which enjoyed the advantage of possessing small windows for the admission of air and light. This was uniformly devoted to females, whenever any were on board; and as Mabel and her companion were alone, they had ample space and accommodation. The main cabin was larger, and lighted from above. It was now appropriated to the uses of the quartermaster, the sergeant, Cap, and Jasper, the Pathfinder roaming through any part of the cutter he pleased, the female compartment excepted. The corporals and common soldiers occupied the space beneath the main hatch, which had a deck for such a purpose; while the crew were berthed, as usual, in the forecastle. Although the cutter did not measure quite fifty tons, the draft of officers and men was so light that there was ample room for all on board, there being space enough to accommodate treble the number, if necessary.

As soon as Mabel had taken possession of her own really comfortable and pretty cabin, in doing which she could not abstain from indulging in the pleasant reflection that some of Jasper's favor had been especially manifested in her behalf, she went on deck again. The men were roving to and fro in quest of their knapsacks and other effects, but method and habit soon reduced things to order, when the stillness on board became even imposing, for it was connected with the idea of future adventure and ominous preparation.

Darkness was now beginning to render objects on shore indistinct, the whole of the land forming one shapeless black outline of even forest summits that was to be distinguished from the impending heavens only by the greater light of the sky. The stars, however, soon began to appear in the latter, one after another, in their usual mild, placid luster, bringing with them that sense of quiet which ordinarily accompanies night. There was something soothing as well as exciting in such a scene; and Mabel, who was seated on the quarter-deck, sensibly felt both influences. The Pathfinder was standing near her, leaning, as usual, on his long rifle, and she fancied that, through the glowing darkness of the hour, she could trace even stronger lines of thought than usual in his rugged countenance.

"To you, Pathfinder, expeditions like this can be no great novelty," she said, "though I am surprised to find how silent and thoughtful the men appear to be."

"We l'arn this by making war ag'in Injins. Your militia are great talkers and little doers, in gin'ral; but the soger who has often met the Mingos l'arns to know the value of a prudent tongue. A silent army, in the woods, is doubly strong; and a noisy one, doubly weak. If tongues made soldiers, the women of a camp would generally carry the day."

"But we are neither an army nor in the woods. There can be no danger of Mingos in the 'Scud.'"

"Ask Jasper how he got to be master of this cutter, and you will find yourself answered as to that opinion! No one is safe from a Mingo who does n't understand his very natur'; and even then he must act up to his own knowledge, and that closely. Ask Jasper how he got command of this very cutter!"

"And how *did* he get the command?" inquired Mabel, with an earnestness and interest that delighted her simple-minded and true-hearted companion, who was never better pleased than when he had an opportunity of saying aught in favor of a friend. "It is honorable to him that he has reached this station while yet so young."

"That it is—but he deserved it all, and more. A frigate would n't have been too much to pay for so much spirit and coolness,—had there been such a thing on Ontario, as there is not, hows'ever, or likely to be."

"But, Jasper, you have not yet told me how he got the command of the schooner?"

"It is a long story, Mabel, and one your father, the sergeant, can tell much better than I, for he was present, while I was off on a distant scoutin'. Jasper is not good at a story, I know; I've heard him questioned about this affair, and he never made a good tale of it, although everybody knows it was a good thing. No—no—Jasper is not good at a story, as his best friends must own. The 'Scud' had near fallen into the hands of the French and the Mingos when Jasper saved her, in a way that none but a quick-witted mind and a bold heart would have attempted. The sergeant will tell the tale better than I can, and I wish you to question him some day when nothing better offers. As for Jasper himself, there will be no use in worrying the lad, since he will make a bungling matter of it, for he do n't know how to make a history at all."

Mabel determined to ask her father to repeat the incidents of the affair that very night, for it struck her young fancy that nothing better could offer than to listen to the praises of one who was a bad historian of his own exploits.

"Will the 'Scud' remain with us when we reach the island?" she asked, after a little hesitation about the propriety of the question, "or shall we be left to ourselves?"

"That's as may be. Jasper does not often keep the cutter idle when anything is to be done, and we may expect activity on his part. My gift, however, runs so little toward the water, and vessels ginrally, unless it be among rapids and falls, and in canoes, that I pretend to know nothing about it. We shall have all right, under Jasper. I make no doubt, who can find a trail on Ontario as well as a Delaware can find one on the land."

"And our own Delaware, Pathfinder, Chingachgook,—the Big Serpent, as you call him,—why is he not with us to-night?"

"Your question would have been more nat'ral had you said, 'Why are *you* here, Pathfinder?' The Sarpent is in his place, while I am not in mine. He is out with two or three more scouting the lake shores, and will join us down among the islands with the tidings he may gather. The sergeant is too good a soldier to forget his rear while he is facing the enemy in front! It's a thousand pities, Mabel, your father wasn't born a gin'ral, as some of the English are who come among us, for I feel sartain he wouldn't leave a Frencher in the Canadas a week, could he have his own way with them."

"Shall we have enemies to face in front?" asked Mabel, smiling, and for the first time feeling a slight apprehension about the dangers of the expedition. "Are we likely to have an engagement?"

"If we have, Mabel, there will be men enough ready and willing to stand atween you and harm. But you are a soldier's daughter, and, we all know, have the spirit of one. Don't let the fear of a battle keep your pretty eyes from sleeping."

"I do feel braver out here in the woods, Pathfinder, than I ever felt before amid the weaknesses of the towns, although I have always tried to remember what I owe to my dear father."

"Ay, your mother was so before you! 'You will find Mabel like her mother,—no screamer or a faint-hearted girl to trouble a man in his need, but one who would encourage her mate, and help to keep his heart up when sorest pressed by danger,' said the sergeant to me, before I ever laid eyes on that sweet countenance of yours—he did!"

"And why should my father have told you this, Pathfinder?" the girl demanded, a little earnestly. "Perhaps he fancied you would think the better of me if you did not believe me a silly coward, as so many of my sex love to make themselves appear."

Deception, unless it were at the expense of his enemies in the field—nay, concealment of even a thought, was so little in accordance with the Pathfinder's very nature that he was not a little embarrassed by this simple question. To own the truth openly and tell the girl that her father wished her to marry the scout would not be proper, of that he felt certain ; and to hide it, agreed with neither his sense of right nor his habits. In such a strait he took refuge in a middle course, not revealing that which he fancied ought not to be told, nor yet absolutely concealing it.

"You must know, Mabel," he said "that the sergeant and I are old friends, and have stood side by side—or if not actually side by side, I a little in advance, as became a scout, and your father with his own men, as better suited a soldier of the king—on many a hard-fought and bloody day. It's the way of us skirmishers to think little of the fight when the rifle has done cracking, and at night, around our fires, or on our marches, we talk of the things we love, just as you young women converse about your fancies and opinions when you get together to laugh over your idees. Now, it was natural that the sergeant, having such a daughter as you, should love her better than anything else, and that he should talk of her oftener than of anything else, while I, having neither daughter, nor sister, nor mother, nor kith nor kin, nor anything but the Delawares to love, I naturally chimed in, as it were, and got to love you, Mabel, before I ever saw you—yes, I did—just by talking about you so much."

"And now you *have* seen me," returned the smiling girl, whose unmoved and natural manner proved how little she was thinking of anything more than parental or fraternal regard, "you are beginning to see the folly of forming friendships for people before you know anything about them, except by hearsay."

"It was n't friendship—it is n't friendship, Mabel, that I feel for you. I am the friend of the Delawares, and have been so from boyhood ; but my feelings for them, or for the best of them, are not the same as them I got from the sergeant for you ; and especially now that I begin to know you better. I'm sometimes afear'd it is n't wholesome for one who is much occupied in a very manly calling, like that of a guide, or a scout, or a soldier even, to form friendships for women,—young women in particular,—as they seem to me to lessen the love of enterprise, and to turn the feelings away from their gifts and natural occupations."

"You surely do not mean, Pathfinder, that friendship for a girl like me would make you less bold, and more unwilling to meet the French than you were before?"

"Not so ; not so. With you in danger, for instance, I fear I might become foolhardy ; but before we became so intimate, as I may say, I loved to think of my scoutin's, and of my marches, and out-lyings, and fights, and other adventures ; but now my mind cares less about them ; I think more of the barracks and of evenings passed in discourse, of feelings in which there are no wranglings and bloodshed, and of young women, and of their laughs and their cheerful, soft voices, their pleasant looks, and their winning ways ! I sometimes tell the sergeant that he and his daughter will be the spoiling of one of the best and most experienced scouts on the lines."

"Not they, Pathfinder ; they will try to make that which is already so excellent, perfect. You do not know us, if you think that either wishes to see you in the least changed. Remain, as at present, the same honest, upright, conscientious, fearless, intelligent guide that you are, and neither my dear father nor myself can ever think of you differently from what we now do."

The Pathfinder's humble nature was encouraged by the directness and strength of the words he had just heard. Unwilling, if not unable to say any more, he walked away, and stood leaning on his rifle and looking up at the stars for quite ten minutes in profound silence.

In the meanwhile, an interview at the Fort took place between Major Duncan and the sergeant.

"Have the men's knapsacks been examined?" demanded Major Duncan, after he had cast his eye at a written report handed to him by the sergeant, but which it was too dark to read.

"All, your honor ; and all are right."

"The ammunition—arms—?"

"All in order, Major Duncan, and fit for any service."

"You have the men named in my own draft, Dunham?"

"Without an exception, sir. Better men could not be found in the regiment."

"You have need of the best of our men, sergeant. This experiment has now been tried three times ; always under one of the ensigns, who have flattered me with success, but have as often failed. After so much preparation and expense, I do not like to abandon the project entirely ; but this will be the last effort, and the result will mainly depend on you and on the Pathfinder."

"You may count on us both, Major Duncan. The duty you have given us is not above our habits and experience, and I think it will be well done. I know that the Pathfinder will not be wanting."

"On that, indeed, it will be safe to rely. He is a most extraordinary man, Dunham—one who long puzzled me ; but who, now that I understand him, commands as much of my respect as any general in his Majesty's service."

"I was in hopes, sir, that you would come to look at the proposed marriage with Mabel as a thing I ought to wish and forward."

"As for that, sergeant, time will show," returned Major Duncan, smiling. "One woman is sometimes more difficult to manage than a whole regiment of men. By the way, you know that your would-be son-in-law, the quartermaster, will be of the party, and I trust you will at least give him an equal chance in the trial for your daughter's smiles."

"If respect for his rank, sir, did not cause me to do this, your honor's wish would be sufficient."

"I thank you, sergeant. We have served much together, and ought to value each other in our several stations. Understand me, however; I ask no more for Davy Muir than a clear field and no favor. In love, as in war, each man must gain his own victories. Are you certain that the rations have been properly calculated?"

"I'll answer for it, Major Duncan; but, if they were not, we can not suffer with two such hunters as Pathfinder and the Serpent in company."

"That will never do, Dunham," interrupted the major sharply; "and it comes of your American birth and American training. No thorough soldier ever relies on anything but his commissary for supplies; and I beg no part of my regiment may be the first to set an example to the contrary."

"You have only to command, Major Duncan, to be obeyed; and yet, if I might presume, sir—"

"Speak freely, sergeant, you are talking with a friend."

"I was merely about to say that I find even the Scotch soldiers like venison and birds quite as well as pork, when they are difficult to be had."

"That may be very true; but likes and dislikes have nothing to do with system. An army can rely on nothing but its commissaries. The irregularity of the provincials has too long hurt the king's service to be winked at any longer."

"General Braddock, your honor, might have been advised by Colonel Washington."

"Out upon your Washington! You're all provincials together, man, and uphold each other as if you were of a sworn confederacy."

"I believe his Majesty has no more loyal subjects than the Americans, your honor."

"In that, Dunham, I'm thinking you're right; and I have been a little too warm, perhaps. I do not consider *you* a provincial, however, sergeant; for, though born in America, a better soldier never shouldered a musket."

"And Colonel Washington, your honor—?"

"Well, and Colonel Washington may be a useful subject, too. He is the American prodigy, and I suppose I may as well give him all the credit you ask. You have no doubt of the skill of Jasper Western?"

"The boy has been tried, sir, and found equal to all that can be required of him."

"He has passed much of his boyhood in the French colonies; has he French blood in his veins, sergeant?"

"Not a drop, your honor. Jasper's father was an old comrade of my own, and his mother came of an honest and loyal family in this very province."

"How came he, then, so much among the French, and whence his name? He speaks the language of the Canadas, too, I find."

"That is easily explained, Major Duncan. The boy was left under the care of one of our mariners in the old war, and he took to the water like a duck. Your honor knows that we have no ports on Ontario, that can be named as such, and he naturally passed most of his time on the other side of the lake, where the French have had a few vessels these fifty years. He learned to speak their language as a matter of course."

"A French master is but a poor instructor for a British sailor, notwithstanding."

"I beg your pardon, sir; Jasper was brought up under a real English seaman,—one that had sailed under the king's pennant, and may be called a thoroughbred: that is to say, a subject born in the colonies, but none the worse at his trade, I hope, Major Duncan, for that."

"Perhaps not, sergeant, perhaps not; nor any better. This Jasper behaved well, too, when I gave him the command of the 'Scud'; no lad could have conducted himself more loyally or better."

"Or more bravely, Major Duncan. I am sorry to see, sir, that you have doubts as to the fidelity of Jasper."

"It is the duty of the soldier who is intrusted with the care of a distant and important post like this, Dunham, never to relax in his vigilance. We have two of the most artful enemies that the world has ever produced, in their several ways, to contend with—the Indians and the French; and nothing should be overlooked that can lead to injury."

"I hope your honor considers me fit to be intrusted with any particular reason that may exist for doubting Jasper, since you have seen fit to intrust me with this command."

"It is not that I doubt you, Dunham, that I hesitate to reveal all I may happen to know, but from a strong reluctance to circulate an evil report concerning one of whom I have hitherto thought well. You must think well of the Pathfinder or you would not wish to give him your daughter?"

"For the Pathfinder's honesty I will answer with my life, sir," returned the sergeant firmly, and not without a dignity of manner that struck his superior. "Such a man does n't know how to be false."

"I believe you are right, Dunham, and yet this last information has unsettled all my old opinions. The truth is, sergeant, I have received an anonymous communication advising me to be on my guard against Jasper Western, who, it alleges, has been bought by the enemy, and giving me reason to expect that further and more precise information will soon be sent."

"Letters without signatures to them, sir, are scarcely to be regarded in war."

"Or in peace, Dunham. No one can entertain a lower opinion of the writer of an anonymous letter, in ordinary matters, than myself. The very act denotes cowardice, meanness, and baseness ; and it usually is a token of falsehood, as well as of other vices. But in matters of war it is not exactly the same thing ; besides, several suspicious circumstances have been pointed out to me—"

"Such as is fit for an orderly to hear, your honor?"

"Certainly; one in whom I confide as much as in yourself, Dunham. It is said, for instance, that your daughter and her party were permitted to escape the Iroquois, when they came in, merely to give Jasper credit with me. I am told that the Frenchmen care more for the capture of the 'Scud,' with Sergeant Dunham and a party of men, together with the defeat of our favorite plan, than for the capture of a girl and the scalp of her uncle."

"I understand the hint, sir ; I do not give it credit. Jasper can hardly be true, and Pathfinder false ; and as for the last, I would as soon distrust your honor as distrust him."

"It would seem so, sergeant ; it would, indeed, seem so. But Jasper is not the Pathfinder after all, and I will own, Dunham, I should put more faith in the lad if he did n't speak French."

"It's no recommendation in my eyes, I assure your honor ; but the boy learned it by compulsion, as it were, and ought not to be condemned too hastily for the circumstance, by your honor's leave. If he does speak French, it's because he can't well help it."

"Well, it never did any one good—at least no British subject ; for I suppose the French themselves must talk together in some language or other. I should have much more faith in this Jasper did he know nothing of their language. This letter has made me uneasy ; and, were there another to whom I could trust the cutter, I would devise some means to detain him here. I have spoken to you already of your brother-in-law, who goes with you, sergeant, and who is a sailor?"

"A real seafaring man, your honor, is Cap, though somewhat prejudiced against fresh water. I doubt if he could be induced to risk his character on a lake, and I'm certain he never could find the station."

"The last is probably true, and, then, the man can not know enough of this treacherous lake to be fit for the employment. You will have to be doubly vigilant, Dunham. I give you full powers, and should you detect this Jasper in any treachery make him a sacrifice at once to offended justice."

"Being in the service of the crown, he is amenable to martial law——"

"Very true—then iron him, from his head to his heels, and send him up here in his own cutter. That brother-in-law of yours must be able to find the way back after he has once traveled the road."

"I make no doubt, Major Dunham, we shall be able to do all that will be necessary, should Jasper turn out as you seem to anticipate ; though I think I would risk my life on his truth."

"I like your confidence ; it speaks well for the fellow—but that infernal letter ! There is such an air of truth about it,—nay, there is so much truth in it, touching other matters——"

"I think your honor said it wanted the name at the bottom ; a great omission for an honest man to make."

"Quite right, Dunham, and no one but a rascal, and a cowardly rascal into the bargain, would write an anonymous letter on private affairs. It *is* different, however, in war. Dispatches are feigned, and artifice is generally allowed to be justifiable."

"Military, manly artifices, sir, if you will ; such as ambushes, surprises, feints, false attacks, and even spies ; but I never heard of a true soldier who could wish to undermine the character of an honest young man by such means as these."

"I have met with many strange events, and some stranger people, in the course of my experience. But fare you well, sergeant ; I must detain you no longer. You are now on your guard, and I recommend to you untiring vigilance. I think Muir means shortly to retire, and should you fully succeed in this enterprise my influence will not be wanting in endeavoring to put you into the vacancy, to which you have many claims."

"I humbly thank your honor," coolly returned the sergeant, who had been encouraged in this manner any time for the preceding twenty years, "and hope I shall never disgrace my station, whatever it may be. I am what nature and Providence have made me, and I hope I'm satisfied."

"You have not forgotten the howitzer?"

"Jasper took it on board this morning, sir."

"Be wary, and do not trust that young man unnecessarily. Make a confidant of Pathfinder at once ; he may be of service in detecting any villainy that may be stirring. His simple honesty will favor his observation by concealing it. *He must* be true."

"For him, sir, my own head shall answer, or even my rank in the regiment. I have seen him too often tried to doubt him."

"Of all wretched sensations, Dunham, distrust, where one is compelled to confide, is the most painful. You have bethought you of the spare flints?"

"A sergeant is a safe commander for all such details, your honor."

"Well, then, give me your hand, Dunham. God bless you, and may you be successful. Have all the ammunition carefully examined and dried as soon as you arrive; the damp of the lake may affect it. And now, once more, farewell, sergeant. Beware of that Jasper, and consult with Muir in any difficulty. I shall expect you to return triumphant this day month."

"God bless your honor; if anything should happen to me I trust to you, Major Duncan, to care for an old soldier's character."

"Rely on me, Dunham—you will rely on a friend. Be vigilant; remember you will be in the very jaws of the lion,—pshaw, of no lion, neither, but of treacherous tigers,—in their very jaws, and beyond support. Have the flints counted and examined in the morning—and—farewell, Dunham, farewell."

So they parted, and soon the "Scud" was sailing on its voyage. The sergeant called Pathfinder into the cabin, and then communicated to him Major Duncan's doubts about Jasper Western.

"Pathfinder," he said, "Major Duncan has received some information which has led him to suspect that Jasper Western is false, and in the pay of the enemy. I wish to hear your opinion on the subject."

"What's that?" asked Pathfinder, greatly surprised.

"I say, the Major suspects Jasper of being a traitor—a French spy—or, what is worse, of being bought to betray us. He has received a letter to this effect, and has been charging me to keep an eye on the boy's actions, for he fears we shall meet with enemies when we least expect it, and by his means."

"Duncan has told you this, Sergeant Dunham?"

"He has, indeed, Pathfinder; and, though I have been loath to believe anything to the injury of Jasper, I have a feeling which tells me I ought to distrust him."

"Ah! You've been talking with Duncan consarning Jasper, and his words have raised misgivin's."

"Not so in the least. For, while conversing with the major, my feelings were altogether the other way; and I endeavored to convince him all I could that he did the boy injustice. But there is no use in holding out. I fear there is something in the suspicion, after all."

"I have known Jasper Western since he was a boy," said Pathfinder, confidently, "and I have as much faith in his honesty as I have in my own, or that of the Sarpent himself."

"But the Serpent, Pathfinder, has his tricks and ambushes in war as well as another!"

"Ay, them are his nat'ral gifts, and such as belong to his people. Neither redskin nor paleface can deny natur'; but Chingachgook is not a man to feel a presentiment ag'in."

"That I believe; nor should I have thought ill of Jasper this very morning. But it seems to me, Pathfinder, that somehow the lad does not bustle about his deck naturally, as he used to do, but that he is silent and moody and thoughtful, like a man who has a load on his conscience."

"Jasper is never noisy, and he tells me noisy ships are generally ill-worked ships. Master Cap agrees in this, too. No, no; I will believe naught against Jasper until I see it. Send for your brother, sergeant, and let us question him in this matter; for to sleep with distrust of one's fri'nd in the heart is like sleeping with lead there. I have no faith in your presentiments."

The sergeant, although he scarce knew himself with what object, complied, and Cap was summoned to join in the consultation. As Pathfinder was more collected than his companion, and felt so strong a conviction of the good faith of the party accused, he assumed the office of spokesman.

"We have asked you to come down, Master Cap," he commenced, "in order to inquire if you have remarked anything out of the common way in the movements of Jasper Western this evening."

"His movements are common enough, I dare say, for fresh water, Master Pathfinder, though we should think most of his proceedings irregular down on the coast."

"Yes, yes; we know you will never agree with the lad about the manner the cutter ought to be managed; but it is on another p'int we wish your opinion."

The Pathfinder then explained to Cap the nature of the suspicions which the sergeant entertained, and the reasons why they had been excited, so far as the latter had been communicated by Major Duncan.

"The youngster talks French, does he?"

"They say he speaks it better than common," returned the sergeant gravely. "Pathfinder knows this to be true."

"I'll not gainsay it, I'll not gainsay it," answered the guide, "at least they tell me such is the fact. But this would prove nothing ag'in a man like Jasper. I speak the Mingo dialect myself, having l'arnt it while a prisoner among the reptyles; but who will say I am their fri'nd? Not that I am an inimy, either, according to Injin notions; though I am their inimy, I will admit, agreeable to Christianity."

"Ay, Pathfinder, but Jasper did not get his French as a prisoner: he took it in, in boyhood, when the mind is easily impressed, and gets its permanent notions; when nature has a presentiment, as it were, which way the character is likely to incline."

"A very just remark," added Cap, "for that is the time of life when we all learn the catechism, and other moral improvements. The sergeant's observation shows that he understands human nature, and I agree with him perfectly; it *is* a bad thing for a youngster, up here, on this bit of fresh water, to talk French. If it were down on the Atlantic, now, where a seafaring man has occasion sometimes to converse with a pilot or a linguister in that language, I should not think so much of it, though we always look with suspicion, even there, at a shipmate who knows too much of the tongue; but up here on Ontario I hold it to be a most suspicious circumstance."

"But Jasper must talk in French to the people on the other shore," said Pathfinder, "or hold his tongue, as there are none but French to speak to."

"You don't mean to tell me, Pathfinder, that France lies hereaway, on the opposite coast?" cried Cap, jerking a thumb over his shoulder in the direction of the Canadas; "that one side of this bit of fresh water is York and the other France!"

"I mean to tell you this is York, and that is Upper Canada; and that English and Dutch and Indian are spoken in the first, and French and Indian in the last. Even the Mingos have got many of the French words in their dialect, and it is no improvement, neither."

"Very true; and what sort of people are the Mingos, my friend?" inquired the sergeant, touching the other on the shoulder, by way of enforcing a remark, the inherent truth of which sensibly increased its value in the eyes of the speaker. "No one knows them better than yourself, and I ask you what sort of a tribe are they?"

"Jasper is no Mingo, sergeant."

"He speaks French, and he might as well be in that particular. Brother Cap, can you recollect no movement of this unfortunate young man, in the way of his calling, that would seem to denote treachery?"

"Not distinctly, sergeant, though he has gone to work wrong end foremost half his time. It is true that one of his hands coiled a rope against the sun, and he called it *curling* a rope, too, when I asked him what he was about; but I am not certain that anything was meant by it; though I dare say the French coil half their running rigging the wrong way, and may call it 'curling it down,' too, for that matter. Then Jasper himself belayed the end of the jib-halyards to a stretcher in the rigging, instead of bringing them in to the mast, where they belong,—at least among British sailors."

"I dare say Jasper may have got some Canada notions about working his craft, from being so much on the other side," Pathfinder interposed, "but catching an idee or a word is n't treachery or bad faith. I sometimes get an idee from the Mingos themselves, but my heart has always been with the Delawares. No, no; Jasper is true; and the king might trust him with his crown, just as he would trust his eldest son, who, as he is to wear it one day, ought to be the last man to wish to steal it."

But still they talked on against Jasper, and even Pathfinder could not convince the others that the young sailor was all right. He talked French, and did not call things by their sea names. These were enough to convict him with the sergeant and the seaman.

For the next day everything that Jasper did was put down against him. The sergeant and Cap watched him closely, and found fault with him so constantly that the poor young sailor felt certain they had noticed how much he looked at Mabel, and were angry with him accordingly.

Toward evening, Cap, who was standing in the forward part of the cutter, saw something on the water.

"Sail, ho!" he shouted—or "Boat, ho!" would be nearer the truth.

Jasper ran forward; and, sure enough, a small object was discernible about a hundred yards ahead of the cutter, and nearly on her lee bow. At the first glance he saw it was a bark canoe; for though the darkness prevented hues from being distinguished, the eye that had got to be accustomed to the night might discern forms at some little distance; and the eye which, like Jasper's, had long been familiar with things aquatic, could not be at a loss in discovering the outlines necessary to come to the conclusion he did.

"This may be an enemy," the young man remarked; "and it may be well to overhaul him."

"He is paddling with all his might, lad," observed the Pathfinder, "and means to cross your bows and get to windward, when you might as well chase a full-grown buck on snow-shoes."

"Let her luff!" cried Jasper, to the man at the helm. "Luff up till she shakes—there, steady, and hold all that."

The helmsman complied, and as the "Scud" was now dashing the water aside merrily, a minute or two put the canoe so far to leeward as to render escape impracticable. Jasper now sprang to the helm. And by judicious and careful handling he got so near the canoe that it was secured by a boat hook. What was his surprise to find that its occupants were Arrowhead and his wife.

Now, Arrowhead, you remember, was the Tuscarora Indian who had guided Mabel and her uncle through the woods until they met Pathfinder. Then he had disappeared suddenly.

Everyone suspected him to be an enemy. So, when he was captured in his canoe, Pathfinder questioned him closely.

"Why has my brother been so long from the Fort?" he asked. "His friends have thought of him often, but have never seen him."

ARROWHEAD AND HIS WIFE TAKEN ON BOARD THE CUTTER.

Arrowhead told him that his wife, June, had been stolen by the Mingos, and that he had gone to rescue her.

"Well, well, all this seems nat'ral, and according to matrimony. But, Tuscarora, how did you get that canoe, and why are you paddling toward the St. Lawrence, instead of the garrison?"

"Arrowhead can tell his own from that of another. This canoe is mine; I found it on the shore, near the Fort."

"That sounds reasonable, too," said the scout, "for the canoe does belong to the man, and an Injin would make few words about taking it. Still, it is extr'ord'nary that we saw nothing of the fellow and his wife, for the canoe must have left the river before we did ourselves."

"One thing more my brother will tell me," continued Pathfinder, "and there will be no cloud between his wigwam and the strong-houses of the Yengeese. If he can blow away this bit of fog his friends will look at him, as he sits by his own fire, and he can look at them, as they lay aside their arms, and forget that they are warriors. Why was the head of Arrowhead's canoe looking toward the St. Lawrence, where there are none but enemies to be found?"

"Why were the Pathfinder and his friends looking the same way?" asked the Tuscarora, calmly. "A Tuscarora may look in the same direction as the Yengeese."

"Why, to own the truth, Arrowhead, we were out scouting like—that is, sailin'; in other words, we are on the king's business, and we have a right to be here, though we may not have a right to say *why* we are here."

"Arrowhead saw the big canoe, and he loves to look on the face of Jasper. He was going toward the sun at evening in order to seek his wigwam; but, finding that the young sailor was going the other way, he turned, that he might look in the same direction. Jasper and Arrowhead were together on the last trail."

"This may all be true, Tuscarora, and you are welcome. You shall eat of our venison, and then we must separate. The setting sun is behind us, and both of us move quick; my brother will get too far from that which he seeks unless he turns round."

Pathfinder now returned to the others and repeated the result of his examination. He appeared himself to believe that the account of Arrowhead might be true, though he admitted that caution would be prudent with one he disliked; but his auditors, Jasper excepted, seemed less disposed to put faith in the explanations.

"This chap must be ironed at once, Brother Dunham," said Cap, as soon as Pathfinder finished his narration; "he must be turned over to the master-at-arms, if there is any such officer on fresh water, and a court-martial ought to be ordered as soon as we reach port."

"I think it wisest to detain the fellow," the sergeant answered, "but irons are unnecessary as long as he remains in the cutter. In the morning the matter shall be inquired into."

Arrowhead was now summoned and told the decision. The Indian listened gravely and made no objections. On the contrary, he submitted with the calm and reserved dignity with which the American aborigines are known to yield to fate; and he stood apart, an attentive, but calm, observer of what was passing. Jasper caused the cutter's sails to be filled, and the "Scud" resumed her course.

It was now getting toward the hour to set the watch, when it was usual to retire for the night. Most of the party went below, leaving no one on deck but Cap, the sergeant, Jasper, and two of the crew. Arrowhead and his wife also remained, the former standing aloof, in proud reserve, and the latter exhibiting, by her attitude and passiveness, the meek humility that characterizes an Indian woman.

"You will find a place for your wife below, Arrowhead, where my daughter will attend to her wants," said the sergeant, kindly, who was himself on the point of quitting the deck; "yonder is a sail, where you may sleep yourself."

"I thank my father. The Tuscaroras are not poor. The woman will look for my blankets in the canoe."

"As you wish, my friend. We think it necessary to detain you, but not necessary to confine or maltreat you. Send your squaw into the canoe for the blankets, and you may follow her yourself and hand us up the paddles. As there may be some sleepy heads in the 'Scud,' Jasper Western," added the sergeant, in a lower tone, "it may be well to secure the paddles."

Jasper assented, and Arrowhead and his wife, with whom resistance appeared to be out of the question, silently complied with the directions. A few expressions of sharp rebuke passed from the Indian to his wife, while both were employed in the canoe, which the latter received with submissive quiet, immediately repairing an error she had made by laying aside the blanket she had taken and selecting another that was more to her tyrant's mind.

"Come, bear a hand, Arrowhead," said the sergeant, who stood on the gunwale, overlooking the movements of the two, which were proceeding too slowly for the impatience of a drowsy man; "it is getting late, and we soldiers have such a thing as reveille. Early to bed and early to rise."

"Arrowhead is coming," was the answer, as the Tuscarora stepped toward the head of his canoe.

One blow of his keen knife severed the rope which held the boat, when the cutter glanced ahead, leaving the light bubble of bark, which instantly lost its way, almost stationary. So suddenly and dexterously was this maneuver performed that the canoe was on the lee quarter of the "Scud" before the sergeant was aware of the artifice, and quite in her wake ere he had time to announce it to his companions.

"Hard-a-lee!" shouted Jasper, letting fly the jib-sheet with his own hands, when the cutter came swiftly up to the breeze, with all her canvas flapping, or was running into the wind's eye, as seamen term it, until the light craft was a hundred feet to windward of her former position. Quick and dexterous as was this movement, and ready as had been the expedient, it was not quicker and more ready than that of the Tuscarora. With an intelligence that denoted some familiarity with vessels, he had seized his paddle, and was already skimming the water, aided by the efforts of his wife. The direction he took was southwesterly, or on a line that led him equally toward the wind and the shore, while it also kept him so far aloof from the cutter as to avoid the danger of the

latter's falling on board of him when she filled on the other tack. Swiftly as the "Scud" had shot into the wind and forged ahead, Jasper knew it was necessary to cast her ere she had lost all her way; and it was not two minutes from the time the helm had been put down before the lively little craft was aback forward, and rapidly falling off, in order to allow her sails to fill on the opposite tack.

"He will escape!" said Jasper, the instant he caught a glimpse of the relative bearings of the cutter and the canoe. "The cunning knave is paddling dead to windward, and the 'Scud' can never overtake him!"

' "You have a canoe!" exclaimed the sergeant, manifesting the eagerness of a boy to join in the pursuit, "let us launch it and give chase!"

"'Twill be useless. If Pathfinder had been on deck there might have been a chance, but there is none now. To launch the canoe would have taken three or four minutes, and the time lost would have been sufficient for the purposes of Arrowhead."

Both Cap and the sergeant saw the truth of this, which would have been nearly self-evident even to one unaccustomed to vessels. The shore was distant less than half a mile, and the canoe was already glancing into its shadows at a rate to show that it would reach the land ere its pursuers could probably get half the distance. The canoe itself might have been seized, but it would have been a useless prize; for Arrowhead in the woods would be more likely to reach the other shore without detection than if he still possessed the means to venture on the lake again, though it might be, and probably would be, a greater bodily labor to himself. The helm of the "Scud" was reluctantly put up again, and the cutter wore short round on her heel, coming up to her course on the other tack as if acting on instinct. All this was done by Jasper in profound silence, his assistants understanding what was necessary and lending their aid in a sort of mechanical imitation. While these maneuvers were in the course of execution, Cap took the sergeant by a button and led him toward the cabin door, where he was out of ear-shot, and began to unlock his stores of thought.

They felt certain, both of them, that Jasper had allowed Arrowhead to escape. They believed, too, that he had come across the "Scud" in order to get word of Jasper, and that he would now go straight to the French and tell them enough to enable them to capture the "Scud" and the English soldiers and stores.

At once, therefore, and without any explanation except that he had let Arrowhead escape, Jasper was told by Sergeant Dunham that he felt it to be his duty to deprive him, temporarily, of the command of the cutter, and to confer it on his own brother-in-law. A natural and involuntary burst of surprise which escaped the young man was met by a quiet remark, reminding him that military service was often of a nature that required concealment, and a declaration that the present was of such a character that this particular arrangement had become indispensable. Although Jasper's astonishment remained undiminished,—the sergeant cautiously abstaining from making any allusion to his suspicions,—the young man was accustomed to obey with military submission ; and he quietly acquiesced, with his own mouth directing the little crew to receive their further orders from Cap until another change should be effected. When, however, he was told the case required that not only he himself, but his principal assistant, who, on account of his long acquaintance with the lake, was usually termed the pilot, were to remain below, there was an alteration in his countenance and manner that denoted deep mortification, though it was so well mastered as to leave even the distrustful Cap in doubt as to its meaning. As a matter of course, however, when distrust exists, it is not long before the worst construction is put upon it.

As soon as Jasper and the pilot were below, the sentinel at the hatch received private orders to pay particular attention to both ; to allow neither to come on deck again without giving instant notice to the person who might then be in charge of the cutter, and to insist on his return below as soon as possible. This precaution, however, was uncalled for, Jasper and his assistant both throwing themselves silently on their pallets, which neither quitted again that night.

But now, when Cap set about sailing the "Scud," he found things so different from on shipboard at sea that he soon got all snarled up. The sailors did not understand his orders ; he did not have the fresh-water names for things, and he did not know which way to steer, as both the captain and pilot had been sent below.

So they had all sorts of troubles. Twice they very nearly ran ashore ; they lost their course so badly that they sailed in the wrong direction, and actually passed the fort which they had left the day before. Then they were nearly captured by a French vessel, and when the wind blew up a storm they would really have been shipwrecked had not the sergeant come to the conclusion that Jasper knew how to sail on the lake better than Cap, and called him up, just in the nick of time to save the "Scud" from going ashore. And so they were saved.

Jasper came about, and headed his vessel for the point which was their original destination, the fort on Station Island, in the St. Lawrence. He had to keep a sharp lookout, however. He knew that the northern shore of the lake was lined with French forts and blockhouses, and that the French vessel they had but barely escaped was somewhere on the lake in search of the "Scud." So he sailed cautiously.

All that day the wind hung to the southward, and the cutter continued her course about a league from the land, running six or eight knots an hour in perfectly smooth water. Although the scene had one feature of monotony, the outline of unbroken forest, it was not without its interest and pleasures. Various headlands presented themselves, and the cutter, in running from one to another, stretched across bays so deep as almost to deserve the name of gulfs, but nowhere did the eye meet with evidences of civilization. Rivers occasionally poured their tribute into the great reservoir of the lake, but their banks could be traced inland for miles by the same outlines of trees ; and even large bays that lay imbosomed in woods, communicating with Ontario only by narrow outlets, appeared and disappeared without bringing with them a single trace of a human habitation.

Of all on board, the Pathfinder viewed the scene with the most unmingled delight. His eyes feasted on the endless line of forest, and, more than once that day, notwithstanding he found it so grateful to be near Mabel, listening to her pleasant voice, and echoing, in feelings, at least, her joyous laugh, did his soul pine to be wandering beneath the high arches of the maples, oaks, and lindens, where his habits had induced him to fancy lasting and true joys were only to be found. Cap viewed the prospect differently. More than once he expressed his disgust at there being no lighthouses, church towers, beacons, or roadsteads, with their shipping. Such another coast, he protested, the world did not contain ; and, taking the sergeant aside, he gravely assured him that the region could never come to anything, as the havens were neglected, the rivers had a deserted and useless look, and that even the breeze had a smell of the forest about it which spoke ill of its properties.

But the humors of the different individuals in her did not stay the speed of the " Scud." When the sun was setting she was already a hundred miles on her route toward Oswego, into which river Sergeant Dunham now thought it his duty to go, in order to receive any communications that Major Duncan might please to make. With a view to effect this purpose, Jasper continued to hug the shore all night ; and though the wind began to fail him toward morning, it lasted long enough to carry the cutter up to a point that was known to be a league or two from the Fort. Here the breeze came out light at the northward, and the cutter hauled a little from the land in order to obtain a safe offing should it come on to blow, or should the weather again get to be easterly.

When the day dawned the cutter had the mouth of the Oswego well under her lee, distant about two miles, and just as the morning gun from the Fort was fired, Jasper gave the order to ease off the sheets and to bear up for his port. At that moment a cry from the forecastle drew all eyes toward the point on the eastern side of the outlet, and there, just without the range of shot from the light guns of the works, with her canvas reduced to barely enough to keep her stationary, lay the French vessel they had escaped, the "Montcalm," as she was called, and evidently in waiting for their appearance. To pass her was impossible, for, by filling her sails, the French ship could have intercepted them in a few minutes, and the circumstances called for a prompt decision. After a short consultation the sergeant again changed his plan, determining to make the best of his way toward the station for which he had been originally destined, trusting to the speed of the "Scud" to throw the enemy so far astern as to leave no clew to her movements.

The cutter accordingly hauled up on the wind with the least possible delay, with everything set that would draw. Guns were fired from the Fort, ensigns shown, and the ramparts were again crowded. But sympathy was all the aid that Major Duncan could lend to his party; and the "Montcalm," also firing four or five guns of defiance, and throwing abroad several of the banners of France, was soon in chase, under a cloud of canvas.

For several hours the two vessels were pressing through the water as fast as possible, making short stretches to windward, apparently with a view to keep the port under their lee, the one to enter it, if possible, and the other to intercept it in the attempt.

At noon the French ship was hull down dead to leeward, the disparity of sailing on a wind being very great, and some islands were nearby, behind which Jasper said it would be possible for the cutter to conceal her future movements. Although Cap and the sergeant, and particularly Lieutenant Muir, to judge by his language, still felt a good deal of distrust of the young man, and though the French lake-port and station of Frontenac was not distant, this advice was followed, for time pressed, and the quartermaster discreetly observed that Jasper could not well betray them without running openly into the enemy's harbor—a step they could at any time prevent, since the only cruiser of force the French possessed at the moment was under their lee, and not in a situation to do them any immediate injury.

Left to himself, Jasper Western soon proved how much was really in him. He weathered upon the islands, passed them, and, on coming out to the eastward, kept broad away, with nothing in sight in his wake or to leeward. By sunset again the cutter was up with the first of the islands that lie in the outlet of the lake, and ere it was dark she was running through the narrow channels on her way to the long-sought station. At nine o'clock, however, Cap insisted that they should anchor, for the maze of the islands, now so famous and popular as a delightful summer resort, became so complicated and obscure that he feared at every opening the party would find themselves under the guns of a French fort. Jasper consented cheerfully, it being a part of his standing instructions to approach the station under such circumstances as would prevent the men from obtaining any very accurate notion of its position, lest a deserter might betray the little garrison to the enemy.

The "Scud" was brought to in a small, retired bay, where it would have been difficult to find her by daylight, and where she was perfectly concealed at night, when all but a solitary sentinel on deck sought their rest. Cap had been so harassed during the previous eight-and-forty hours that his slumbers were long and deep, nor did he awake from his first nap until the day was just beginning to dawn. His eyes were scarcely open, however, when his nautical instinct told him that the cutter was under way. Springing up, he found the "Scud" threading the islands again, with no one on deck but Jasper and the pilot, unless the sentinel be excepted, who had not in the least interfered with movements that he had every reason to believe were as regular as they were necessary.

"How's this, Master Western?" demanded Cap, with sufficient fierceness for the occasion. "Are you running us into Frontenac at last, and we all asleep below, like so many marines waiting for the 'sentry go'?"

"This is according to orders, Master Cap, Major Duncan having commanded me never to approach the station unless at a moment when the people were below; for he does not wish there should be more pilots in these waters than the king has need of."

"Whe-e-w! A pretty job I should have made of running down among these bushes and rocks with no one on deck! Why, a regular York branch could make nothing of such a channel."

"I always thought, sir," said Jasper, smiling, "you would have done better had you left the cutter in my hands until she had safely reached her place of destination."

"We should have done it, Jasper; we should have done it, had it not been for a circumstance—these circumstances are serious matters, and no prudent man will overlook them."

"Well, sir, I hope there is now an end of them. We shall arrive in less than an hour, if the wind holds, and then you'll be safe from any circumstances that I can contrive."

"Humph!"

Cap was obliged to acquiesce, and as everything around him had the appearance of Jasper's being sincere, there was not much difficulty in making up his mind to submit. It would not have been easy, indeed, for a person the most sensitive on the subject of circumstances to fancy that the "Scud" was anywhere in the vicinity of a port as long established and as well known on the frontiers as Frontenac. The islands might not have been literally a thousand in number, but they were so numerous and small as to baffle calculation, though occasionally one of larger size than common was passed. Jasper had quitted what might have been termed the main channel, and was winding his way with a good stiff breeze and a favorable current through passes that were sometimes so narrow that there appeared to be barely room sufficient for the "Scud's" spars to clear the trees, while at other moments he shot across little bays, and buried the cutter again amid rocks, forests, and bushes. The water was so transparent that there was no occasion for the lead, and being of equal depth little risk was actually run, though Cap, with his maritime habits, was in a constant fever lest they should strike.

"I give it up! I give it up, Pathfinder!" the old seaman at length exclaimed, when the little vessel emerged in safety from the twentieth of these narrow inlets through which she had been so boldly carried; "this is defying the very nature of seamanship, and sending all its law and rules to Davy Jones."

"Nay, nay, Saltwater," for so the scout called the seaman; "'tis the parfection of the art. You perceive that Jasper never falters, but, like a hound with a true nose, he runs with his head high, as if he had a strong scent. My life on it the lad brings us out right in the ind, as he would have done in the beginning had we given him leave."

"No pilot, no lead, no beacons, buoys, or lighthouses, no——"

"Trail!" interrupted Pathfinder, "for that to me is the most mysterious part of the business. Water leaves no trail, as every one knows, and yet here is Jasper moving ahead as boldly as if he had before his eyes the prints of moccasins on leaves as plainly as we can see the sun in the heavens."

"Stand by to haul down the jib," called out Jasper, who merely smiled at the remarks of his companion. "Haul down—starboard your helm—starboard hard—so—meet her—gently there with the helm—touch her lightly—now jump ashore with the fast, lad—no, heave—there are some of our people ready to take it."

All this passed so quickly as barely to allow the spectators time to note the different evolutions ere the "Scud" had been thrown into the wind until her mainsail shivered, next cast a little by the use of the rudder only, and then she set bodily alongside of a natural rocky quay, where she was immediately secured by good fasts run to the shore. In a word, the station was reached, and the soldiers were greeted by their expectant comrades with the satisfaction that a relief usually brings.

Mabel sprang upon the shore with a delight which she did not care to express, and her father led his men after her with an alacrity which proved how wearied he had become of the cutter. The station, as the place was familiarly termed by the soldiers of the 55th, was indeed a spot to raise expectations of enjoyment among those who had been cooped up so long in a vessel of the dimensions of the "Scud." None of the islands were high, though all lay at a sufficient elevation above the water to render them perfectly healthy and secure. Each had more or less wood, and the greater number, at that distant day, were clothed with the virgin forest. The one selected by the troops for their purpose was small, containing about twenty acres of land, and by some of the accidents of the wilderness it had been partly stripped of its trees, probably centuries before the period of which we are writing, and a little grassy glade covered nearly half its surface. It was the opinion of the officer who had made the selection of this spot for a military post, that a sparkling spring nearby had early caught the attention of the Indians, and that they had long frequented this particular place in their hunts or when fishing for salmon—a circumstance that had kept down the second growth and given time for the natural grasses to take root and to gain dominion over the soil. Let the cause be what it might, the effect was to render this island far more beautiful than most of those around it, and to lend it an air of civilization that was then wanting in so much of that vast region of country.

The shores of Station Island were completely fringed with bushes, and great care had been taken to preserve them, as they answered as a screen to conceal the persons and things collected within their circle. Favored by this shelter, as well as by that of several thickets of trees and different copses, some six or eight low huts had been erected to be used as quarters for the officer and his men, to contain stores, and to serve the purposes of kitchen, hospital, etc. These huts were built of logs in the usual manner, had been roofed by bark brought from a distance, lest the signs of labor should attract attention, and, as they had now been inhabited some months, were as comfortable as dwellings of that description usually get to be.

At the eastern extremity of the island, however, was a small, densely wooded peninsula, with a thicket of underbrush so closely matted as nearly to prevent the possibility of seeing across it so long as the leaves remained on the branches. Near the narrow neck that connected this acre with the rest of the island, a small blockhouse had been erected with some attention to its means of resistance. The logs were bullet-proof, squared, and jointed with a care to leave no defenseless points ; the windows were loop-holes ; the door massive and small ; and the roof, like the rest of the structure, was framed of hewn timber, covered properly with bark to exclude the rain. The lower apartment, as usual, contained stores and provisions ; here, indeed, the party kept all their supplies ; the second story was intended for a dwelling as well as for the citadel, and a low garret was subdivided into two or three rooms, and could hold the pallets of some ten or fifteen persons. All the arrangements were exceedingly simple and cheap, but they were sufficient to protect the soldiers against the effects of a surprise. As the whole building was considerably less than forty feet high, its summit was concealed by the tops of trees, except from the eyes of those who had reached the interior of the island. On that side the view was open from the upper loops, though bushes, even there, more or less concealed the base of the wooden tower.

The object being purely defense, care had been taken to place the blockhouse so near an opening in the limestone rock that formed the base of the island as to admit of a bucket being dropped into the water in order to obtain that great essential in the event of a siege. In order to facilitate this operation, and to enfilade the base of the building, the upper stories projected several feet beyond the lower, in the manner usual to blockhouses, and pieces of wood filled the apertures cut in the log flooring, which were intended as loops and traps. The communications between the different stories were by means of ladders. If we add that these blockhouses were intended as citadels, for garrisons or settlements to retreat to in case of attack, the general reader will obtain a sufficiently correct idea of the arrangements it is our wish to explain.

But the situation of the island itself formed its principal merit as a military position. Lying in the midst of twenty others, it was not an easy matter to find it, since boats might pass quite near, and, by the glimpses caught through the openings, this particular island would be taken for a part of some other. Indeed, the channels between the islands that lay around the one we have been describing were so narrow that it was even difficult to say which portions of the land were connected or which separated, even as one stood in their center, with the express desire of ascertaining the truth. The little bay in particular that Jasper used as a harbor, was so embowered with bushes and shut in with islands that, the sails of the cutter being lowered, her own people, on one occasion, had searched for hours before they could find the "Scud" on their return from a short excursion among the adjacent channels in quest of fish. In short, the place was admirably adapted to its present uses, and its natural advantages had been as ingeniously improved as economy and the limited means of a frontier post would very well allow.

The hour that succeeded the arrival of the "Scud" was one of hurried excitement. The party in possession had done nothing worthy of being mentioned, and, wearied with their seclusion, they were all eager to return to Oswego. The sergeant and the officer he came to relieve had no sooner gone through the little ceremonies of transferring the command than the latter hurried on board the "Scud" with his whole party, and Jasper, who would gladly have passed the day on the island, was required to get under way forthwith, the wind promising a quick passage up the river and across the lake. Before separating, however, Lieutenant Muir, Cap, and the sergeant had a private conference with the ensign who had been relieved, in which the latter was made acquainted with the suspicions that existed against the fidelity of the young sailor. Promising due caution the officer embarked, and in less than three hours from the time when she had arrived the cutter was again in motion. Mabel had taken possession of a hut, and, with female readiness and skill, she made all the simple little domestic arrangements of which the circumstances would admit, not only for her own comfort but for that of her father. To save labor a mess table was prepared in a hut set apart for that purpose, where all the heads of the detachments were to eat, the soldier's wife performing the necessary labor. The hut of the sergeant, which was the best on the island, being thus freed from any of the vulgar offices of a

MABEL AND PATHFINDER ON STATION ISLAND.

household, admitted of such a display of womanly taste that, for the first time since her arrival on the frontier, the girl felt proud of her home. As soon as these important duties were discharged she strolled out on the island, taking a path that led through the pretty glade, and which conducted to the only point that was not covered with bushes. Here she stood gazing at the limpid water which lay, with scarcely a ruffle on it, at her feet, musing on the novel situation in which she was placed, and permitting a pleasing and deep excitement to steal over her feelings as she remembered the scenes through which she had so lately passed, and conjectured those which still lay veiled in the future.

Lieutenant Muir came to call on Mabel, and to talk as sweetly as he could to her; but she did not care to listen to him, and was well pleased when Pathfinder came and with some difficulty succeeded in taking his place. For some little time they sat enjoying the beautiful scene, talking over the exciting experiences of the recent journey, and the events which had transpired at the Fort. Among the later, one which interested Mabel most was a shooting match between the officers and men of the 55th, which had taken place on the day before their departure, and in which Jasper Western, through the self-denial of Pathfinder, had been allowed to come off victor. But Jasper was now in turn called away by the lieutenant, who seemed to have something of importance to communicate.

"We occupy," he said, "an exceedingly precarious and uncertain position here,—almost in the jaws of the lion, as it were."

"Do you mean the Frenchers, by the lion, and this island as his jaws, lieutenant?"

"Only in a way, my friend," said the lieutenant; "for the French are no lions, and this island is not a jaw—unless, indeed, it may prove to be what I greatly fear may come true, the jaw-bone of an ass."

Here the quartermaster indulged in a sneering laugh that proclaimed anything but respect and admiration for the wisdom of his friend, Major Duncan, in selecting that particular spot for his operations.

"The post is as well chosen as any I ever put foot in," said Pathfinder, looking around him as one surveys a picture.

"I'll no deny it—I'll no deny it. Duncan is a great soldier in a small way. I have followed the major so long that I've got to reverence all he says and does. That's just my weakness, ye'll know, Pathfinder. Well, this post may be the post of an ass, or of a Solomon, as men fancy; but it's most critically placed, as is apparent by all Duncan's precautions and injunctions. There are savages out, scouting through these thousand islands and over the forest, searching for this very spot, as is known to Duncan himself on certain information, and the greatest service you can render the regiment is to discover their trails and lead them off on a false scent. Unhappily, Sergeant Dunham has taken up the notion that the danger is to be apprehended from up-stream, because Frontenac lies above us; whereas all experience tells us that Indians come on the side that is most contrary to reason, and consequently are to be expected from below. Take your canoe, therefore, and go down stream among the islands, that we may have notice if any danger approaches from that quarter. If you should look a few miles on the main, especially on the York side, the information you'd bring in would be all the more accurate, and consequently the more valuable."

"The Big Sarpent is on the lookout in that quarter," said Pathfinder, "and as he knows the station well, no doubt he will give us timely notice should any wish to sarcumvent us in that direction."

"He is but an Indian, after all, Pathfinder, and this is an affair that calls for the knowledge of a white man. Major Duncan will be eternally grateful to the man that shall help the little enterprise to come off with flying colors. To tell you the truth, my friend, he is conscious it should never have been attempted; but he has too much obstinacy about him to own an error, though it be as manifest as the morning star."

The quartermaster then continued to reason with his companion in order to induce him to quit the island without delay, using such arguments as first suggested themselves, sometimes contradicting himself and not infrequently urging at one moment a motive that at the next was directly opposed by another. The Pathfinder, simple as he was, detected these flaws in the lieutenant's philosophy, though he was far from suspecting that they proceeded from a desire to clear the coast of Mabel's suitor. He met bad reasons by good ones, resisted every inducement that was not legitimate by his intimate acquaintance with his peculiar duties, and was blind, as usual, to the influence of every incentive that could not stand the test of integrity. He did not exactly suspect the secret objects of Muir, but he was far from being blind to his sophistry. The result was that the two parted, after a long dialogue, unconvinced and distrustful of each other's motives, though the distrust of the guide, like all that was connected with the man, partook of his own upright, disinterested, and ingenuous nature.

A conference that took place soon after between Sergeant Dunham and the lieutenant led to more consequences. When it was ended secret orders were issued to the men, the blockhouse was taken possession of, the huts were occupied, and one accustomed to the movements of soldiers might have detected that an expedition was in the wind. In fact, just as the sun was setting, the sergeant, who had been much occupied at what was called the harbor, came into his own hut, followed by Pathfinder and Cap, and, as he took his seat at the neat table that Mabel had prepared for him, he opened the budget of his intelligence.

"You are likely to be of some use here, my child," the old soldier commenced, "as this tidy and well-ordered supper can testify; and I trust when the proper moment arrives you will show yourself to be the descendant of those who know how to face their enemies."

"Why, father," cried Mabel, "I am not expected to fall in with the men and help defend the island, am I?"

"And yet women often have done such things in this quarter of the world, girl, as our friend the Pathfinder here will tell you. But lest you should be surprised at not seeing us when you awake in the morning, it is proper that I now tell you we intend to march in the course of this very night."

"*We*, father—and leave me and Jennie on this island alone!"

"No, my daughter, not quite as unmilitary as that. We shall leave Lieutenant Muir, Brother Cap, Corporal McNab, and three men, to compose the garrison during our absence. Jennie will remain with you in this hut and Brother Cap will occupy my place."

Mabel did not like the idea of having Lieutenant Muir as a companion, but her father continued:

"Neither you nor Mabel, Brother Cap," he said, "can have any legal authority with the garrison I leave behind on the island, but you may counsel and influence. Strictly speaking, Corporal McNab will be the commanding officer, and I have endeavored to impress him with a sense of his dignity, lest he might give way too much to the superior rank of Lieutenant Muir, who, being a volunteer, can have no right to interfere with the duty. I wish you to sustain the corporal, Brother Cap, for should the quartermaster once break through the regulations of the expedition he may pretend to command me as well as McNab."

"Of course, sergeant, you'll leave everything that is afloat under my care. The greatest confusion has grown out of misunderstandings between commanders-in-chief ashore and afloat."

"In one sense, brother, though in a general way the corporal is commander-in-chief. History does indeed tell us that a division of command leads to difficulties, and I shall avoid that danger. The corporal must command, but you can counsel freely, particularly in all matters relating to the boats, of which I shall leave one behind to secure your retreat should there be occasion. I know the corporal well—he is a brave man and a good soldier, and one that may be relied on, if the Santa Cruz can be kept from him. But then, he is a Scotchman, and will be liable to the quartermaster's influence, against which I desire both you and Mabel to be on your guard."

"But why leave us behind, dear father? I have come thus far to be a comfort to you, and why not go farther?"

"You are a good girl, Mabel, and very like the Dunhams! But you must halt here. We shall leave the island to-morrow before the day dawns, in order not to be seen by any prying eyes, and shall take the two largest boats, leaving you the other and one bark canoe. We are about to go into the channel used by the French, where we shall lie in wait perhaps a week to intercept their supply boats that are about to pass up on their way to Frontenac, loaded in particular with a heavy amount of Indian goods.

"It is of vast importance to his majesty's interests in this part of the world that the boats in question should be captured and carried into Oswego. They contain the blankets, trinkets, rifles, ammunition—in short, all the stores with which the French bribe their accursed savage allies to commit their unholy acts, setting at naught our holy religion and its precepts, the laws of humanity, and all that is sacred and dear among men. By cutting off these supplies we shall derange their plans and gain time on them, for the articles can not be sent across the ocean again this autumn."

"But, father, does not his majesty employ Indians also?" asked Mabel, with some curiosity.

"Certainly, girl, and he has a right to employ them—God bless him! It's a very different thing whether an Englishman or a Frenchman employs a savage, as everybody can understand."

"But I do not see the difference, father, between an Englishman and a Frenchman employing savages in war."

"All the odds in the world, child, though you may not be able to see it. In the first place, an Englishman is naturally humane and considerate, while a Frenchman is naturally ferocious and timid."

"And you may add, brother," said Cap, "that he will dance from morning till night, if you'll let him."

"Very true," gravely returned the sergeant.

"But, father, I can not see that all this alters the case. If it be wrong in a Frenchman to hire savages to fight his enemies, it would seem to be equally wrong in an Englishman. *You* will admit this, Pathfinder?"

"It's reasonable—it's reasonable," replied the scout, "and I have never been one of them that has raised a cry ag'in the Frenchers for doing the very thing we do ourselves. Still, it is worse to consort with a Mingo than to consort with a Delaware. If any of that just tribe were left, I should think it no sin to send them out ag'in the foe."

" And yet they scalp and slay young and old, women and children!"

"They have their gifts, Mabel, and are not to be blamed for following them. Natur' is natur', though the different tribes have different ways of showing it. For my part, I am white, and indeavour to maintain white feelings."

"I do not understand it, at all," said Mabel. "What is right in King George it would seem ought to be right in King Louis."

As all parties, Mabel excepted, seemed satisfied with the course the discussion had taken, no one appeared to think it necessary to pursue the subject. The trio of men, indeed, in this particular, so much resembled the great mass of their fellow-creatures, who usually judge of character equally without knowledge and without justice, that we might not have thought it necessary to record the discourse, had it not some bearing in its facts on the incidents of the legend, and in its opinions on the motives of the characters.

Supper was no sooner ended than the sergeant dismissed his guests, and then held a long and confidential dialogue with his daughter. He was little addicted to giving way to the gentler emotions, but the novelty of his present situation awakened feelings that he was unused to experience. The soldier, or the sailor, so long as he acts under the immediate supervision of a superior, thinks little of the risks he runs; but the moment he feels the responsibility of command, all the hazards of his undertaking begin to associate themselves in his mind with the chances of success or failure. While he dwells less on his own personal danger, perhaps, than when that is the principal consideration, he has more lively general perceptions of all the risks, and submits more to the influence of the feelings which doubt creates. Such was now the case with Sergeant Dunham, who, instead of looking forward to victory as certain, according to his usual habits, began to feel the possibility that he might be parting with his child forever.

The talk between father and daughter was long and affectionate, and when it was over the old sergeant kissed her fondly.

"God bless and protect you, girl," he said, "you are a good daughter."

Mabel threw herself in her father's arms, and sobbed on his bosom like an infant. The stern old soldier's heart was melted, and the tears of the two mingled; but Sergeant Dunham soon started, as if ashamed of himself, and gently forcing his daughter from him, bade her good-night, and sought his pallet. Mabel went sobbing to the rude corner that had been prepared for her reception, and in a few minutes the hut was undisturbed by any sound save the heavy breathing of the veteran.

It was not only broad daylight when she awoke, but the sun had actually been up some time. Her sleep had been tranquil, for she rested on an approving conscience, and fatigue contributed to render it sweet, and no sound of those who had been so early in motion had interfered with her rest. Springing to her feet, and rapidly dressing herself, the girl was soon breathing the fragrance of the morning in the open air. For the first time she was sensibly struck with the singular beauties, as well as with the profound retirement, of her present situation. The day proved to be one of those of the autumnal glory so common to a climate that is more abused than appreciated, and its influence was in every way inspiriting and genial. Mabel was benefited by this circumstance, for, as she fancied, her heart was heavy on account of the dangers to which a father, whom she now began to love, as women love when confidence is created, was about to be exposed.

But the island seemed absolutely deserted. The previous night the bustle of the arrival had given the spot an appearance of life that was now entirely gone, and our heroine had turned her eyes around on nearly every object in sight before she caught a view of a single human being to remove the sense of utter solitude. Then, indeed, she beheld all who were left behind, collected in a group, around a fire which might be said to belong to the camp. The person of her uncle, to whom she was so much accustomed, reassured the girl, and she examined the remainder with a curiosity natural to her situation. Beside Cap and the quartermaster, there were the corporal, the three soldiers, and the woman who was cooking. The huts were silent and empty, and the low but tower-like summit of the blockhouse rose above the bushes, by which it was half concealed, in picturesque beauty. The sun was just casting its brightness in the open places of the glade, and the vault over her head was impending in the soft sublimity of the blue void. Not a cloud was visible, and she secretly fancied the circumstance might be taken as a harbinger of peace and security.

Perceiving that all the others were occupied with that great concern of human nature, a breakfast, Mabel walked unobserved toward an end of the island where she was completely shut out of view by the trees and bushes. Here she got a stand on the very edge of the water by forcing aside the low branches, and stood watching the barely perceptible flow and re-flow of the miniature waves that laved the shore—a sort of physical echo to the agitation that prevailed on the lake fifty miles above her. The glimpses of natural scenery that offered were very pleasing, and our heroine, who had a quick and true eye for all that was lovely in nature, was not slow in selecting the most striking bits of landscape. She gazed through the different vistas formed by the openings between the islands, and thought she had never looked on aught more lovely.

While thus occupied, Mabel was suddenly alarmed by fancying that she caught a glimpse of a human form among the bushes that lined the shore of the island that lay directly before her. The distance across the water was not a hundred yards, and though she might be mistaken, and her fancy be wandering when the form passed before her sight, still she did not think she could be deceived. Aware that her sex would be no protection against a rifle-bullet, should an Iroquois get a view of her, the girl instinctively drew back, taking care to conceal her person as much as possible by the leaves, while she kept her own look riveted on the opposite shore, vainly awaiting for some time in the expectation of seeing the stranger. She was about to quit her post in the bushes and hasten to her uncle in order to acquaint him of her suspicions, when she saw the branch of an alder thrust beyond the bushes on the other island, and waved toward her significantly, and, as she fancied, in token of amity. This was a breathless and trying moment to one as inexperienced in frontier warfare as our heroine, and yet she felt the great necessity that existed for preserving her recollection and of acting with steadiness and discretion.

It was one of the peculiarities of the exposure to which those who dwelt on the frontiers of America were liable, to bring out the moral qualities of the women to a degree that they must themselves, under other circumstances, have believed they were incapable of manifesting, and Mabel well knew that the borderers loved to dwell in their legends on the presence of mind, fortitude, and spirit that their wives and sisters had displayed under circumstances the most trying. Her emulation had been awakened by what she had heard on such subjects, and it at once struck her that now was the moment for her to show that she was truly Sergeant Dunham's child. The motion of the branch was such as, she believed, indicated amity; and, after a moment's hesitation, she broke off a twig, fastened it to a stick, and, thrusting it through an opening, waved it in return, imitating as closely as possible the manner of the other.

This dumb show lasted two or three minutes on both sides, when Mabel perceived that the bushes opposite were cautiously pushed aside, and a human face appeared at an opening. A glance sufficed to let Mabel see that it was the countenance of a redskin, as well as that of a woman. A second and a better look satisfied her that it was the face of June, the wife of Arrowhead, the Tuscarora. During the time she had traveled in company with this woman, Mabel had been won by the gentleness of manner, the meek simplicity, and the mingled awe and affection with which she regarded her husband. Once or twice, in the course of the journey, she fancied the Tuscarora had manifested toward herself an unpleasant degree of attention, and on those occasions it had struck her that his wife exhibited sorrow and mortification. As Mabel, however, had more than compensated for any pain she might, in this way, unintentionally have caused her companion, by her own kindness of manner and attentions, the woman had shown much attachment to her, and they had parted with a deep conviction on the mind of our heroine that in June she had lost a friend.

It is useless to attempt to analyze all the ways by which the human heart is led into confidence. Such a feeling, however, had the young Tuscarora woman awakened in the breast of our heroine; and the latter, under the impression that this extraordinary visit was for her own good, felt every disposition to have a closer communication. She no longer hesitated about showing herself clear of the bushes, and was not sorry to see June imitate her confidence by stepping fearlessly out of her own cover. The two girls—for the Tuscarora, though married, was even younger than Mabel—now openly exchanged signs of friendship, and the latter beckoned to her friend to approach, though she knew not the manner, herself, in which this object could be effected. But June was not slow in letting it be seen that it was in her power; for, disappearing a moment, she soon showed herself again in the end of a bark canoe, the bows of which she had drawn to the edge of the bushes, and of which the body still lay in a sort of covered creek. Mabel was about to invite her to cross, when her own name was called aloud in the stentorian voice of her uncle. Making a hurried gesture for the Tuscarora girl to conceal h e r s e l f, Mabel sprang from the bushes, and tripped up the glade toward the sound, and perceived that the whole party had just seated themselves at breakfast, Cap having barely put his appetite under sufficient restraint to summon her to join them. That this was the most favorable instant for the interview flashed on the mind of Mabel; and excusing herself on the plea of not being prepared for the meal, she bounded back to the thicket, and soon renewed her communications with the young Indian woman.

MABEL AND JUNE ON STATION ISLAND.

June was quick of comprehension; and with half a dozen noiseless strokes of the paddle her canoe was concealed in the bushes of Station Island. In another minute Mabel held her hand, and was leading her through the grove toward her own hut. Fortunately the latter was so placed as to be completely hidden from the sight of those at the fire, and they both entered it unseen. Hastily explaining to her guest, in the best manner she could, the necessity of quitting her for a short time, Mabel, first placing June in her own room, with a full certainty that she would not quit it until told to do so, went to the fire and took her seat among the rest, with all the composure it was in her power to command.

"Late come, late served, Mabel," said her uncle, between two mouthfuls of broiled salmon, for though the cooking might be very unsophisticated on that remote frontier, the viands were generally delicious; "late come, late served: it is a good rule, and keeps laggards up to their work."

"I am no laggard, uncle, for I have been stirring near an hour, and exploring our island."

That was the only explanation that Mabel gave of her lateness, and, in fact, to most of the conversation during breakfast she paid but little attention, though she felt some surprise that Lieutenant Muir, an officer whose character for courage stood well, should openly recommend, as he did in his talk, an abandonment of what appeared to her to be a double duty, her father's character being connected with the defense of the island. Her mind, however, was so much occupied with her guest, that, seizing the first favorable moment, she left the table, and was soon in her own hut again. Carefully fastening the door, and seeing that the simple curtain was drawn before the single little window, Mabel led June into the outer room, making signs of affection and confidence.

"I am glad to see you, June," said Mabel, with one of her sweetest smiles, and in her own winning voice; "very glad to see you. What has brought you hither, and how did you discover the island?"

"Talk slow," said June, returning smile for smile, and pressing the little hand she held with one of her own, that was scarcely larger, though it had been hardened by labor, "more slow—too quick."

Mabel repeated her questions, endeavoring to repress the impetuosity of her feelings, and she succeeded in speaking so distinctly as to be understood.

"June, friend," returned the Indian woman.

"I believe you, June—from my soul I believe you; what has this to do with your visit?"

"Friend come to see friend," answered June, again smiling openly in the other's face.

"There is some other reason, June, else would you never run this risk, and alone—you are alone, June?"

"June wid you—no one else. June come alone, paddle canoe."
"I hope so—I think so—nay, I *know* so. You would not be treacherous with me, June?"
"What treacherous?"
"You would not betray me—would not give me to the French—to the Iroquois—to Arrowhead"—June shook her head earnestly—"you would not sell my scalp?"

Here June passed her arm fondly around the slender waist of Mabel, and pressed her to her heart, with a tenderness and affection that brought tears into the eyes of our heroine. It was done in the fond caressing manner of a woman, and it was scarcely possible that it should not obtain credit for sincerity with a young and ingenuous person of the same sex. Mabel returned the pressure, and then held the other off at the length of her arm, looking her steadily in the face, and continued her inquiries.

"If June has something to tell her friend, let her speak plainly," she said. "My ears are open."

"June 'fraid Arrowhead kill her."

"But Arrowhead will never know it." Mabel's blood mounted to her temples as she said this, for she felt that she was urging a wife to be treacherous to her husband. "That is, Mabel will not tell him."

"He bury tomahawk in June's head."

"That must never be, dear June; I would rather you should say no more than run this risk."

"Blockhouse good place to sleep—good place to stay."

"Do you mean that I may save my life by keeping in the blockhouse, June? Surely, surely, Arrowhead will not hurt you for telling me that. He can not wish me any great harm, for I never injured him."

"Arrowhead wish no harm to handsome paleface," returned June, averting her face, and, though she always spoke in the soft, gentle voice of an Indian girl, permitting its notes to fall so low as to cause them to sound melancholy and timid. "Arrowhead love paleface girl."

Mabel blushed, she knew not why, and for a moment her questions were repressed by a feeling of inherent delicacy. But it was necessary to know more, for her apprehensions had been keenly awakened, and she resumed her inquiries.

"Arrowhead can have no reason to love or hate *me*," she said. "Is he near you?"

"Husband always near wife, here," said June, laying her hand on her heart.

"But, tell me, June, ought I keep in the blockhouse to-day—this morning—now?"

"Blockhouse very good; good for squaw. Blockhouse got no scalp."

"I fear I understand you only too well, June. Do you wish to see my father?"

"No here; gone away."

"You can not know that, June; you see the island is full of his soldiers."

"No full; gone away"—here June held up four of her fingers—"so many redcoats."

"And Pathfinder—would you not like to see the Pathfinder? He can talk to you in the Iroquois tongue."

"Tongue gone wid him," said June, laughing; "keep tongue in his mout'."

There was something so sweet and contagious in the infantile laugh of an Indian girl that Mabel could not refrain from joining in it, much as her fears were aroused by all that had passed.

"You appear to know, or think you know, all about us, June. But, if Pathfinder be gone, Jasper Westen can speak French, too. You know Jasper Western; shall I run and bring *him* to talk with you?"

"Jasper gone, too; all but heart; that there." As June said this, she laughed again, looked in different directions, as if unwilling to confuse the other, and laid her hand on Mabel's bosom.

Our heroine had often heard of the wonderful sagacity of the Indians, and of the surprising manner in which they noted all things, while they appeared to regard none, but she was scarce prepared for the direction the discourse had so singularly taken. Willing to change it, and, at the same time, truly anxious to learn how great the danger that impended over them might really be, she arose from the camp-stool on which she had been seated, and, by assuming an attitude of less affectionate confidence, she hoped to hear more of what she really desired to learn, and to avoid allusions to that which she found so embarrassing.

"You know how much or how little you ought to tell me, June," she said, "and I hope you love me well enough to give me the information I ought to hear. My dear uncle, too, is on the island, and you are, or ought to be, his friend, as well as mine; and both of us will remember your conduct when we get back to Oswego."

"Maybe never get back—who know?" This was said doubtingly, or as one lays down an uncertain proposition, and not with a taunt, or desire to alarm.

"No one knows what will happen, but God. Our lives are in His hands. Still, I think you are to be His instrument in saving us."

This passed June's comprehension, and she only looked her ignorance, for it was evident she wished to be of use.

"Blockhouse very good," she repeated, as soon as her countenance ceased to express uncertainty, laying strong emphasis on the two last words.

"Well, I understand this, June, and will sleep in it to-night. Of course, I am to tell my uncle what you have said?"

June started, and she discovered a very manifest uneasiness at the interrogatory.

"No—no—no—no," she answered, with a volubility and vehemence that was imitated from the French of the Canadas; "no good to tell Saltwater. He much talk and long tongue. Think woods all water; understand not'ing. Tell Arrowhead, and June die."

"You do my dear uncle injustice, for he would be as little likely to betray you as any one."

"No understand. Saltwater got tongue, but no eye, no ear, no nose—not'ing but tongue, tongue, tongue."

Although Mabel did not exactly coincide in this opinion, she saw that Cap had not the confidence of the young Indian woman, and that it was idle to expect she would consent to his being admitted to their interview.

"You appear to think you know our situation pretty well, June," Mabel continued. "Have you been on the island before this visit?"

"Just come."

"How, then, do you know that what you say is true? My father, the Pathfinder, and Jasper may all be here within the sound of my voice, if I choose to call them."

"All gone," said June, positively, smiling good-humoredly at the same time.

"Nay, this is more than you *can* say certainly, not having been over the island to examine it."

"Got good eyes; see boat with men go away—see ship with Jasper."

"Then you have been some time watching us; I think, however, you have not counted them that remain."

June laughed, held up her four fingers, and then pointed to her two thumbs; passing her finger over the first, she repeated the word "redcoats," and, touching the last, she added, "Saltwater," "Quartermaster." All this was being very accurate, and Mabel began to entertain serious doubts of the propriety of her permitting her visitor to depart without her becoming more explicit. Still, it was so repugnant to her feelings to abuse the confidence this gentle and affectionate creature had evidently reposed in her, that Mabel had no sooner admitted the thought of summoning her uncle than she rejected it as unworthy of herself and unjust to her friend. To aid this good resolution, too, there was the certainty that June would reveal nothing, but take refuge in a stubborn silence if any attempt were made to coerce her.

"You think, then, June," Mabel continued, as soon as these thoughts had passed through her mind, "that I had better live in the blockhouse?"

"Good place for squaw. Blockhouse got no scalp. Logs t'ick."

"You speak confidently, June, as if you had been in it, and had measured its walls."

June laughed, and she looked knowing, though she said nothing.

"Does anyone but yourself know how to find this island? Have any of the Iroquois seen it?"

June looked sad, and she cast her eyes warily about her, as if distrusting a listener.

"Tuscarora everywhere—Oswego here, Frontenac, Mohawk—everywhere. If he see June, kill her."

"But we thought that no one knew of this island, and that we had no reason to fear our enemies while on it."

"Much eye, Iroquois."

"Eyes will not always do, June. This spot is hid from ordinary sight, and few of even our own people know how to find it."

"One man can tell—some English talk French."

Mabel felt a chill at her heart. All the suspicions against Jasper, which she had hitherto disdained entertaining, crowded in a body on her thoughts, and the sensation that they brought was so sickening that for an instant she imagined she was about to faint. Arousing herself, and remembering her promise to her father, she arose and walked up and down the hut for a minute, fancying that Jasper's delinquencies were naught to her, though her inmost heart yearned with the desire to think him innocent.

"I understand your meaning, June," she then said. "You wish me to know that someone has treacherously told your people where and how to find the island."

June laughed, for in her eyes artifice in war was oftener a merit than a crime; but she was too true to the tribe herself to say more than the occasion required. Her object was to save Mabel, and Mabel only, and she saw no sufficient reason for "traveling out of the record," as the lawyers express it, in order to do anything else.

"Paleface know now," she added. "Blockhouse good for girl—no matter for men and warriors."

"But it is much matter with me, June, for one of these men is my uncle, whom I love, and the others are my countrymen and friends. I must tell them what has passed."

"Then June be kill," returned the young Indian quietly, though she spoke with concern.

"No—they shall not know that you have been here. Still, they must be on their guard, and we can all go into the blockhouse."

"Arrowhead know—see everything, and June be kill. June come to tell young paleface friend, not to tell men. Every warrior watch his own scalp. June squaw, and tell squaw; no tell men."

Mabel was greatly distressed at this declaration of her wild friend, for it was now evident the young creature understood that her communication was to go no farther. She was ignorant how far these people considered the point of honor interested in her keeping the secret; and, most of all, was she unable to say how far any indiscretion of her own might actually commit June and endanger her life. All these considerations flashed on her mind, and reflection only rendered their influence more painful. June, too, manifestly viewed the matter gravely, for she began to gather up the different little articles she had dropped in taking Mabel's hand, and was preparing to depart. To attempt detaining her was out of the question, and to part from her, after all she had hazarded to serve her, was repugnant to all the just and kind feelings of our heroine's nature.

"June," she said eagerly, folding her arms round the gentle but uneducated being, "we are friends. From me you have nothing to fear, for no one shall know of your visit. If you could give me some signal just before the danger comes, some sign by which to know when to go into the blockhouse—how to take care of myself."

June paused, for she had been in earnest in her intention to depart; and then she said quietly:

"Bring June pigeon."

"A pigeon! Where shall I find a pigeon to bring you?"

"Next hut—bring old one—June go to canoe."

"I think I understand you, June; but had I not better lead you back to the bushes, lest you meet some of the men?"

"Go out first—count men—one—two—t'ree—four—five—six"—here June held up her fingers and laughed—"all out of way—good—all but one—call him one side. Then sing, and fetch pigeon."

Mabel smiled at the readiness and ingenuity of the girl, and prepared to execute her requests. At the door, however, she stopped, and looked back entreatingly at the Indian woman.

"Is there no hope of your telling me more, June?" she said.

"Know all now—blockhouse good—pigeon tell—Arrowhead kill."

The last words sufficed; for Mabel could not urge further communications, when her companion herself told her that the penalty of her revelations might be death by the hand of her husband. Throwing open the door, she made a sign of adieu to June, and went out of the hut. Mabel resorted to the simple expedient of the young Indian girl to ascertain the situation of the different individuals on the island. Instead of looking about her with the intention of recognizing faces and dresses, she merely counted them; and found that three still remained at the fire, while two had gone to the boat, one of whom was Mr. Muir. The sixth man was her uncle, and he was coolly arranging some fishing-tackle, at no great distance from the fire. The woman was just entering her own hut; and this accounted for the whole party. Mabel now, affecting to have dropped something, returned nearly to the hut she had left, warbling an air, stooped as if to pick up some object from the ground, and hurried toward the hut June had mentioned. This was a dilapidated structure, and it had been converted by the soldiers of the last detachment into a sort of storehouse for their live stock. Among other things, it contained a few dozen pigeons, which were regaling on a pile of wheat that had been brought off from one of the farms plundered on the Canada shore. Mabel had not much difficulty in catching one of these pigeons, although they fluttered, and flew about the hut, with a noise like that of drums; and, concealing it in her dress, she stole back toward her own hut with the prize. It was empty; and, without doing more than cast a glance in at the door, the eager girl hurried down to the shore. She had no difficulty in escaping observation, for the trees and bushes made a complete cover to her person. At the canoe she found June, who took the pigeon, placed it in a basket of her own manufacturing, and repeating the words, "Blockhouse good," glided out of the bushes and across the narrow passage as noiselessly as she had come. Mabel waited some time to catch a signal of leave-taking or amity, after her friend had landed, but none was given. The adjacent islands, without exception, were as quiet as if no one had ever disturbed the sublime repose of nature; and nowhere could any sign or symptom be discovered, as Mabel then thought, that might denote the proximity of the sort of danger of which June had given notice.

On returning, however, from the shore, Mabel was struck with a little circumstance that, in an ordinary situation, would have attracted no attention, but which, now that her suspicions had been aroused, did not pass before her uneasy eye unnoticed. A small piece of red bunting, such as is used in the ensigns of ships, was fluttering at the lower branch of a small tree, fastened in a way to permit it to blow out, or to droop like a vessel's pennant.

Now that Mabel's fears were awakened, June herself could not have manifested greater quickness in analyzing facts that she believed might affect the safety of the party. She saw at a glance that this bit of cloth could be observed from an adjacent island; that it lay so near the line between her own hut and the canoe, as to leave no doubt that June had passed near it, if not directly under it; and that it might be a signal to communicate some important fact connected with the mode of attack to those who were probably lying in ambush near them. Tearing the little strip of bunting from the tree, Mabel hastened on, scarce knowing what duty next required. June might be false to her; but her manner, her looks, her affection, and her disposition, as Mabel had known it in the journey, forbade the idea.

As she walked toward the blockhouse she met Lieutenant Muir, who, after a few words of compliment, said suddenly: "What is that you're twisting round your slender finger, Mistress Mabel, as you may be said to twist hearts?"

"It is nothing but a bit of cloth—a sort of flag—a trifle that is hardly worth our attention at this grave moment—if—"

"A trifle! It's not so trifling as you may imagine, Mistress Mabel," taking the bit of bunting from her and stretching it at full length with both his arms extended, while his face grew grave and his eye watchful. "You didn't find this, Mabel Dunham, in the breakfast, did you?"

Mabel simply acquainted him with the spot where, and the manner in which she had found the bit of cloth. While she was speaking the eye of the quartermaster was not quiet for a moment, glancing from the rag to the face of our heroine, then back again to the rag. That his suspicions were awakened was easy to be seen, nor was he long in letting it be known what direction they had taken.

"We are not in a part of the world where our ensigns ought to be spread abroad to the wind, Mabel Dunham!" he said, with an ominous shake of the head.

"I thought as much myself, Mr. Muir, and brought away the little flag, lest it might be the means of betraying our presence here to the enemy, even though nothing is intended by its display. Ought not my uncle to be made acquainted with the circumstances?"

"I don't see the necessity for that, Mabel, for, as you justly say, it is a circumstance, and circumstances sometimes worry the worthy mariner. But this flag, if flag it can be called, belongs to a seaman's craft. You may perceive that it is made of what is called bunting, and that is a description of cloth used only by vessels for such purposes, *our* colors being of silk, as you may understand, or painted canvas. It's surprisingly like the fly of the 'Scud's' ensign! And now I recollect me to have observed that a piece had been cut from that very flag!"

Mabel felt her heart sink, but she had sufficient self-command not to attempt an answer.

"It must be looked to," Muir continued, "and after all, I think it may be well to hold a short consultation with Master Cap, than whom a more loyal subject does not exist in the British Empire."

"I have thought the warning so serious," Mabel rejoined, "that I am about to remove to the blockhouse and to take the woman with me."

"I do not see the prudence of that, Mabel. The blockhouse will be the first spot assailed, should there really be an attack, and it's not well provided for a seige—that must be allowed. If I might advise in so delicate a contingency, I would recommend your taking refuge in the boat, which, as you may now perceive, is most favorably placed to retreat by that channel opposite, where all in it would be hid by the islands in one or two minutes. Water leaves no trail, as Pathfinder well expresses it, and there appear to be so many different passages in that quarter, that escape would be more than probable. I've always been of the opinion that the major hazarded too much in occupying a post as far advanced, and as much exposed, as this."

"It's too late to regret it now, Mr. Muir, and we have only to consult our own security."

"And the King's honor, Mabel. Yes; His Majesty's arms and his glorious name are not to be overlooked on any occasion."

"Then I think it might be better if we all turned our eyes toward the place that has been built to maintain them, instead of the boat," said Mabel, smiling; "and so, Mr. Muir, I am for the blockhouse, with a disposition to await there the return of my father and his party. He would be sadly grieved at finding we had fled when he got back, successful himself, and filled with the confidence of our having been as faithful to our duties as he has been to his own."

"Nay, nay, for heaven's sake, do not misunderstand me, Mabel!" Muir interrupted, with some alarm of manner; "I am far from intimating that any but you females ought to take refuge in the boat. The duty of us men is sufficiently plain, no doubt, and my resolution has been formed from the first to stand or fall by the blockhouse."

Mabel had heard enough. Her mind was too much occupied with what had passed that morning, and with her fears, to wish to linger further to listen to love speeches, that, in her most joyous and buoyant moments, she would have found unpleasant. She took a hasty leave of her companion, and was about to trip away toward the hut of the other woman, when Muir arrested the movement by laying a hand on her arm.

"One word, Mabel," he said, "before you leave me. This little flag may, or it may not, have a particular meaning; if it has, now that we are aware of its being shown, may it not be better to put it back again, while we watch vigilantly for some answer that may betray the conspiracy; and if it mean nothing, why, nothing will follow."

"This may be all right, Mr. Muir, though, if the whole is accidental, the flag might be the occasion of the Fort being discovered."

Mabel stayed to utter no more, but she was soon out of sight, running into the hut toward which she had been first proceeding. The quartermaster remained on the very spot, and in the precise attitude in which she had left him, for quite a minute, first looking at the bounding figure of the girl, and then at the bit of bunting, which he still held before him, in a way to denote indecision. His irresolution lasted but for this minute, however, for he was soon beneath the tree, where he fastened the mimic flag to a branch again; though from his ignorance of the precise spot from which it had been taken by Mabel, he left it fluttering from a part of the oak where it was still more exposed than before to the eyes of any passenger on the river, though less in view from the island itself.

Removing at once into the blockhouse, as June had advised, Mabel left Jennie, the soldier's wife, in charge, and went, herself, to see how matters stood.

But, even as she stood talking with Corporal McNab, whom her father had left in charge, the sharp crack of a rifle sounded from the thicket, and the corporal fell dead at her feet.

Then came over Mabel the full consciousness of her situation, and of the necessity of exertion. She cast a rapid glance at the body at her feet, saw that it had ceased to breathe, and fled. It was but a few minutes' run to the blockhouse, the door of which Mabel had barely gained when it was closed violently in her face by Jennie, the soldier's wife, who, in blind terror, thought only of her own safety. The reports of five or six rifles were heard while Mabel was calling out for admittance; and the additional terror they produced prevented the woman within from undoing quickly the very fastenings she had been so very expert in applying. After a minute's delay, however, Mabel found the door reluctantly yielding to her constant pressure, and she forced her slender body through the opening the instant it was large enough to allow of its passage. By this time, Mabel's heart ceased to beat tumultuously, and she gained sufficient self-command to act collectedly. Instead of yielding to the almost convulsive efforts of her companion to close the door again, she held it open long enough to ascertain that none of her own party was in sight, or likely, on the instant, to endeavor to gain admission; she then allowed the opening to be shut. Her orders and proceedings now became more calm and rational. But a single bar was crossed, and Jennie was directed to stand in readiness to remove even that, at any application from a friend. She then ascended the ladder to the room above, where, by means of loopholes, she was enabled to get as good a view of the island as the surrounding bushes would allow. Admonishing her associate below to be firm and steady, she made as careful an examination of the environs as her situation permitted.

To her great surprise, Mabel could not, at first, see a living soul on the island, friend or enemy. Neither Frenchman nor Indian was visible, though a small, straggling white cloud, that was floating before the wind, told her in which quarter she ought to look for them. The rifles had been discharged from the direction of the island whence June had come, though whether the enemy were on that island, or had actually landed on her own, Mabel could not say. Going to the loop that commanded a view of the spot where McNab lay, her blood curdled at perceiving all three of his soldiers lying apparently lifeless at his side. These men had rushed to a common center at the first alarm, and had been shot down almost simultaneously by the invisible foe, whom the corporal had affected to despise.

Neither Cap nor Lieutenant Muir were to be seen. With a beating heart, Mabel examined every opening through the trees, and ascended even to the upper story, or garret, of the blockhouse, where she got a full view of the whole island, so far as its covers would allow, but with no better success. She had expected to see the body of her uncle lying on the grass, like those of the soldiers, but it was nowhere visible. Turning toward the spot where the boat lay, Mabel saw that it was still fastened to the shore; and then she supposed that, by some accident, Muir had been prevented from effecting his retreat in that quarter. In short, the island lay in the quiet of the grave, the bodies of the soldiers rendering the scene as fearful as it was extraordinary.

Jennie, fearing for the safety of her husband, peered out of the blockhouse door. Again the rifles cracked, and, as the war-whoop of the Iroquois rang out, Jennie fell dead across the body of her murdered husband. The savages had surrounded the blockhouse.

Mabel was alone in the blockhouse. But she bravely secured the door and waited for what was to come.

Long and painfully melancholy hours passed, during which Mabel heard the yells of the savages; for the liquor which they had found in the stores had carried them beyond the bounds of precaution. Toward the middle of the day she fancied she saw a white man on the island, though his dress and wild appearance at first made her take him for a newly arrived savage. A view of his face, although it was swarthy naturally and much darkened by exposure, left no doubt that her conjecture was true, and she felt as if there was now one of a species more like her own present, and one to whom she might appeal for succor in the last emergency. Mabel little knew, alas! how small was the influence exercised by the whites over their savage allies when the latter had begun to taste of blood; or how slight, indeed, was the disposition to divert them from their cruelties.

The day seemed a month by Mabel's computation, and the only part of it that did not drag were the minutes spent in prayer. She had recourse to this relief from time to time; and at each effort she found her spirit firmer, her mind more tranquil, and her tendency to resignation more confirmed.

While the light lasted, the situation of our heroine was sufficiently alarming, but as the shades of evening gradually gathered over the island it became fearfully appalling. By this time the savages had wrought themselves up to the point of fury, for they had possessed themselves of all the liquor of the English, and their outcries and gesticulations were those of men truly possessed of evil spirits. All the efforts of their French leader to restrain them were entirely fruitless, and he had wisely withdrawn to an adjacent island, where he had a sort of bivouac, that he might keep at a safe distance from friends so apt to run into excesses. Before quitting the spot, however, this officer, at great risk to his own life, succeeded in extinguishing the fire and in securing the ordinary means to relight it. This precaution he took lest the Indians should burn the blockhouse, the preservation of which was necessary to the success of his future plans. He would gladly have removed all the arms also, but this he found impracticable, the warriors clinging to their knives and tomahawks with the tenacity of men who regarded a point of honor as long as a faculty was left; and to carry off the rifles, and leave behind him the very weapons that were generally used on such occasions, would have been an idle expedient.

Morning had almost come, when a light footstep was audible below, and one of those gentle pushes at the door was heard which just moved the massive beams on the hinges.

"Who wishes to enter? Is it you, dear, dear uncle?" whispered Mabel.

"Saltwater no here. St. Lawrence sweet water," was the answer. "Open quick—want to come in."

It was June, the faithful Tuscarora woman.

The step of Mabel was never lighter, or her movements more quick and natural, than while she was descending the ladder and turning the bars, for all her motions were earnest and active. This time she thought only of her escape, and she opened the door with a rapidity that did not admit of caution. Her first impulse was to rush into the open air, in the blind hope of quitting the blockhouse, but June repulsed the attempt, and entering, she coolly barred the door again, before she would notice Mabel's eager efforts to embrace her.

"Bless you—bless you, June," cried our heroine most fervently—"you are sent by Providence to be my guardian angel!"

"No hug so tight—" answered the Tuscarora woman. "Paleface woman all cry or all laugh. Let June fasten door."

Mabel became more rational, and in a few minutes the two were in the upper room, seated, hand in hand, distrust or rivalry between them being banished on the one side by the consciousness of favors received, and on the other by the consciousness of favors conferred.

"Now, tell me, June," Mabel commenced, as soon as she had given and received one warm embrace, "have you seen or heard aught of my poor uncle?"

"Do n't know. No one see him; no one hear him; no one know anyt'ing. Saltwater run into river, I t'ink, for I no find him; quartermaster gone too. I look, and look, and look; but no see 'em, one, t'other, nowhere."

"Blessed be God! They must have escaped, though the means are not known to us. I thought I saw a Frenchman on the island, June?"

"Yes—French captain come, but he go away, too. Plenty of Injin on island."

"Oh! June, June, are there no means to prevent my beloved father from falling into the hands of his enemies?"

"Do n't know; t'ink dat warriors wait in ambush, and Yengeese must lose scalp."

But June determined to do her best to save Mabel from the Iroquois, and the night passed quietly, for the Indians had gone away, evidently to carouse or watch in ambush for the sergeant's return.

The night was far more quiet than that which had preceded it, and Mabel slept with an increasing confidence, for she now felt satisfied that her own fate would not be decided until the return of her father. The following day he was expected, however, and when our heroine awoke, she ran eagerly to the loops in order to ascertain the state of the weather and the skies, as well as the condition of the island. The weather had changed. The wind blew fresh from the southward, and though the air was bland, it was filled with the elements of storm.

"This grows more and more difficult to bear, June," Mabel said, when she left the window.

"Hush! Here they come! June thought hear a cry, like a warrior's shout when he take a scalp."

"What mean you? There is no more butchery! There *can* be no more."

"Saltwater!" exclaimed June, laughing, as she stood peeping through a loophole.

"My dear uncle! Thank God, he then lives. Oh! June, June, *you* will not let them harm *him?*"

"June poor squaw. What warrior t'ink of what she say? Arrowhead bring him here."

By this time Mabel was at a loop, and, sure enough, there were Cap and the quartermaster in the hands of the Indians, eight or ten of whom were conducting them to the foot of the block; for by this capture the enemy now well knew that there could be no man in the building. Mabel scarcely breathed until the whole party stood ranged directly before the door, when she was rejoiced to see that the French officer was among them. A low conversation followed, in which both the white leader and Arrowhead spoke earnestly to their captives, when the quartermaster called out to her, in a voice loud enough to be heard.

"Mabel! Pretty Mabel!" he said. "Look out of one of the loopholes and pity our condition. We are threatened with instant death, unless you open the door to the conquerors. Relent, then, or we'll no be wearing our scalps half an hour from this blessed moment."

Mabel thought there were mockery and levity in this appeal, and its manner rather fortified than weakened her resolution to hold the place as long as possible.

"Speak to me, uncle," she said, with her mouth at a loop, "and tell me what I ought to do."

"Thank God! Thank God!" ejaculated Cap. "The sound of your sweet voice, Mabel, lightens my heart of a heavy load, for I feared you had shared the fate of poor Jennie. My breast has felt, the last four-and-twenty hours, as if a ton of kentledge had been stowed in it. You ask me what you ought to do, child, and I do not know how to advise you, though you are my own sister's daughter! The most I can say just now, my poor girl, is most heartily to curse the day you or I ever saw this bit of fresh water."

"But, uncle, is your life in danger—do *you* think I ought to open the door?"

"A round turn and two half-hitches make a fast belay; and I would counsel no one who is out of the hands of these Frenchers and redskins to unbar or unfasten anything, in order to fall into them. As to the quartermaster and myself, we are both elderly men, and not of much account to mankind in general, as honest Pathfinder would say; and it can make no great odds to him whether he balances the purser's books this year or the next; and as for myself, why, if I were on the seaboard I should know what to do—but up here in this watery wilderness, I can only say that if I were behind that bit of a bulwark, it would take a good deal of Indian logic to rouse me out of it."

But the quartermaster advised surrender.

"If nothing but your convenience were concerned, Mabel," he said, "we should all cheerfully acquiesce in your wishes; but these gentlemen fancy that the work will aid their operations, and they have a strong desire to possess it. To be frank with you, finding myself and your uncle in a very peculiar situation, I acknowledge that, to avert consequences, I have assumed the power that belongs to His Majesty's commission, and entered into a verbal capitulation, by which I have engaged to give up the blockhouse and the whole island. It is the fortune of war, and must be submitted to; so open the door, pretty Mabel, forthwith, and confide yourself to the care of those who know how to treat beauty and virtue in distress. There's no courtier in Scotland more complaisant than this chief, or who is more familiar with the laws of decorum."

"No leave blockhouse," muttered June, who stood at Mabel's side, attentive to all that passed. "Blockhouse good; got no scalp."

Our heroine might have yielded, but for this appeal. Now, however, she replied bravely—

"I shall remain as I am, Mr. Muir, until I get some tidings of my father. He will return in the course of the next ten days."

"Ah! Mabel, this artifice will no deceive the enemy, who, by means that would be unintelligible did not our suspicions rest on an unhappy young man with too much plausibility, are familiar with all our doings and plans, and well know that the sun will not set before the worthy sergeant and his companions will be in their power. Aweel! Submission to Providence is truly a Christian virtue!"

"Mr. Muir, you appear to be deceived in the strength of this work, and to fancy it weaker than it is. Do you desire to see what I can do in the way of defense, if so disposed?"

"I do n't mind if I do," answered the quartermaster.

"What you think of that, then? Look at the loop of the upper story."

As soon as Mabel had spoken all eyes were turned upward, and beheld the muzzle of a rifle cautiously thrust through a hole. The result did not disappoint expectation. No sooner did the Indians catch a sight of the fatal weapon, than they leaped aside, and in less than a minute every man among them had sought a cover. The French officer kept his eye on the barrel of the piece, in order to ascertain that it was not pointed in his particular direction, and he coolly took a pinch of snuff. As neither Muir nor Cap had anything to apprehend from the quarter in which the others were menaced, they kept their ground.

"Be wise, my pretty Mabel, be wise," exclaimed the former, "and no be provoking useless contention."

"What do ye think of the Pathfinder, Master Muir, for a garrison to so strong a post!" cried Mabel, resorting to a ruse that the circumstances rendered very excusable. "What will your French and Indian companions think of the aim of the Pathfinder's rifle?"

"Bear gently on the unfortunate, pretty Mabel, and do not confound the king's servants—may heaven bless him and all his royal lineage—with the king's enemies. If Pathfinder be, indeed, in the blockhouse, let him speak, and we will hold our negotiations directly with him. He knows us as friends, and we fear no evil at his hands, and least of all to myself; for a generous mind is apt to render rivalry in a certain interest a sure ground of respect and amity; since admiration of the same woman proves a community of feeling and tastes."

The reliance on Pathfinder's friendship did not extend beyond the quartermaster and Cap, however, for even the French officer, who had hitherto stood his ground so well, shrunk at the sound of the terrible name. So unwilling, indeed, did this individual, a man of iron nerves, and one long accustomed to the dangers of the peculiar warfare in which he was engaged, appear to be to remain exposed to the assaults of Killdeer, Pathfinder's famous rifle, that he did not disdain to seek a cover, insisting that his two prisoners should follow him. Mabel was too glad to be rid of her enemies to lament the departure of her friends, though she kissed her hand to Cap through the loop, and called out to him in terms of affection as he moved slowly and unwillingly away.

The enemy now seemed disposed to abandon all attempts on the block-house for the present, and June, who had ascended to a trap in the roof, whence the best view was to be obtained, reported that the whole party had assembled to eat on a distant and sheltered part of the island, where Muir and Cap were quietly sharing in the good things that were going, as if they had no concern on their minds. This information greatly relieved Mabel, and she began to turn her thoughts again to the means of effecting her own escape, or at least of letting her father know of the danger that awaited him. The sergeant was expected to return that afternoon, and she knew that a moment gained or lost might decide his fate.

Three or four hours flew by. The island was again buried in a profound quiet, the day was wearing away, and yet Mabel had decided on nothing. June was in the basement preparing their frugal meal, and Mabel herself had ascended to the roof, which was provided with a trap that allowed her to go out on the top of the building, whence she commanded the best view of surrounding objects that the island possessed.

The sun had actually set, no intelligence had been received from the boats, and Mabel ascended to the roof, to take a last look, hoping that the party would arrive in the darkness; which would at least prevent the Indians from rendering their ambuscade as fatal as it might otherwise prove, and which possibly might enable her to give some more intelligible signal, by means of fire, than it would otherwise be in her power to do. Her eye had turned carefully round the whole horizon, and she was just on the point of drawing in her person, when an object that struck her as new caught her attention. The islands lay grouped so closely that six or eight different channels or passages between them were in view; and in one of the most covered, concealed in a great measure by the bushes of the shore, lay, what a second look assured her, was a bark canoe. It contained a human being beyond question. Confident that, if an enemy, her signal could do no harm, and, if a friend, that it might do good, the eager girl waved a little flag toward the stranger, which she had prepared for her father, taking care that it should not be seen from the island.

Mabel had repeated her signal eight or ten times in vain, and she began to despair of its being noticed, when a sign was given in return, by the wave of a paddle, and the man so far discovered himself as to let her see it was Chingachgook. Here, then, at last, was a friend; one, too, who was able, and she doubted not would be willing, to aid her! From that instant her courage and her spirits revived. The Mohican had seen her—must have recognized her, as he knew that she was of the party; and, no doubt, as soon as it was sufficiently dark, he would take the steps necessary to release her. That he was aware of the presence of the enemy was apparent by the great caution he observed, and she had every reliance on his prudence and address. The principal difficulty now existed with June, for Mabel had seen too much of her fidelity to her own people, relieved as it was by sympathy for herself, to believe she would consent to a hostile Indian entering the blockhouse, or, indeed, to her leaving it with a view to defeat Arrowhead's plans. The half hour that succeeded the discovery of the presence of the Great Serpent was the most painful of Mabel Dunham's life. She saw the means of effecting all she wished, as it might be within reach of her hands, and yet it eluded her grasp. She knew June's decision and coolness, notwithstanding all her gentleness and womanly feeling, and at last she came to the conclusion that there was no other way of attaining her end than by deceiving her tried companion and protector. It was revolting to one as sincere and natural, as pure of heart, and as much disposed to ingenuousness as Mabel Dunham, to practise deception on a friend like June; but her own father's life was at stake, her companion would receive no positive injury, and she had feelings and interests directly touching herself that would have removed greater scruples.

As soon as it was dark, Mabel's heart began to beat with violence, and she adopted and changed her plan of procedure at least a dozen times in the course of a single hour. June was always the source of her greatest embarrassment, for she did not well see, firstly, how she was to ascertain when Chingachgook was at the door, where she doubted not he would soon appear; and, secondly, how she was to admit him without giving the alarm to her watchful companion. Time pressed, however; for the Mohican might come and go away again, unless she were ready to receive him. It would be too hazardous for the Delaware to remain long on the island; and it became absolutely necessary to determine on some course, even at the risk of choosing one that was indiscreet. After running over various projects in her mind, therefore, Mabel came to her companion and said, with as much calmness as she could assume—

"Are you not afraid, June, now your people believe Pathfinder is in the blockhouse, that they will come and try to set it on fire?"

"No t'ink such t'ink. No burn blockhouse. Blockhouse good; got no scalp."

"June, we can not know. They hid because they believed what I told them of Pathfinder's being with us."

"Believe fear. Fear come quick, go quick. Fear make run away; wit make come back. Fear make warrior fool, as well as young girl."

Here June laughed, as her sex is apt to laugh when anything particularly ludicrous crosses their youthful fancies.

"I feel uneasy, June, and wish you yourself would go up again to the roof and look out upon the island to make certain that nothing is plotting against us; you know the signs of what your people intend to do better than I."

"June go, Lily wish; but very well know that Indian sleep; wait for fader. Warrior eat, drink, sleep, all time, when do n't fight, and go on war-trail. Den never sleep, eat, drink—never feel. Warrior sleep, now."

"God send it may be so; but go up, dear June, and look well about you. Danger may come when we least expect it."

June arose and prepared to ascend to the roof, but she paused with her foot on the first round of the ladder. Mabel's heart beat so violently that she was fearful its throbs would be heard, and she fancied that some gleamings of her real intentions had crossed the mind of her friend. She was right, in part, the Indian woman having actually stopped to consider whether there was any indiscretion in what she was about to do. At first, the suspicion that Mabel intended to escape flashed across her mind; then she rejected it, on the ground that the paleface had no means of getting off the island, and that the blockhouse was much the most secure place she could find. The next thought was, that Mabel had detected some sign of the near approach of her father. This idea, too, lasted but an instant; for June entertained some such opinion of her companion's ability to understand symptoms of this sort—symptoms that had escaped her own sagacity—as a woman of high fashion entertains of the accomplishments of her maid. Nothing else in the same way offering, she began slowly to mount the ladder.

Just as she reached the upper floor a lucky thought suggested itself to our heroine, and, by expressing it in a hurried but natural manner, she gained a great advantage in executing her projected scheme.

"I will go down," she said, "and listen by the door, June, while you are on the roof, and we will thus be on our guard, at the same time, above and below."

Though June thought this savored of unnecessary caution, well knowing that no one could enter the building unless aided from within, nor any serious danger menace them from the exterior without giving sufficient warning, she attributed the proposition to Mabel's ignorance and alarm, and, as it was made apparently with frankness, it was received without distrust. By these means our heroine was enabled to descend to the door as her friend ascended to the roof. The distance between the two was now too great to admit of conversation, and for three or four minutes one was occupied in looking about her as well as the darkness would allow, and the other listening at the door with as much intentness as if all her senses were absorbed in the single faculty of hearing.

June discovered nothing from her elevated stand ; the obscurity, indeed, almost forbade the hope of such a result, but it would not be easy to describe the sensation with which Mabel thought she perceived a slight and guarded push against the door. Fearful that all might not be as she wished, and anxious to let Chingachgook know that she was near, she began, though in tremulous and low notes, to sing. So profound was the stillness of the moment that the sound of the unsteady warbling ascended to the roof, and in a minute June began to descend. A slight tap at the door was heard immediately after. Mabel was bewildered, for there was no time to lose. Hope proved stronger than fear, and with unsteady hands she commenced unbarring the door. The moccasin of June was heard on the floor above her when only a single bar was turned. The second was released as her form reached half-way down the lower ladder.

"What you do?" exclaimed June, angrily. "Run away—mad—leave blockhouse? Blockhouse good." The hands of both were on the last bar, and it would have been cleared from the fastenings but for a vigorous shove from without which jammed the wood. A short struggle ensued, though both were disinclined to violence. June would probably have prevailed had not another and more vigorous push from without forced the door past the trifling impediment that held it, when the door opened. The form of a man was seen to enter, and both the females rushed up the ladder as if equally afraid of the consequences. The stranger secured the door, and, first examining the lower room with great care, he cautiously ascended the ladder. June, as soon as it became dark, had closed the loops of the principal floor and lighted a candle. By means of this dim taper, then, the two females stood in expectation, waiting to ascertain the person of their visitor, whose wary ascent of the ladder was distinctly audible though sufficiently deliberate. It would not be easy to say which was the more astonished on finding, when the stranger had got through the trap, that the Pathfinder stood before them.

" God be praised ! " Mabel exclaimed, for the idea that the blockhouse would be impregnable with such a garrison at once crossed her mind. "Oh! Pathfinder, what has become of my father?"

"The sergeant is safe as yet, and victorious, though it is not in the gift of man to say what will be the ind of it. Is not that the wife of Arrowhead, skulking in the corner there?"

"Speak not of her reproachfully, Pathfinder; I owe her my life—my present security. Tell me, what has happened to my father's party, why you are here, and I will relate all the horrible events that have passed upon this island."

"Few words will do the last, Mabel; for one used to Indian deviltries needs but little explanation on such a subject. Everything turned out as we had hoped with the expedition, for the Sarpent was on the lookout, and he met us with all the information heart could desire. We ambushed three boats, druv the Frenchers out of them, got possession and sunk them, according to orders, in the deepest part of the channel; and the savages of Upper Canada will fare badly for Indian goods this winter. Both powder and ball, too, will be scarcer among them than keen hunters and actyve warriors may relish. We did not lose a man, or have even a skin barked; nor do I think the inimy suffered to speak of. In short, Mabel, it has been just such an expedition as the major likes—much harm to the foe, and little harm to ourselves."

"Ah! Pathfinder, I fear, when Major Duncan comes to hear the whole of the sad tale, he will find reason to regret he ever undertook the affair!"

"I know what you mean—I know what you mean; but by telling my story straight you will understand it better. As soon as the sergeant found himself successful, he sent me and the Sarpent off in canoes to tell you how matters had turned out, and he is following with the two boats; which, being so much heavier, can not arrive before morning. I parted from Chingachgook this forenoon, it being agreed that he should come up one set of channels and I another, to see that the path was clear. I've not seen the chief since."

Mabel now explained the manner in which she had discovered the Mohican, and her expectation that he would yet come to the blockhouse.

"Not he—not he! A regular scout will never get behind walls or logs so long as he can keep the open air and find useful employment. I should not have come myself, Mabel, but I promised the sergeant to comfort you, and look a'ter your safety. Ah's me! I reconnoitered the island with a heavy heart this forenoon, and there was a bitter hour when I fancied you might be among the slain."

"By what lucky accident were you prevented from paddling up boldy to the island and from falling into the hands of the enemy?"

"By such an accident, Mabel, as Providence employs to tell the hound where to find the deer, and the deer how to throw off the hound. We never come in upon a post blindly ; and I have lain outside a garrison a whole night, because they had changed their sentries and their mode of standing guard. Neither the Sarpent nor myself would be likely to be taken in by these contrivances, which were most probably intended for the Scotch, who are cunning enough in some particulars, though anything but witches when Indian sarcumventions are in the wind."

"Can we not get into your canoe and go and meet my father?" Mabel asked.

"That is not the course I advise. I do n't know by which channel the sergeant will come, and there are twenty ; rely on it, the Sarpent will be winding his way through them all. No, no ; my advice is to remain here. The logs of this blockhouse are still green, and it will not be easy to set them on fire ; and I can make good the place, bating a burning, ag'in a tribe. The Iroquois nation can not dislodge me from this fortress, so long as we can keep the flames off it. The sergeant is now camped on some island, and will not come in until morning. If we hold the block, we can give him timely warning—by firing rifles, for instance ; and should he determine to attack the savages, as a man of his temper will be very likely to do, the possession of this building will be of great account in the affair. No, no ; my judgment says remain, if the object be to sarve the sergeant ; though escape for our two selves will be no very difficult matter."

"Stay," murmured Mabel, "stay, for God's sake, Pathfinder. Anything— everything, to save my father!"

"Yes, that is natur'. I am glad to hear you say this, Mabel, for I own a wish to see the sergeant fairly supported. As the matter now stands, he has gained himself credit ; and could he once drive off these miscreants and make an honorable retreat, laying the huts and block in ashes, no doubt, the major would remember it and sarve him accordingly. Yes, yes, Mabel, we must not only save the sergeant's life, but we must save his reputation."

"No blame can rest on my father on account of the surprise of this island."

"There's no telling—there's no telling ; military glory is a most unsartain thing. I've seen the Delawares routed when they desarved more credit than at other times when they've carried the day. A man is wrong to set his head on success of any sort, and worst of all on success in war. The principal thing with a soldier is, never to be whipt ; nor do I think mankind stops long to consider by whom the day was won or lost."

"My father could not have suspected that the position of the island was known to the enemy," resumed Mabel, whose thoughts were running on the probable effect of the recent events on the sergeant.

"That is true ; nor do I well see how the Frenchers found it out. The spot is well chosen, and it is not an easy matter, even for one who has traveled the road to and from it, to find it again. There has been treachery, I fear; yes, yes, there must have been treachery."

"Oh, Pathfinder, can this be?"

"Nothing is easier, Mabel, for treachery comes as nat'ral to some men as eating. Now, when I find a man all fair words, I look close to his deeds; for when the heart is right, and raally intends to do good, it is generally satisfied to let the conduct speak, instead of the tongue."

"Jasper Western is not one of these," said Mabel, impetuously. "No youth can be more sincere in his manner, or less apt to make the tongue act for the head."

"Jasper Western!—tongue and heart are both right with that lad, depend on it, Mabel; and the notion taken up by the major, and the quartermaster, and the sergeant, and your uncle, too, is as wrong as it would be to think that the sun shone by night and the stars shone by day. No, no; I'll answer for Jasper's honesty with my own scalp, or, at need, with my own rifle."

"Bless you—bless you, Pathfinder!" exclaimed Mabel, extending her own hand, and pressing the iron fingers of her companion under a state of feeling that far surpassed her own consciousness of its strength. "You are all that is generous—all that is noble."

"I've been thinking about the woman, for it will not be safe to shut our eyes and leave hers open on this side of the blockhouse door. If we put her in the upper room and take away the ladder, she'll be a prisoner at least."

"I can not treat one thus who has saved my life. It would be better to let her depart; I think she is too much my friend to do anything to harm me."

"You do not know the race, Mabel; you do not know the race. It's true she's not a full-blooded Mingo, but she consorts with the vagabonds and must have learned some of their tricks. What is that?"

"It sounds like oars,—some boat is passing through the channel."

Pathfinder closed the trap that led to the lower room, to prevent June from escaping, extinguished the candle, and went hastily to a loop, Mabel looking over his shoulder in breathless curiosity. These several movements consumed a minute or two, and by the time the eye of the scout had got a view of things without, two boats had swept past and shot up to the shore, at a spot some fifty yards beyond the block, where there was a regular landing. The obscurity prevented more from being seen; and Pathfinder whispered to Mabel that the new-comers were as likely to be foes as friends, for he did not think her father could possibly have arrived so soon. A number of men were now seen to quit the boats, and then followed three hearty English cheers, leaving no further doubts of the character of the party.

Pathfinder sprang to the trap, raised it, glided down the ladder, and began to unbar the door with an earnestness that proved how critical he deemed the moment. Mabel had followed, but she rather impeded than aided his exertions, and but a single bar was turned when a heavy discharge of rifles was heard. They were still standing in breathless suspense as the war-whoop rang in all the surrounding thickets. The door now opened, and both Pathfinder and Mabel rushed into the open air. All human sounds had ceased. After listening half a minute, however, Pathfinder thought he heard a few stifled groans near the boats; but the wind blew so fresh, and the rustling of the leaves mingled so much with the murmurs of the passing air, that he was far from certain. But Mabel was borne away by her feelings, and she rushed by him, taking the way toward the boats.

"This will not do, Mabel," said the scout in an earnest but low voice, seizing her by the arm, "this will never do. Sartain death would follow, and that without sarving anyone. We must return to the block."

"Father!—my poor, dear, murdered father!" said the girl wildly, though habitual caution, even at that trying moment, induced her to speak low. "Pathfinder, if you love me, let me go to my dear father!"

"This will not do, Mabel. It is singular that no one speaks; no one returns the fire from the boats—and I have left Killdeer in the block. But of what use would a rifle be when no one is to be seen."

At that moment the quick eye of Pathfinder, which, while he held Mabel firmly in his grasp, had never ceased to roam over the dim scene, caught an indistinct view of five or six dark, crouching forms endeavoring to steal past him, doubtless with the intention of intercepting their retreat to the blockhouse. Catching up Mabel, and putting her under an arm as if she were an infant, the sinewy frame of the woodsman was exerted to the utmost, and he succeeded in entering the building. The tramp of his pursuers seemed immediately at his heels. Dropping his burden, he turned, closed the door, and fastened one bar, as a rush against the solid mass threatened to force it from its hinges. To secure the other bar was the work of an instant.

Mabel now ascended to the first floor, while Pathfinder remained as a sentinel below. Our heroine was in that state in which the body exerts itself apparently without the control of the mind. She re-lighted the candle mechanically, as her companion had desired, and returned with it below, where he was waiting her reappearance. No sooner was Pathfinder in possession of the light than he examined the place carefully, to make certain no one was concealed in the fortress, ascending to each floor in succession after assuring himself that he left no enemy in his rear. The result was the conviction that the blockhouse now contained no one but Mabel and himself, June having escaped. When perfectly convinced on this material point, Pathfinder rejoined our heroine in the principal apartment, setting down the light and examining the priming of Killdeer before he seated himself.

"Our worst fears are realized," said Mabel, to whom the hurry and excitement of the last five minutes appeared to contain the emotions of a life. "My beloved father and all his party are slain or captured!"

"We do n't know that; morning will tell us all. I do not think the affair as settled as that, or we should hear the vagabond Mingos yelling out their triumph around the blockhouse. Of one thing we may be sartain: if the inimy has really got the better he will not be long in calling upon us to surrender. The squaw will let him into the secret of our situation, and, as they well know the place can not be fired by daylight so long as Killdeer continues to deserve his reputation, you may depend on it that they will not be backward in making their attempt while darkness helps them."

"Surely, I hear a groan! Surely some one is below, and in pain!"

Pathfinder was compelled to own that the quick senses of Mabel had not deceived her. He cautioned her, however, to repress her feelings, and reminded her that the savages were in the practice of resorting to every artifice to attain their ends, and that nothing was more likely than that the groans were feigned with a view to lure them from the blockhouse, or at least to induce them to open the door.

"No—no—no," said Mabel, hurriedly, "there is no artifice in those sounds, and they come from anguish of body, if not of spirit. They are fearfully natural."

"Well, we shall soon know whether a friend is there or not. Hide the light again, Mabel, and I will speak the person from a loop."

Not a little precaution was necessary, according to Pathfinder's judgment and experience, in performing even this simple act, for he had known the careless slain by their want of proper attention to what might have seemed to the ignorant supererogatory means of safety. He did not place his mouth to the loop itself, but so near it that he could be heard without raising his voice, and the same precaution was observed as regards his ear.

"Who is below?" Pathfinder demanded, when his arrangements were made to his mind. "Is any one in suffering? If a friend, speak boldly, and depend on our aid."

"Pathfinder!" answered a voice that both Mabel and the person addressed at once knew to be the sergeant's, "Pathfinder, in the name of God, tell me what has become of my daughter!"

"Father I am here—unhurt—safe—and, oh! that I could think the same of you!"

The ejaculation of thanksgiving that followed was distinctly audible to the two, but it was clearly mingled with a groan of pain.

"My worst forebodings are realized!" said Mabel, with a sort of desperate calmness. "Pathfinder, my father must be brought within the block, though we hazard everything to do it."

"This is natur', and it is the law of God. But, Mabel, be calm, and indeavour to be cool. All that can be effected for the sergeant by human invention shall be done. I only ask you to be cool."

"I am—I am—Pathfinder. Never in my life was I more calm, more collected, than at this moment. But remember how perilous may be every instant; for heaven's sake, what we do, let us do without delay."

Pathfinder was struck with the firmness of Mabel's tones, and perhaps he was a little deceived by the forced tranquility and self-possession she had assumed. At all events, he did not deem any further explanation necessary, but descended forthwith and began to unbar the door. This delicate process was conducted with the usual precaution, but as he warily permitted the mass of timber to swing back on the hinges, he felt an impression against it that nearly induced him to close it again. But, catching a glimpse of the cause through a crack, the door was permitted to swing back, when the body of Sergeant Dunham, which was propped against it, fell partly within the block. To draw in the legs and secure the fastenings occupied the Pathfinder but a moment. Then there existed no obstacle to their giving their undivided care to the wounded man.

Mabel, in this trying scene, conducted herself with the sort of unnatural energy that her sex when aroused is apt to manifest. She got the light, administered water to the parched lips of her father, and assisted Pathfinder in forming a bed of straw for his body and a pillow of clothes for his head. All this was done earnestly, and almost without speaking; nor did Mabel shed a tear until she heard the blessings of her father murmured on her head for this tenderness and care. All the time Mabel had merely conjectured the condition of her parent. Pathfinder, however, showed greater attention to the physical danger of the sergeant. He ascertained that a rifle ball had passed through the body of the wounded man, and he was sufficiently familiar with injuries of this nature to be certain that the chances of his surviving the hurt were very trifling, if any.

At once Mabel and Pathfinder made the sergeant as comfortable as possible, but they could not calm his disquieted mind, which was troubled at the thought that all these disasters to his post had been brought about through treachery—whose, he could not say, for his suspicion of Jasper had long since disappeared.

As they looked to their defenses another knock for admission came to the blockhouse door. This time it was Cap, who had escaped his captors, and made his way to the blockhouse in the hope of saving Mabel.

Still another summons came on the blockhouse door. It was Lieutenant Muir, sent by the Frenchman to advise surrender. But nothing was farther from the thoughts of Pathfinder and Cap. They absolutely refused, and Pathfinder assured the lieutenant that those in the blockhouse would defend it to the last.

Throughout this dialogue Pathfinder kept his body covered, lest a treacherous shot should be aimed at the loop; and he now directed Cap to ascend to the roof in order to be in readiness to meet the first assault. Although the latter used sufficient diligence, he found no less than ten blazing arrows sticking to the bark, while the air was filled with the yells and whoops of the enemy. A rapid discharge of rifles followed, and the bullets came pattering against the logs in a way to show that the struggle had indeed seriously commenced.

These were sounds, however, that appalled neither Pathfinder nor Cap, while Mabel was too much absorbed in her affliction to feel alarm. She had good sense enough, too, to understand the nature of the defenses, and fully to appreciate their importance.

At that instant the heavy report of a gun burst on the night, and the crashing of rending wood was heard as a heavy shot tore the logs in the room above, and the whole block shook with the force of the shell that lodged in the work. The Pathfinder narrowly escaped the passage of this formidable missle as it entered, but when it exploded Mabel could not suppress a shriek, for she supposed all over her head, whether animate or inanimate, destroyed. To increase her horror, her father shouted, in a frantic voice, "Charge!"

"Mabel," said Pathfinder, with his head at the trap, "this is true Mingo work—more noise than injury. The vagabonds have got the howitzer we took from the French, and have discharged it ag'in the block; but, fortunately, they have fired off the only shell we had, and there is an end of its use for the present. There is some confusion among the stores up in this loft, but no one is hurt. Your uncle is still on the roof, and as for myself, I've run the gantlet of too many rifles to be skeary about such a thing as a howitzer, and that in Injin hands."

Mabel murmured her thanks, and tried to give all her attention to her father, whose efforts to rise were only counteracted by his weakness. During the fearful minutes that succeeded, she was so much occupied with the care of the invalid that she scarce heeded the clamor that reigned around her. Indeed, the uproar was so great that, had not her thoughts been otherwise employed, confusion of faculties, rather than alarm, would probably have been the consequence.

Cap preserved his coolness admirably. He had a profound and increasing respect for the power of the savages, and even for the majesty of fresh water, it is true; but his apprehensions of the former proceeded more from his dread of being scalped and tortured than from any unmanly fear of death; and as he was now on the deck of a house, if not on the deck of a ship, and knew that there was little danger of boarders, he moved about with a fearlessness and a rash exposure of his person that Pathfinder, had he been aware of the fact, would have been the first to condemn. Instead of keeping his body covered, agreeably to the usages of Indian warfare, he was seen on every part of the roof, dashing the water right and left with the apparent steadiness and unconcern he would have manifested had he been a sail-trimmer exercising his art in a battle afloat. His appearance was one of the causes of the extraordinary clamor among the assailants, who, unused to see their enemies so reckless, opened upon him with their tongues like a pack that has the fox in view. Still he appeared to possess a charmed life; for, though the bullets whistled around him on every side, and his clothes were several times torn, nothing cut his skin. When the shell passed through the logs below, the old sailor dropped his bucket, waved his hat, and gave three cheers; in which heroic act he was employed as the dangerous missile exploded. This characteristic feat probably saved his life; for from that instant the Indians ceased to fire at him, and even to shoot their flaming arrows at the block—having taken up the notion simultaneously and by common consent that the "Saltwater was mad"; and it was a singular effect of their magnanimity never to lift a hand against those whom they imagined devoid of reason.

The conduct of Pathfinder was very different. Everything he did was regulated by the most exact calculation—the result of long experience and habitual thoughtfulness. His person was kept carefully out of a line with the loops, and the spot that he selected for his lookout was one that was quite removed from danger. This celebrated guide had often been known to lead forlorn hopes; he had once stood at the stake, suffering under the cruelties and taunts of savage ingenuity and savage ferocity without quailing; and legends of his exploits, coolness, and daring were to be heard all along that extensive frontier, or wherever men dwelt and men contended. But on this occasion one who did not know his history and character might have thought his exceeding care and studied attention to self-preservation proceeded from an unworthy motive. But such a judge would not have understood his subject. The Pathfinder bethought him of Mabel, and of what might possibly be the consequences to that poor girl should any casualty befall himself. But the recollection rather quickened his intellect than changed his customary prudence.

"There is one riptyle the less," Pathfinder muttered to himself, as he discharged his rifle from a loop; "I've seen that vagabond afore, and know him to be a merciless devil. Well, well; the man acted according to his gifts, and he has been rewarded according to his gifts. One more of the knaves, and that will sarve the turn for to-night. When daylight appears we may have hotter work."

All this time another rifle was getting ready, and as Pathfinder ceased a second savage fell. This, indeed, sufficed; for, indisposed to wait for a third visitation from the same hand, the whole band, which had been crouching in the bushes around the block, ignorant of who was and who was not exposed to view, leaped from their covers and fled to different places for safety.

"Now, pour away, Master Cap," said Pathfinder; "I've made my mark on the blackguards, and we shall have no more fires lighted to-night."

"Scaldings!" cried Cap, upsetting the barrel with a care that at once and completely extinguished the flames.

This ended the singular conflict, and the remainder of the night passed in peace. Pathfinder and Cap watched alternately, though neither can be said to have slept. Sleep, indeed, scarcely seemed necessary to them, for both were accustomed to protracted watchings; and there were seasons and times when the former appeared to be literally insensible to the demands of hunger and thirst, and callous to the effects of fatigue.

As the light returned Pathfinder and Cap ascended again to the roof, with a view once more to reconnoiter the state of things on the island. This part of the blockhouse had a low battlement around it, which afforded a considerable protection to those who stood in its center, the intention having been to enable marksmen to lie behind it and to fire over its top. By making proper use, therefore, of these slight defenses,—slight as to height, though abundantly ample as far as they went,—the two lookouts commanded a pretty good view of the island, its covers excepted, and of most of the channels that led to the spot.

The gale was still blowing very fresh from the south, and there were places in the river where its surface looked green and angry, though the wind had hardly sweep enough to raise the water into foam. The shape of the little island was generally oval, and its greatest length was from east to west. By keeping in the channels that washed it, in consequence of their several courses and of the direction of the gale, it would have been possible for a vessel to range past the island on either of its principal sides and always to keep the wind very nearly abeam. These were the facts first noticed by Cap, and explained to his companion, for the hopes of both now rested on the chances of relief sent from the Fort. At this instant, while they stood gazing anxiously about them, Cap cried out in his lusty, hearty manner: "Sail, ho!"

Pathfinder turned quickly in the direction of his companion's face, and there, sure enough, was just visible the object of the old sailor's exclamation. The elevation enabled the two to overlook the low land of several of the adjacent islands, and the canvas of a vessel was seen through the bushes that fringed the shore of one that lay to the southward and westward. The stranger was under what seamen call low sail, but so great was the power of the wind that her white outlines were seen flying past the openings in the verdure with the velocity of a fast-traveling horse, resembling a cloud driving in the heavens.

Anxiety and suspense prevented Pathfinder from attempting to make any signal. It was not easy, truly, to see how it could be done, for the "Scud" came foaming through the channel on the weather side of the island at a rate that scarce admitted of the necessary time. Nor was any one visible on her deck to make signs to; even her helm seemed deserted, though her course was as steady as her progress was rapid.

Cap stood in silent admiration of a spectacle so unusual. But, as the "Scud" drew nearer, his practised eye detected the helm in play by means of tiller-ropes, though the person who steered was concealed. As the cutter had weather-boards of some little height, the mystery was explained, no doubt remaining that her people lay behind the latter in order to be protected from the rifles of the enemy. As this fact showed that no force beyond that of the small crew could be on board, Pathfinder received his companion's explanation with an ominous shake of the head.

"This proves that the Sarpent has not reached the Fort," he said, "and that we are not to expect succor from the garrison. I hope the major has not taken it into his head to displace the lad, for Jasper Western would be a host of himself in such a strait. We three, Master Cap, ought to make a manful warfare—you, as a seaman, to keep up the intercourse with the cutter; Jasper, as a laker, who knows all that is necessary to be done on the water; and I, with gifts that are as good as any among the Mingos, let me be what I may in other particulars. I say we ought to make a manful fight in Mabel's behalf."

"That we ought—and that we will," answered Cap heartily, for he began to have more confidence in the security of his scalp now that he saw the sun again; "I set down the arrival of the 'Scud' as one circumstance, and the chances of Jasper's honesty as another. This Jasper is a young man of prudence, you find, for he keeps a good offing, and seems determined to know how matters stand on the island before he ventures to bring up."

"I have it, I have it," exclaimed Pathfinder with exultation ; "there lies the canoe of the Sarpent on the cutter's deck, and the chief has got on board, and no doubt has given a true account of our condition ; unlike a Mingo, a Delaware's sartain to get a story right or to hold his tongue."

So it proved, and as the "Scud" came up the channel and abreast of the blockhouse Jasper sprang upon his feet and gave three hearty cheers. Regardless of all risk, Cap leaped upon the rampart of logs and returned the greeting, cheer for cheer. Happily, the policy of the enemy saved the latter, for they still lay quiet, not a rifle being discharged. On the other hand, Pathfinder kept in view the useful, utterly disregarding the mere dramatic part of warfare. The moment he beheld his friend Jasper, he called out to him with stentorian lungs :

"Stand by us, lad, and the day's our own ! Give 'm a grist in yonder bushes, and you'll put 'm up like partridges."

Part of this reached Jasper's ears, but most was borne off to leeward on the wings of the wind. By the time this was said the "Scud" had driven past, and the next moment she was hidden from view by the grove in which the blockhouse was partially concealed.

Two anxious minutes succeeded, but at the expiration of that brief space

SERGEANT DUNHAM'S DEATH.

the sails were again gleaming through the trees, Jasper having wore, jibed, and hauled up under the lee of the island on the other tack. The wind was free enough, as has been already explained, to admit of this maneuver, and the cutter, catching the current under her lee bow, was breasted up to her course in a way that showed she would come out to windward of the island again without any difficulty. This whole evolution was made with the greatest facility, not a sheet being touched, the sails trimming themselves, the rudder alone controlling the admirable machine. The object appeared to be a reconnaissance. When, however, the "Scud" had made the circuit of the entire island, and had again got her weatherly position in the channel by which she had first approached, her helm was put down, and she tacked. The noise of the mainsail flapping when it filled, close-reefed as it was, sounded like the report of a gun, and Cap trembled lest the seams should open.

"His Majesty gives good canvas, it must be owned," muttered the old seaman; "and it must be owned, too, that that boy handles his boat as if he were thoroughly bred! Why, Master Pathfinder, I believe, after all that has been reported in the matter, that this Jasper got his trade on this bit of fresh water."

"He did; yes, he did. He never saw the ocean, and has come by his calling altogether up here on Ontario. I have often thought he has a nat'ral gift in the way of schooners and sloops, and have respected him accordingly. As for treason, and lying, and blackhearted vices, friend Cap, Jasper Western is as free as the most virtuousest of the Delaware warriors; and if you crave to see a truly honest man you must go among that tribe to discover him."

"There he comes round!" exclaimed the delighted Cap, the "Scud" at this moment filling on her original tack, "and now we shall see what the boy would be at; he can not mean to keep running up and down these passages like a girl footing it through a country dance."

The "Scud" now kept so much away that for a moment the two observers on the blockhouse feared Jasper meant to come to, and the savages in their lairs gleamed out upon her with the sort of exultation that the crouching tiger may be supposed to feel as he sees his unconscious victim approach his bed. But Jasper had no such intention. Familiar with the shore, and acquainted with the depth of water at every part of the island, he well knew that the "Scud" might be run against the bank with impunity, and he ventured fearlessly so near that as he passed through the little cove he swept the two boats of the soldiers from their fastenings and forced them out into the channel, towing them with the cutter. As all the canoes were fastened to the two Dunham boats, by this bold and successful attempt the savages were at once deprived of the means of quitting the island, unless by swimming, and they appeared to be instantly aware of the very important fact. Rising in a body, they filled the air with yells, and poured in a harmless fire. While up in this unguarded manner two rifles were discharged by their adversaries. One came from the summit of the block, and an Iroquois fell dead in his tracks, shot through the brain. The other came from the "Scud." The last was the piece of the Delaware, but, less true than that of his friend, it only maimed an enemy for life. The people of the "Scud" shouted, and the savages sank again to a man, as it might be into the earth.

"That was the Sarpent's voice," said Pathfinder, as soon as the second piece was discharged. "I know the crack of his rifle as well as I do that of Killdeer. 'Tis a good barrel, though not sartain death. Well, well; with Chingachgook and Jasper on the water, and you and I in the block, friend Cap, it will be hard if we do n't teach these Mingo scamps the rationality of a fight."

All this time the "Scud" was in motion. As soon as she had reached the end of the island, Jasper sent his prizes adrift, and they went down before the wind until they stranded on a point more than a mile to leeward. He then wore, and came, stemming the current again, through the other passage. Those on the summit of the block could now perceive that something was in agitation on the deck of the "Scud"; and to their great delight, just as the cutter came abreast of the principal cove, on the spot where most of the enemy lay, the howitzer, which composed her sole armament, was unmasked, and a shower of case-shot was sent hissing into the bushes. A bevy of quail would not have risen quicker than this unexpected discharge of iron hail put up the Iroquois; when a second savage fell by a messenger sent from Killdeer, and another went limping away by a visit from the rifle of Chingachgook. New covers were immediately found, however, and each party seemed to prepare for the renewal of the strife in another form. But the appearance of June, bearing a white flag, and accompanied by the French officer and Muir, stayed the hands of all, and was the forerunner of another parley.

The negotiation that followed was held beneath the blockhouse, and so near it as at once to put those who were uncovered completely at the mercy of Pathfinder's unerring aim. Jasper anchored directly abeam, and the howitzer, too, was kept trained upon the negotiators, so that the besieged and their friends, with the exception of the man who held the match, had no hesitation about exposing their persons. Chingachgook alone lay in ambush; more, however, from habit than distrust.

"You've triumphed, Pathfinder," called out the quartermaster, "and Captain Sanglier has come himself to offer terms. You'll no be denying a brave enemy an honorable retreat, when he has fought ye fairly and done all the credit he could to king and country. Ye are too loyal a subject yourself to visit loyalty and fidelity with a heavy judgment. I am authorized to offer on the part of the enemy an evacuation of the island, a mutual exchange of prisoners, and a restoration of scalps. In the absence of baggage and artillery, little more can be done."

As the conversation was necessarily carried on in a high key, both on account of the wind and on account of the distance, all that was said was heard equally by those on the block and those in the cutter.

"What do you say to that, Jasper?" called out Pathfinder. "You hear the tarms; shall we let the vagabonds go, or shall we mark them, as they mark their sheep in the settlement, that we may know them again?"

"What has befallen Mabel Dunham?" demanded the young man, with a frown on his handsome face that was visible even to those in the block. "If a hair of her head has been touched it will go hard with the whole Iroquois tribe."

"Nay, nay, she is safe below, nursing a dying parent as becomes her sex. We owe no grudge on account of the sergeant's hurt, which comes of lawful warfare; and as for Mabel——"

"She is here!" exclaimed the girl herself, who had mounted to the roof the moment she found the direction things were taking. "She is here; and in the name of our holy religion, and of that God whom we profess to worship in common, let there be no more bloodshed! Enough has been spilled already, and if these men will go away, Pathfinder,—if they will depart peaceably, Jasper,—oh! do not detain one of them. My poor father is approaching his end, and it were better that he should draw his last breath in peace with the world. Go, go, Frenchmen and Indians; we are no longer your enemies, and will harm none of you."

By this time both Pathfinder and Cap doubted the loyalty of Lieutenant Muir. They thought that the Frenchman, perhaps, had offered the quartermaster life and freedom in exchange for good terms from the blockhouse. But they talked the matter over, and, after a short discussion, all the savages on the island were collected in a body, without arms, at the distance of a hundred yards from the block, and under the gun of the "Scud," while Pathfinder descended to the door of the blockhouse and settled the terms on which the island was to be finally evacuated by the enemy. Considering all the circumstances, the conditions were not very discreditable to either party. The Indians were compelled to give up all their arms, even to their knives and tomahawks, as a measure of precaution, their force being still quadruple that of their foes. The French officer, Monsieur Sanglier, as he chose to call himself, remonstrated against this act as one likely to reflect more discredit on his command than any other part of the affair; but Pathfinder, who had witnessed one or two Indian massacres, and knew how valueless pledges became when put in opposition to interest where a savage was concerned, was obdurate. The second stipulation was of nearly the same importance. It compelled Captain Sanglier to give up all his prisoners, who had been kept, well guarded, in the very hole or cave in which Cap and Muir had taken refuge. When these men were produced, four of them were found to be unhurt; they had fallen merely to save their lives, a common artifice in that species of warfare; and of the remainder, two were so slightly injured as not to be unfit for service. As they brought their muskets with them, this addition to his force immediately put Pathfinder at his ease, for having collected all the arms of the enemy in the blockhouse, he directed these men to take possession of the building, stationing a regular sentinel at the door. The remainder of the soldiers were dead, the badly wounded having been instantly dispatched in order to obtain the much-coveted scalps.

As soon as Jasper was made acquainted with the terms, and the preliminaries had been so far observed as to render it safe for him to be absent, he got the "Scud" under way, and, running down to the point where the boats had stranded, he took them in tow again, and making a few stretches brought them into the leeward passage. Here all the savages instantly embarked, when Jasper took the boats in tow a third time, and running off before the wind he soon set them adrift, quite a mile to leeward of the island. The Indians were furnished with but a single oar in each boat to steer with, the young sailor well knowing that by keeping before the wind they would land on the shores of Canada in the course of the morning.

Captain Sanglier, Arrowhead, and June alone remained when this disposition had been made of the rest of the party; the former having certain papers to draw up and sign with Lieutenant Muir, who, in his eyes, possessed the virtues which are attached to a commission, and the latter preferring, for reasons of his own, not to depart in company with her late friends, the Iroquois. Canoes were retained for the departure of these three when the proper moment should arrive.

In the meantime, or while the "Scud" was running down with the boats in tow, Pathfinder and Cap, aided by proper assistants, busied themselves with preparing a breakfast, most of the party not having eaten for four-and-twenty hours. The brief space that passed in this manner, before the "Scud" came to again, was little interrupted by discourse, though Pathfinder found leisure to pay a visit to the sergeant, to say a few friendly words to Mabel, and to give such directions as he thought might smooth the passage of the dying man. As for Mabel herself, he insisted on her taking some light refreshment, and there no longer existing any motive for keeping it there, he had the guard removed from the block, in order that the daughter might have no impediment to her attentions to her father. These little arrangements completed, the scout returned to the fire, around which he found all the remainder of the party assembled, including Jasper.

When this was accomplished and the party assembled at the blockhouse, Lieutenant Muir, by virtue of his commission, and because of the condition of Sergeant Dunham, assumed command of the post, and his first order to his soldiers was to arrest Jasper Western for treason.

Pathfinder sprang to his feet.

"What does that mean, indeed?" he cried, stepping forward, and shoving the two soldiers away with a power of muscle that would not be denied. "Who has the heart to do this to Jasper Western, and who has the boldness to do it before my eyes?"

"It is by my orders, Pathfinder," answered the quartermaster, "and I command it on my own responsibility. Ye'll no tak' on yourself to dispute the legality of orders given by one who bears the king's commission to the king's soldiers?"

"I'd dispute the king's words if they came from the king's own mouth, did they say that Jasper deserves this. Has not the lad just saved all our scalps?—taken us from defeat and given us victory? No, no, lieutenant; if this is the first use that you make of your authority, I for one will not respect it."

"This savors a little of insubordination," answered Muir; "but we can bear much from Pathfinder. It is true this Jasper has *seemed* to serve us in this affair, but we ought not to overlook past transactions. Did not Major Duncan himself dénounce him to Sergeant Dunham before we left the post? Have we not seen sufficient with our own eyes to make sure of having been betrayed? And is it not natural and almost necessary to believe that this young man has been the traitor? Ah! Pathfinder, ye'll not be makin' yourself a great statesman or a great captain if you put too much faith in appearances. Lord bless me! Lord bless me! if I do not believe, could the truth be come at, as you often say yourself, Pathfinder, that hypocrisy is a more common vice than even envy, and that's the bane o' human nature."

"I care not for your envy or your hypocrisy, or even for your human natur'," returned Pathfinder. "Jasper Western is my friend; Jasper is a brave lad, and an honest lad, and a loyal lad; and no man shall lay hands on him short of Major Duncan's own orders while I'm in the way to prevent it. You may have authority over your soldiers, but you have none over Jasper or me, Master Muir."

"Will ye no hearken to reason, Pathfinder? Ye'll no be forgetting our suspicions and judgments; and here is another circumstance to augment and aggravate them all. Ye can see this little bit of bunting; well, where should it be found but by Mabel Dunham, on the branch of a tree on this very island, just an hour or so before the attack of the enemy; and if ye'll be at the trouble to look at the fly of the 'Scud's' ensign, ye'll just say that the cloth has been cut from it. Evidence was never stronger."

"Talk to me of no ensigns and signals when I know the heart," continued the Pathfinder. "Jasper has the gift of honesty; and it is too rare a gift to be trifled with like a Mingo's conscience. No, no; off hands, or we shall see which can make the stoutest battle—you and your men of the 55th, or the Sarpent, here, and the Killdeer, with Jasper and his crew. You overrate your force, Lieutenant Muir, as much as you underrate Jasper's truth."

"Well, if I must speak plainly, Pathfinder, I e'en must. Captain Sanglier, here, and Arrowhead, this brave Tuscarora, have both informed me that this unfortunate boy is the traitor. After such testimony you can no longer oppose my right to correct him, as well as the necessity of the act."

"Captain Sanglier is a brave soldier, and will not gainsay the conduct of an honest sailor," put in Jasper. "Is there any traitor here, Captain?"

"Ay," added Muir, "let him speak out, then, since ye wish it, unhappy youth, that the truth may be known. I only hope that ye may escape the last punishment when a court will be sitting on your misdeeds. How is it, Captain; do ye or do ye not see a traitor among us?"

"Yes, sir. I do, sir," replied the Frenchman.

"Too much lie," said Arrowhead, in a voice of thunder, striking the breast of Muir with the back of his own hand in a sort of ungovernable gesture. "Where my warriors? Where the English scalp? Too much lie."

Muir wanted not for personal courage, nor for a certain sense of personal honor. The violence which had been intended only for a gesture he mistook for a blow, for conscience was suddenly aroused within him; and he stepped back a pace, extending a hand toward a gun. His face was livid with rage, and his countenance expressed the fell intention of his heart. But Arrowhead was too quick for him. With a wild glance of the eye the Tuscarora looked about him; then, thrusting a hand beneath his own girdle, drew forth a concealed knife, and in the twinkling of an eye buried it in the body of the quartermaster to the handle. As the latter fell at his feet, gazing into his face with the vacant stare of one surprised by death, Sanglier took a pinch of snuff, and said in a calm voice:

"That ends the affair, but it is the death of a traitor."

The act was too sudden to be prevented, and when Arrowhead, uttering a yell, bounded into the bushes, the white men were too confounded to follow. Chingachgook, however, was more collected, and the bushes had scarcely closed on the passing body of the Tuscarora than they were again opened by that of the Delaware in full pursuit.

Jasper Western spoke French fluently, and the words and manner of Sanglier struck him.

"Speak, sir," he said, "*am* I the traitor?"

"See!" answered the cool Frenchman; "that is our spy—our agent—our friend—but a fine traitor. See here!"

As he spoke Sanglier bent over the dead body, and thrust a hand into a pocket of the quartermaster, out of which he drew a purse. Emptying the contents on the ground, several double-louis rolled toward the soldiers, who were not slow in picking them up. Casting the purse from him in contempt, the soldier of fortune turned toward the soup he had been preparing with so much care, and finding it to his liking he began to break his fast, with an air of indifference that the most stoical Indian warrior might have envied.

It was the truth; Lieutenant Muir had been in the pay of the French for months, and had deliberately accompanied the party with the intention of surrendering all, and the island fort, into the hands of the enemy.

But Jasper was freed of all suspicion. His innocence, his loyalty, and his courage had all been proved after a hard and cruel test, and Mabel and Pathfinder both rejoiced.

And when, on that green island in the great river, the brave sergeant breathed his last, leaving Mabel as a charge to Pathfinder, the true and gentle scout, although loving Mabel dearly, saw that she cared the most for Jasper, and, acting in her father's place, put his own wishes aside and bade Jasper take Mabel as his wife.

Then he bade them good-by.

"Good-by!" cried Jasper. "Why, you do not mean to leave us, dear friend?"

"'Tis best, Mabel and Jasper; best and wisest," Pathfinder replied. "I could live and die in your company if I only followed feeling; but if I follow reason I shall quit you here. You will go back to the Fort and become man and wife as soon as you arrive; for all that is determined with Master Cap, who hankers after the sea again, and who knows what is to happen; while I shall return to the wilderness and my Maker. Come, Mabel," continued Pathfinder, rising and drawing nearer to our heroine with grave decorum, "kiss me. Jasper will not grudge me one kiss; then we'll part."

"Oh, Pathfinder!" exclaimed Mabel, falling into the arms of the guide and kissing his cheeks again and again with a freedom and warmth she had been far from manifesting while held to the bosom of Jasper; "God bless you, dearest Pathfinder! You will come to us hereafter. We shall see you again. When old you will come to our dwelling and let me be a daughter to you?"

"Yes—that's it," returned the guide, almost gasping for breath; "I'll try to think of it in that way. You're more befitting to be my daughter than to be my wife, you are. Farewell, Jasper. Now we'll go to the canoe ; it's time you were on board."

The manner in which Pathfinder led the way to the shore was solemn and calm. As soon as he reached the canoe he again took Mabel by the hands, held her at the length of his own arms, and gazed wistfully into her face, until the unbidden tears rolled out of the fountains of feeling and trickled down his rugged cheeks in streams.

"Bless me, Pathfinder," said Mabel, kneeling reverently at his feet. "Oh! at least bless me before we part."

That untutored but noble-minded being did as she desired, and, aiding her to enter the canoe, seemed to tear himself away as one snaps a strong and obstinate cord. Before he retired, however, he took Jasper by the arm, and led him a little aside, when he spoke as follows :

"You're kind of heart and gentle by natur', Jasper; but we are both rough and wild in comparison with that dear creatur'. Be careful of her, and never show the roughness of man's natur' to her soft disposition. You'll get to understand her in time, and the Lord, who governs the lake and the forest alike, who looks upon virtue with a smile and upon vice with a frown, keep you happy and worthy to be so!"

Pathfinder made a sign for his friend to depart, and he stood leaning on his rifle until the canoe had reached the side of the " Scud." Mabel wept as if her heart would break ; nor did her eyes once turn from the open spot in the glade where the form of the Pathfinder was to be seen, until the cutter had passed a point that completely shut out the island. When last in view, the sinewy frame of this extraordinary man was as motionless as if it were a statue set up in that solitary place to commemorate the scenes of which it had so lately been the witness.

Jasper soon after married Mabel Dunham, but neither he nor his wife ever beheld the Pathfinder again. They remained for another year on the banks of Ontario, and then the pressing solicitations of Cap induced them to join him in New York, where Jasper eventually became a successful and respected merchant. Thrice Mabel received valuable presents of furs, at intervals of years, and her feelings told her whence they came, though no name accompanied the gift. Later in life still, when the mother of several sons, she had occasion to visit the interior, and found herself on the banks of the Mohawk, accompanied by her boys, the eldest of whom was capable of being her protector. On that occasion she observed a man in a singular guise watching her in the distance with an intentness that induced her to inquire into his pursuits and character. She was told he was the most renowned hunter of that portion of the State—a being of great purity of character and of as marked peculiarities, and that he was known in that region of country by the name of the Leatherstocking. Further than that Mrs. Western could not ascertain, though the distant glimpse and singular deportment of this unknown hunter gave her the assurance that it might indeed be her brave defender on the island in the St. Lawrence; her more than father, her true and loyal friend; loyal and true, also, to Jasper in his days of trial— the noble, generous, and valiant Pathfinder.

THE PIONEERS

A TALE OF THE NEW YORK FORESTS.

BY JAMES FENIMORE COOPER.

O N a bright December day, years ago, when the beautiful lake district of Central New York was a border-land between civilization and the wilderness, Judge Temple and his daughter, Elizabeth, were journeying home from Elizabeth's school in New York city.

Judge Temple was a great landholder, who had obtained a large tract, or patent, of land near to Lake Otsego. His daughter had just finished a four-years' course of schooling in New York, and was coming home in the care of her father.

Their sleigh was driven by their black coachman, Aggy, but as they neared their home at Templeton, on the shores of the lake, the judge heard the barking of dogs in the forest.

He knew that meant game, and he was very fond of hunting.

"Hold up, Aggy," he said, "there is old Hector; I should know his bay among ten thousand! The Leatherstocking has put his hounds into the hills, this clear day, and they have started their game. There is a deer track a few rods ahead; and now, Bess, if you can muster courage enough to stand fire, I will give you a saddle for your Christmas dinner."

The black drew up, with a cheerful grin upon his chilled features, and began thrashing his arms together in order to restore the circulation to his fingers; while the speaker stood erect, and, throwing aside his outer covering, stepped from the sleigh upon a bank of snow, which sustained his weight without yielding.

In a few moments the speaker succeeded in extricating a double-barreled fowling-piece from among a multitude of trunks and bandboxes. After throw ing aside the thick mittens which had encased his hands, that now appeared in a pair of leather gloves tipped with fur, he examined his priming, and was about to move forward, when the light, bounding noise of an animal plunging through the woods was heard, and a fine buck darted into the path a short distance ahead of him. The appearance of the animal was sudden, and his flight inconceivably rapid ; but the traveler appeared to be too keen a sportsman to be disconcerted by either. As it came first into view he raised the fowling-piece to his shoulder, and, with a practised eye and steady hand, drew a trigger. The deer dashed forward undaunted, and apparently unhurt. Without lowering his piece, the traveler turned its muzzle toward his victim and fired again. Neither discharge, however, seemed to have taken effect.

JUDGE TEMPLE AND HIS DAUGHTER ELIZABETH IN THE SLEIGH.

The whole scene had passed with a rapidity that confused the girl, who was unconsciously rejoicing in the escape of the buck, as he darted like a meteor across the road, when a sharp, quick sound struck her ear, quite different from the full, round reports of her father's gun, but still sufficiently distinct to be known as the concussion produced by firearms. At the same instant that she heard this unexpected report, the buck sprung from the snow to a great height in the air, and directly a second discharge, similar in sound to the first, followed, when the animal came to the earth, falling headlong, and rolling over on the crust with its own velocity. A loud shout was given by the unseen marksmen, and a couple of men instantly appeared from behind the trunks of two of the pines, where they had evidently placed themselves in expectation of the passage of the deer.

"Ha! Leatherstocking, had I known you were in ambush I should not have fired," cried the traveler, moving toward the spot where the deer lay, near to which he was followed by the delighted black with his sleigh; "but the sound of old Hector was too exhilarating to be quiet, though I hardly think I struck him, either."

"No, no, Judge," returned the hunter, with an inward chuckle, and with that look of exultation that indicates a consciousness of superior skill; "you burned your powder only to warm your nose this cold evening. Did ye think to stop a full-grown buck, with Hector and the pup open upon him within sound, with that pop-gun in your hand? There's plenty of pheasants among the swamps, and the snow-birds are flying round your own door, where you may feed them with crumbs and shoot them at pleasure, any day; but if you're for a buck or a little bear's meat, Judge, you'll have to take the long rifle, with a greased wadding, or you'll waste more powder than you'll fill stomachs, I'm thinking."

As the speaker concluded he drew his bare hand across the bottom of his nose, and again opened his enormous mouth, with a kind of inward laugh.

"The gun scatters well, Leatherstocking, and it has killed a deer before now," said the traveler, smiling good-humoredly. "One barrel was charged with buckshot, but the other was loaded for birds only. Here are two hurts, one through the neck and the other directly through the heart. It is by no means certain, Leatherstocking, but that I gave him one of the two."

"No, no, judge," said the hunter called Leatherstocking; "the creature came to his death by a younger hand than yours or mine," and he nodded toward his companion.

The judge tried pleasantly to decide the question by lot, and next to buy from the young hunter, who accompanied Leatherstocking, the slaughtered deer. But the young man refused.

"First let us determine the question of right to the satisfaction of us both," he said firmly but respectfully, and with a pronunciation and language vastly superior to his appearance; "with how many shot did you load your gun?"

"With five, sir," said the judge, a little struck with the other's manner; "are they not enough to slay a buck like this?"

"One would do it; but," moving to the tree from behind which he had appeared, "you know, sir, you fired in this direction—here are four of the bullets in the tree."

The judge examined the fresh marks in the bark of the pine, and, shaking his head, said, with a laugh—

"You are making out the case against yourself, my young advocate; where is the fifth?"

"Here," said the youth, throwing aside the rough overcoat that he wore, and exhibiting a hole in his undergarment through which large drops of blood were oozing.

"Great Heavens!" exclaimed the judge with horror; "have I been trifling here about an empty distinction, and a fellow-creature suffering from my hands without a murmur? But hasten—quick—get into my sleigh—it is but a mile to the village, where surgical aid can be obtained—all shall be done at my expense, and you shall live with me until your wound is healed, aye, and for ever afterward."

"I thank you for your good intention, but I must decline your offer. I have a friend who would be uneasy were he to hear that I am hurt and away from him. The injury is but slight, and the bullet has missed the bones, but I believe, sir, you will now admit my title to the venison."

"Admit it!" repeated the agitated judge: "I here give you a right to shoot deer, or bears, or anything you please in my woods forever. Leatherstocking is the only other man that I have granted the same privilege to, and the time is coming when it will be of value. But I buy your deer—here, this bill will pay you, both for your shot and my own."

The old hunter gathered his tall person up into an air of pride during this dialogue, but he waited until the other had done speaking.

"There's them living who say that Nathaniel Bumpo's right to shoot on these hills is of older date than Marmaduke Temple's right to forbid him," he said. "But if there's a law about it at all,—though who ever heard of a law that a man shouldn't kill deer where he pleased! But if there is a law at all, it should be to keep people from the use of smooth-bores. A body never knows where his lead will fly when he pulls the trigger of one of them uncertain firearms."

Without attending to the soliloquy of Leatherstocking, the youth bowed his head silently to the offer of the bank-note, and replied:

"Excuse me; I have need of the venison."

"But this will buy you many deer," said the judge; "take it, I entreat you," and lowering his voice to a whisper he added, "it is for a hundred dollars."

For an instant only the youth seemed to hesitate, and then, blushing even through the high color that the cold had given to his cheeks, as if with inward shame at his own weakness, he again declined the offer.

During this scene the girl in the sleigh arose; regardless of the cold air she threw back the hood which concealed her features, and now spoke with great earnestness.

"Surely, surely—young man—sir—you would not pain my father so much as to have him think that he leaves a fellow-creature in this wilderness whom his own hand has injured. I entreat you will go with us and receive medical aid."

The young man hesitated. Leatherstocking advised him to go, as that was the quickest way to get aid, and the wounded hunter, thus persuaded, at last entered the sleigh. Aggy threw the dead buck across the baggage and took up the reins.

The judge invited the old hunter to accompany them, but Leatherstocking declined.

"No, no," said the old man, shaking his head; "I have work to do at home this Christmas eve. Drive on with the boy, and let your doctor look to the shoulder; though, if he will only cut out the shot, I have yarbs that will heal the wound quicker than all his foreign 'intments." He turned and was about to move off, when, suddenly recollecting himself, he again faced the party and added: "If you see anything of Indian John about the foot of the lake, you had better take him with you and let him lend the doctor a hand, for, old as he is, he is curious at cuts and bruises, and it's likelier than not he'll be in with brooms to sweep your Christmas ha'arths."

Suddenly he held up his finger, with an expressive gesture for silence. Then, moving softly along the margin of the road, he kept his eyes steadfastly fixed on the branches of a pine. When he had obtained such a position as he wished, he stopped, and, cocking his rifle, threw one leg far behind him, and stretching his left arm to its utmost extent along the barrel of his piece, he began slowly to raise its muzzle in a line with the straight trunk of the tree. The eyes of the group in the sleigh naturally preceded the movement of the rifle, and they soon discovered the object of Leatherstocking's aim. On a small, dead branch of the pine, which, at a distance of seventy feet from the ground, shot out horizontally, immediately beneath the living members of the tree, sat a bird that in the vulgar language of the country was indiscriminately called a pheasant or a partridge. In size it was but little smaller than a common barnyard fowl. The baying of the dogs and the conversation that had passed near the root of the tree on which it was perched had alarmed the bird, which was now drawn up near the body of the pine, with a head and neck so erect as to form nearly a straight line with its legs. As soon as the rifle bore on the victim Natty drew his trigger, and the partridge fell from its height with a force that buried it in the snow.

"Lie down, you old villain," exclaimed Leatherstocking, shaking his ramrod at Hector as he bounded toward the foot of the tree, "lie down, I say." The dog obeyed, and Natty proceeded with great rapidity, though with the nicest accuracy, to reload his piece. When this was ended he took up his game, and, showing it to the party without a head, he cried: "Here is a tidbit for an old man's Chris'mas; never mind the venison, boy, and remember Indian John; his yarbs are better than all the foreign 'intments. Here, Judge," holding up the bird again, "do you think a smooth-bore would pick game off their roost and not ruffle a feather?" The old man gave another of his remarkable laughs, which partook so largely of exultation, mirth, and irony, and, shaking his head, he turned, with his rifle at a trail, and moved into the forest with steps that were between a walk and a trot. At each movement he made his body lowered several inches, his knees yielding with an inclination inward; but as the sleigh turned at a bend in the road, the youth cast his eyes in quest of his old companion, and he saw that he was already nearly concealed by the trunks of the trees, while his dogs were following quietly in his footsteps, occasionally scenting the deer track, that they seemed to know instinctively was now of no further use to them. Another jerk was given to the sleigh, and Leatherstocking was hid from view.

The judge and his sleigh drove over the crisp snow until the roofs of the little village of Templeton, near his own mansion, were in sight. Then the cheerful sound of sleigh-bells attracted the attention of the whole party as they came jingling up the sides of the mountain, at a rate that announced a powerful team and a hard driver. The bushes which lined the highway interrupted the view, and the two sleighs were close upon each other before either was seen.

A large lumber-sleigh, drawn by four horses, was soon seen dashing through the leafless bushes which fringed the road. The leaders were of gray and the pole horses of a jet black. Bells innumerable were suspended from every part of the harness where a tinkling bell could be placed.

In the sleigh were four men. The judge knew them. They were connected in one way or another with his great estate or its neighboring settlement. The driver was a reckless, boisterous, good-natured man named Richard Jones—the chief agent and assistant of Judge Temple.

He called out in greeting to the judge and his daughter and then prepared to turn his team and accompany the judge homeward.

It was in the quarry only, into which he had turned, that he could effect this object, without ascending to the summit of the mountain. A very considerable excavation had been made in the side of the hill, at the point where Richard had succeeded in stopping the sleighs, from which the stones used for building in the village were ordinarily quarried, and in which he now attempted to turn his team. Passing itself was a task of difficulty, and frequently of danger, in that narrow road; but Richard had to meet the additional risk of turning his four-in-hand. Aggy civilly volunteered his services to take off the leaders, and the judge very earnestly seconded the measure with his advice. Richard treated both proposals with great disdain:

"Why," he exclaimed, a little angrily, "the horses are as gentle as lambs. You know that I broke the leaders myself, and the pole horses are too near my whip to be restive."

Richard, by a sudden application of the whip, succeeded in forcing the leaders into the snow-bank that covered the quarry; but the instant that the impatient animals suffered by the crust, through which they broke at each step, they positively refused to move an inch further in that direction. On the contrary, finding that the cries and blows of their driver were redoubled at this juncture, the leaders backed upon the pole horses, who, in their turn, backed the sleigh. Only a single log lay above the pile which upheld the road, on the side toward the valley, and this was now buried in the snow. The sleigh was easily forced across so slight an impediment; and before Richard became conscious of his danger, one-half of the vehicle was projected over a precipice which fell, perpendicularly, more than a hundred feet.

"Get up, you obstinate brutes!" cried Richard, catching a bird's-eye view of his situation, and, in his eagerness to move forward, kicking the stool on which he sat. "Get up, I say. Judge, I shall have to sell the grays, too; they are the worst broken horses—"

"Merciful Providence!" exclaimed the judge, "they will be all killed!"

Elizabeth gave a piercing shriek, and the black of Aggy's face changed to a muddy white.

At this critical moment, the young hunter, who, during the salutations of the two parties, had sat in rather sullen silence, sprung from the judge's sleigh to the heads of the refractory leaders. The horses, which were yet suffering under the injudicious and somewhat random blows of Richard, were dancing up and down with that ominous movement that threatened a sudden and uncontrollable start, still pressing backward. The youth gave the leaders a powerful jerk, and they plunged aside, and re-entered the road in the position in which they were first halted. The sleigh was whirled from its dangerous position, and upset, with the runners outward. The four occupants were thrown, rather unceremoniously, into the highway, but without danger to their bones. Richard landed at the distance of some fifteen feet, in that snow-bank which the horses had dreaded, right end uppermost. Here, as he instinctively grasped the reins, he rose unsteadily to his feet; then, as the mist gradually cleared from before his eyes, he saw that all was safe, and with an air of great self-satisfaction he cried, "Well, that was neatly saved, anyhow! It was a lucky thought in me to hold on the reins, or the fiery brutes would have been over the mountain by this time. How well I recovered myself, eh, Judge? Another moment would have been too late, but I knew just the spot where to touch the off leader; that blow under the right flank, and the sudden jerk I gave the rein, brought them round quite in rule, I must confess."

"You, sir?" cried the judge. "Why, had it not been for this brave young man in my sleigh, you and your horses would surely have been dashed to pieces. The best thing for you to do, I should say, would be to learn to drive."

Richard protested loudly, and soon, all being replaced, they drove on to Templeton.

The wound of the young hunter, whose name, he said, was Oliver Edwards, was duly attended to in Judge Temple's home, where the country doctor operated upon him in the presence of a number of the most substantial villagers, but he was compelled to remain there for some little time, and so interested the judge, that, in spite of the young man's reluctance to accept favors, he tried to induce him to live in his home instead of being the companion of a hunter and an Indian in a forest hut. And one day, when Leatherstocking and the young hunter were at the mansion, the plan was proposed.

"I have greatly injured you, Mr. Edwards," said the judge, "but, fortunately, it is in some measure in my power to compensate you. My kinsman, Richard Jones, has received an appointment that will, in future, deprive me of his assistance, and leaves me, just now, destitute of one who might greatly aid me with his pen. Your manner, notwithstanding appearances, is a sufficient proof of your education, nor will your shoulder suffer you to labor for some time to come. My doors are open to you, my young friend, for in this infant country we harbor no suspicions, little offering to tempt the cupidity of the evil-disposed. Become my assistant, for at least a season, and receive such compensation as your services will deserve."

There was nothing in the manner or the offer of the judge to justify the reluctance with which the youth listened to his speech, but after a powerful effort for self-command, he replied:

"I would serve you, sir, or any other man, for an honest support, for I do not affect to conceal that my necessities are very great, even beyond what appearances would indicate; but I am fearful that such new duties would interfere too much with more important business, so that I must decline your offer and depend on my rifle, as before, for subsistence."

"It is a precarious life," observed the judge, "and one that brings more evils with it than present suffering. Trust me, young friend (my experience is greater than yours) when I tell you that the unsettled life of these hunters is of vast disadvantage for temporal purposes, and it totally removes one from the influence of more sacred things."

"No, no, Judge," interrupted Leatherstocking, who was hitherto unseen or disregarded; "take him into your shanty in welcome, but tell him truth. I have lived in the woods for forty long years, and have spent five at a time without seeing the light of a clearing bigger than a wind-row in the trees; and I should like to know where you'll find a man in his sixty-eighth year who can get an easier living, for all your betterments and your deer laws; and as for honesty, or doing what's right between man and man, I'll not turn my back to the longest-winded deacon on your patent."

"You are an exception, Leatherstocking," returned the judge, nodding good-naturedly at the hunter, "or you have a temperance unusual in your class and a hardihood exceeding your years. But this youth is made of materials too precious to be wasted in the forest. I entreat you to join my family, if it be but till your arm be healed. My daughter, here, who is mistress of my dwelling, will tell you that you are welcome."

THE COUNTRY DOCTOR OPERATES UPON EDWARDS.

THE PIONEERS.

"Certainly," said Elizabeth, whose earnestness was a little checked by female reserve. "The unfortunate would be welcome at any time, but doubly so when we feel that we have occasioned the evil ourselves."

"Yes," said Richard, "and if you relish turkey, young man, there are plenty in the coops, and of the best kind, I can assure you."

Finding himself thus ably seconded, the judge pushed his advantage to the utmost. He entered into a detail of the duties that would attend the situation, and circumstantially mentioned the reward, and all those points which are deemed of importance among men of business. The youth listened in extreme agitation. There was an evident contest in his feelings; at times he appeared to wish eagerly for the change, and then again the incomprehensible expression of disgust would cross his features, like a dark cloud obscuring a noonday sun.

Near them stood the old redskin whom they all called "Indian John, the Mohican." He stood listening to the offers of the judge with an interest that increased with each syllable. Gradually he drew nigher to the group, and when, with his keen glance, he detected the most marked evidence of yielding in the countenance of his young companion, he changed to the front of an Indian warrior, and moving, with great dignity, closer to the parties, he spoke:

"Listen to your father," he said; "his words are old. Let the Young Eagle and the great Land Chief eat together; let them sleep without fear near each other. The children of Mohican love not blood; they are just, and will do right. The sun must rise and set often before men can make one family; it is not the work of a day, but of many winters. The Mingos and the Delawares are born enemies; their blood can never mix in the wigwam: it will never run in the same stream in the battle. What makes the brother of Mohican and the Young Eagle foes? They are of the same tribe; their fathers and mothers are one. Learn to wait, my son: you are a Delaware, and an Indian warrior knows how to be patient."

This figurative address seemed to have great weight with the young man, who gradually yielded to the representations of the judge, and eventually consented to his proposal. It was, however, to be an experiment only; and if either of the parties thought fit to rescind the engagement, it was left at his option to do so.

Once outside the mansion, the foresters—for the three hunters, notwithstanding their difference in character, well deserved this common name—pursued their course along the skirts of the village in silence. It was not until they had reached the lake, and were moving over its frozen surface toward the foot of the mountain where stood the hut of Leatherstocking, in which they lived, that the youth exclaimed:

"Who could have foreseen this a month since? I have consented to serve

Marmaduke Temple—to be an inmate in the dwelling of the greatest enemy of my race ; yet what better could I do ? The servitude can not be long, and when the motive for submitting to it ceases to exist, I will shake it off, like the dust from my feet."

"Is he a Mingo, that you will call him enemy?" said the Mohican. "The Delaware warrior sits still and waits the time of the Great Spirit. He is no woman, to cry out like a child."

"Well, I'm mistrustful, John," said Leatherstocking, in whose air there had been during the whole business a strong expression of doubt and uncertainty. "They say that there's new laws in the land, and I am sartain that there's new ways in the mountains. One hardly knows the lakes and streams, they've altered the country so much. I must say I'm mistrustful of such smooth speakers, for I've known the whites talk fair when they wanted the Indian lands most. This I will say, though I'm white myself and was born nigh York, and of honest parents, too."

"I will submit," said the youth, "I will forget who I am. Cease to remember, old Mohican, that I am the descendant of a Delaware chief who once was master of these noble hills, these beautiful vales, and of this water over which we tread. Yes, yes, I will become his bondsman—his slave. Is is not an honorable servitude, old man?"

"Old man!" repeated the Indian, solemnly, and pausing in his walk, as usual when much excited ; "Yes, John is old. Son of my brother! if the Mohican were young, when would his rifle be still? Where would the deer hide and he not find him? But John is old ; his hand is the hand of a squaw ; his tomahawk is a hatchet, brooms and baskets are his enemies—he strikes no other. Hunger and old age come together. See, Hawkeye! when young he would go days and eat nothing ; but should he not put the brush on the fire now, the blaze would go out. Take the great Land Chief by the hand, my son, and he will help you."

"I'm not the man I was, I own, Chingachgook," returned the Leatherstocking, "but I can go without a meal now, on occasion. When we tracked the Iroquois through the 'Beechwoods' they drove the game afore them, for I had n't a morsel to eat from Monday morning come Wednesday sundown, and then I shot as fat a buck, on the Pennsylvany line, as ever mortal laid eyes on. It would have done your heart good to have seen the Delaware eat, for I was out scouting and scrimmaging with their tribe at the time. Lord! the Indians, lad, lay still and just waited till Providence should send them their game, but I foraged about and put a deer up, and put him down, too, afore he had made a dozen jumps. I was too weak and too ravenous to stop for his flesh, so I took a good drink of his blood, and the Indians ate of his meat raw. John was there, and John knows. But then, starvation would be apt to be too much for me now, I will own, though I'm no great eater at any time."

"Enough is said, my friends," cried the youth. "I feel that everywhere the sacrifice is required at my hands, and it shall be made; but say no more, I entreat you; I can not bear this subject now."

His companions were silent, and they soon reached the hut, which they entered after removing certain complicated and ingenious fastenings that were put there apparently to guard a property of but very little value. Immense piles of snow lay against the log walls of this secluded habitation on one side, while fragments of small trees, and branches of oak and chestnut, that had been torn from their parent stems by the winds, were thrown into a pile on the other. A small column of smoke rose through a chimney of sticks, cemented with clay, along the side of the rock, and marked the snow above with its dark tinges in a wavy line, from the point of emission to another where the hill receded from the brow of a precipice, and held a soil that nourished trees of a gigantic growth, that overhung the little bottom beneath.

So the young man came into the household of the judge and began the life of a gentleman; but, though earnestly engaged in the service of Judge Temple during the days, his nights were often spent in the hut of Leatherstocking. The intercourse between the three hunters was maintained with a certain air of mystery, it is true, but with much zeal and apparent interest to all the parties. Even John, the Mohican, whom Leatherstocking sometimes called Chingachgook and sometimes the Serpent, seldom came to the mansion-house; Leatherstocking never came. But Oliver Edwards sought every leisure moment to visit his former abode, from which he would often return in the gloomy hours of the night, through the snow, or, if detained beyond the time at which the family retired to rest, with the morning sun. These visits certainly excited much speculation in those to whom they were known, but no comments were made, excepting occasionally, in whispers from Richard, who would say:

"It is not at all remarkable; a half-breed can never be weaned from the savage ways; and, for one of his lineage, the boy is much nearer civilization than could, in reason, be expected."

Elizabeth Temple, who had been away from her father so long, was interested in all the people and plans she was brought in contact with, and one day questioned her father about Leatherstocking.

Her father told her that it was on his first visit to the forest section in which they now lived, that, tired and hungry, he was descending the mountains, when he saw, on the eastern bank of the lake, a line of curling smoke.

"It was," he said, "the only indication of the vicinity of man that I had then seen. After much toil I made my way to the spot, and found a rough cabin of logs built against the foot of a rock and bearing the marks of a tenant, though I found no one within it—"

"It was the hut of Leatherstocking," said Edwards, quickly.

"It was, though I at first supposed it to be a habitation of the Indians. But while I was lingering around the spot, Natty, as I soon came to call Leatherstocking, made his appearance, staggering under the carcass of a buck that he had slain. Our acquaintance began at that time; before, I had never heard that such a being tenanted the woods. He launched his bark canoe and set me across the foot of the lake, to the place where I had fastened my horse, and pointed out a spot where he might get a scanty browsing until the morning, when I returned and passed the night in the cabin of the hunter."

Miss Temple was so much struck by the deep attention of young Edwards, who had listened closely during this speech, that she forgot to resume her interrogatories; but the youth himself continued the discourse by asking:

"And how did Leatherstocking discharge the duties of a host, sir?"

"Why, simply but kindly, until late in the evening, when he discovered my name and object, and the cordiality of his manner very sensibly diminished, or, I might better say, disappeared. He considered the introduction of the settlers as an innovation on his rights, I believe, for he expressed much dissatisfaction at the measure, though it was in his confused and ambiguous manner. I hardly understood his objections, myself, but supposed they related chiefly to an interruption of the hunting."

"Had you then purchased the estate, or were you examining it with an intent to buy?" asked Edwards, a little abruptly.

"It had been mine for several years. It was with a view to people the land that I visited the lake. Natty treated me hospitably, but coldly, I thought, after he learned the nature of my journey. I slept on his own bearskin, however, and in the morning joined my surveyors again."

"Said he nothing of the Indian rights, sir? The Leatherstocking is much given to impeach the justice of the tenure by which the whites hold the country."

"I remember that he spoke of them, but I did not clearly comprehend him, and may have forgotten what he said; for the Indian title was extinguished so far back as the close of the old war, and if it had not been at all, I hold under the patents of the Royal Governors, confirmed by an act of our own State Legislature, and no court in the country can affect my title."

"Doubtless, sir, your title is both legal and equitable," returned the youth, coldly, and remained silent till the subject was changed.

This question of whether the land belonged to the Indians or to the pioneers who occupied and cleared it, was a question of hot debate in those days; but

Leatherstocking, as those words of Oliver Edwards showed, took the side of the Indians as the real owners.

Indeed, he found fault with the pioneers even for cutting down trees and clearing the land, and one day in April, soon after the talk between Elizabeth and her father, Leatherstocking walked into the clearing where the pioneers were indulging in a pigeon-shooting match.

So prodigious was the number of the birds that the scattering fire of the guns, with the hurling of the missiles and the cries of the boys, had no other effect than to break off small flocks from the immense masses that continued to dart along the valley, as if the whole of the feathered tribe were pouring through that one pass. None pretended to collect the game, which lay scattered over the fields in such profusion as to cover the very ground with the fluttering victims.

Leatherstocking was a silent but uneasy spectator of all these proceedings, but was able to keep his sentiments to himself.

"This comes of settling a country!" he said; " here have I known the pigeons to fly for forty long years, and, till you made your clearings, there was nobody to skear or to hurt them. I loved to see them come into the woods, for they were company to a body; hurting nothing, being, as it was, as harmless as a garter-snake. But now it gives me sore thoughts when I hear the frighty things whizzing through the air, for I know it's only a motion to bring out all the brats in the village. Well! the Lord won't see the waste of his creatures for nothing, and right will be done to the pigeons, as well as others, by and by. There's Mr. Oliver, as bad as the rest of them, firing into the flocks as if he was shooting down nothing but Mingo warriors."

Among the sportsmen was one Billy Kirby, a wood-chopper, who had lately been in a shooting match for the prize of a turkey, and had been beaten by Leatherstocking. Now he was armed with an old musket, which he was loading, and, without even looking into the air, was firing and shouting as his victims fell even on his own person. He heard the speech of Natty, and took it upon himself to reply:

"What! old Leatherstocking," he cried, "grumbling at the loss of a few pigeons! If you had to sow your wheat twice and three times, as I have done, you would n't be so massyfully feeling toward the divils. Hurrah, boys! scatter the feathers! This is better than shooting at a turkey's head and neck, old fellow."

"It's better for you, maybe, Billy Kirby," replied the indignant old hunter; "and all them that do n't know how to put a ball down a rifle-barrel, or how to bring it up again with a true aim; but it's wicked to be shooting into flocks in this wasty manner, and none do it who know how to knock over a single bird. If a body has a craving for pigeon's flesh, why, it's made the same as all other creatures—for man's eating; but not to kill twenty and eat one. When I want such a thing I go into the woods till I find one to my liking, and then I shoot him off the branches, without touching the feather of another, though there might be a hundred on the same tree. You couldn't do such a thing, Billy Kirby —you couldn't do it if you tried."

"What's that, old cornstalk! you sapless stub!" cried the woodchopper. "You have grown wordy since the affair of the turkey; but if you are for a single shot, here goes at that bird which comes on by himself."

The fire from the distant part of the field had driven a single pigeon below the flock to which it belonged, and, frightened with the constant reports of the muskets, it was approaching the spot where the disputants stood, darting first from one side and then to the other, cutting the air with the swiftness of lightning, and making a noise with its wings not unlike the rushing of a bullet. Unfortunately for the woodchopper, notwithstanding his vaunt, he did not see this bird until it was too late to fire as it approached, and he pulled his trigger at the unlucky moment when it was darting immediately over his head. The bird continued its course with the usual velocity.

Natty lowered the rifle from his arm when the challenge was made, and

THE SHOOTING MATCH FOR THE PRIZE OF A TURKEY.

waiting a moment, until the terrified victim had got in a line with his eye, and had dropped near the bank of the lake, he raised it again with uncommon rapidity, and fired. It might have been chance, or it might have been skill, that produced the result: it was probably a union of both; but the pigeon whirled over in the air, and fell into the lake, with a broken wing. At the sound of his rifle, both his dogs started from his feet, and in a few minutes the pup brought out the bird, still alive.

The wonderful exploit of Leatherstocking was noised through the field with great rapidity, and the sportsmen gathered in to learn the truth of the report.

"What!" said young Edwards. "Have you really killed a pigeon on the wing, Natty, with a single ball?"

"Have n't I killed loons before now, lad, that dive at the flash?" returned the hunter. "It's much better to kill only such as you want, without wasting your powder and lead, than to be firing into God's creatures in this wicked manner. But I came out for a bird, and you know the reason why I like small game, Mr. Oliver; and now I have got one I will go home, for I do n't relish these wasty ways that you are all practising, as if the least thing was n't made for use, and not to destroy."

"You say well, Leatherstocking," cried the judge, "and I begin to think it time to put an end to this work of destruction."

"Put an ind, Judge, to your clearings. An't the woods His work, as well as the pigeons? Use, but do n't waste. Was n't the woods made for the beasts and birds to harbor in? And when man wanted their flesh, their skins, or their feathers, there's the place to seek them. But I'll go to the hut with my own game, for I would n't touch one of the harmless things that cover the ground here, looking up with their eyes on me as if they only wanted tongues to say their thoughts."

With this sentiment in his mouth, Leatherstocking threw his rifle over his arm, and, followed by his dogs, stepped across the clearing with great caution, taking care not to tread on one of the wounded birds in his path. He soon entered the bushes on the margin of the lake and was hid from view. But for some time the pigeon slaughter went on.

But though Leatherstocking was so particular about the woods and the birds, there was another pioneer way that he could not understand nor agree to, —that was the law that made it wrong to kill deer at certain times of the year only.

This law was, of course, to protect the game and keep it from being quite killed off. But Natty could not understand it.

"When I am hungry I must eat," he said, "law or no law." And so he would frequently have got into trouble had it not been for Judge Temple's protection, which made an exception in favor of Leatherstocking.

But there was one man, the constable of the village, named Hiram Doolittle, who was determined to get Leatherstocking into trouble whether the judge protected him or not.

It was because he had seen this man prowling about Natty's hut, as if he were trying to spy what was inside, that young Oliver Edwards hunted out the old man one day to warn him.

Standing on the shore of the lake, he saw the light-colored bark canoe of his companions riding on the water, and containing two figures that he at once knew to be the Mohican and the Leatherstocking. He pulled, in a very few minutes, to the place where his friends were fishing, and fastened his boat to the light vessel of the Indian.

The old men received Oliver with welcoming nods, but neither drew his line from the water nor in the least varied his occupation. When Edwards had secured his own boat, he baited his hook and threw it into the lake, without speaking.

"Did you stop at the wigwam, lad, as you rowed past?" asked Natty.

"Yes, and I found all safe; but that carpenter and constable, Mr., or, as they call him, Squire, Doolittle, was prowling through the woods. I made sure of the door before I left the hut, and I think he is too great a coward to approach the hounds."

"There's little to be said in favor of that man," said Natty, while he drew in a perch and baited his hook. "He craves dreadfully to come into the cabin, and has as good as asked me as much to my face; but I put him off with unsartain answers, so that he is no wiser than Solomon. This comes of having so many laws that such a man may be called on to intarpret them."

"I fear he is more knave than fool," cried Edwards. "I dread that his impertinent curiosity may yet give us much trouble."

"If he harbors too much about the cabin, lad, I'll shoot the creater," said the Leatherstocking, quite simply.

"No, no, Natty; you must remember the law," said Edwards, "or we shall have you in trouble; and that would be an evil day, and sore tidings to all."

"Would it, boy?" exclaimed the hunter, raising his eyes with a look of friendly interest toward the youth. "You have the true blood in your veins, Mr. Oliver, and I'll support it to the face of Judge Temple or in any court in the country. How is it, John? Do I speak the true word? Is the lad stanch, and of the right blood?"

"He is a Delaware," said the Mohican, "and my brother. The Young Eagle is brave, and he will be a chief. No harm can come."

THE PIONEERS.

"Well, well," cried the youth impatiently, "say no more about it, my good friends; if I am not all that your partiality would make me, I am yours through life, in prosperity as in poverty. We will talk of other matters."

The old hunters yielded to his wish, which seemed to be their law. For a short time a profound silence prevailed, during which each man was very busy with his hook and line ; but Edwards, probably feeling that it remained with him to renew the discourse, soon observed, with the air of one who knew not what he said:

"How beautifully tranquil and glassy the lake is! Saw you it ever more calm and even than at this moment, Natty?"

"I have known the Otsego water for five-and-forty years," said Leatherstocking, "and I will say that for it, which is, that a cleaner spring or better fishing is not to be found in the land. Yes, yes ; I had the place to myself once, and a cheerful time I had of it. The game was plenty as heart could wish, and there was none to meddle with the ground, unless there might have been a hunting party of the Delawares crossing the hills, or, maybe, a rifling scout of them thieves, the Iroquois. There was one or two Frenchmen that squatted in the flats, further west, and married squaws; and some of the Scotch-Irishers from the Cherry Valley would come on to the lake and borrow my canoe to take a mess of perch, or drop a line for salmon-trout ; but, in the main, it was a cheerful place, and I had but little to disturb me in it. John would come, and John knows."

The Mohican turned his dark face at this appeal, and, moving his hand forward with a graceful motion of assent, he spoke, using the Delaware language :

"The land was owned by my people ; we gave it to my brother in council— to the fire-eater ; and what the Delawares give lasts as long as the waters run. Hawkeye smoked at that council, for we loved him."

"No, no, John," said Natty, "I was no chief, seeing that I know'd nothing of scholarship, and had a white skin. But it was a comfortable hunting-ground then, lad, and would have been so to this day, but for the money of Marmaduke Temple and the twisty ways of the law."

"I see no more reason," said Edwards, "for a law against deer-shooting than for one forbidding fishing, and certainly catching thousands of fish with a seine will shortly make it impossible to catch fish at all."

"You're right, my boy," replied Leatherstocking, "if people would only fish with the spear, and kill no more than they require, it would be vastly better for all."

"But that they will not," returned Edwards. "You saw how the judge tried to stop seining the other day, and how interested his daughter was in your spearing the great fish, but the constable and the others would listen to nothing."

This was in reference to a great catch of fish which had been made a few evenings before by the villagers, when Leatherstocking and the Mohican had appeared on the scene engaged in spearing fish for their own use. Miss Temple had expressed an interest in the unusual sight, and, with Edwards, had been taken into the canoe, and had seen Leatherstocking display his skill by spearing an enormous fish.

The hunter was about to reply, when, bending his ear near the water, he sat holding his breath and listening attentively, as if to some distant sound. At length he raised his head and said :

"If I hadn't fastened the hounds with my own hands with a fresh leash of green buckskin, I'd take a Bible oath that I heard old Hector ringing his cry on the mountain."

"It is impossible," said Edwards ; "it is not an hour since I saw him in his kennel."

By this time the attention of the Mohican was attracted to the sounds ; but although the youth was both silent and attentive, he could hear nothing but the lowing of some cattle from the western hills. He looked at the old men, Natty sitting with his hand to his ear, like a trumpet, and the Mohican bending forward with an arm raised to a level with his face, holding the forefinger elevated as a signal for attention, and laughed aloud at what he deemed to be their imaginary sounds.

"Laugh, if you will, boy," said Leatherstocking ; "the hounds be out, and are hunting a deer. No man can deceive me in such a matter. I wouldn't have had the thing happen for a beaver's skin. Not that I care for the law, but the venison is lean now, and the dumb things run the flesh off their own bones for no good. Now do you hear the hounds?"

Edwards started as a full cry broke on his ear, changing from the distant sounds that were caused by some intervening hill to confused echoes that rang among the rocks that the dogs were passing, and then directly to a deep and hollow baying that pealed under the forest on the lake shore. These variations in the tones of the hounds passed with amazing rapidity ; and while his eyes were glancing along the margin of the water, a tearing of the branches of the alder and dog-wood caught his attention, at a spot near them, and at the next moment a noble buck sprang from the shore and buried himself in the lake. A full-mouthed cry followed, when Hector and the pup shot through the opening in the bushes and darted into the lake also, bearing their breasts gallantly against the water.

"I know'd it—I know'd it!" cried Natty, when both deer and hounds were in full view; "the buck has gone by them with the wind, and it has been too much for the poor rogues; but I must break them of these tricks or they'll give me a deal of trouble. He-re, he-re—'shore with you, rascals—'shore with you—will ye? Oh! off with you, old Hector, or I'll hatchel your hide with my ramrod when I get ye."

The dogs knew their master's voice, and after swimming in a circle, as if reluctant to give over the chase, and yet afraid to persevere, they finally obeyed, and returned to the land, where they filled the air with their cries.

In the meantime the deer, urged by his fears, had swum over half the distance between the shore and the boats before his terror permitted him to see the new danger. But at the sound of Natty's voice he turned short in his course, and for a few moments seemed about to rush back again and brave the dogs. His retreat in this direction was, however, effectually cut off, and, turning a second time, he urged his course obliquely for the center of the lake, with an intention of landing on the western shore. As the buck swam by the fishermen, raising his nose high into the air, curling the water before his slim neck like the bead of a galley, the Leatherstocking began to sit very uneasy in his canoe.

"'Tis a noble creater!" he exclaimed; "what a pair of horns! A man

LEATHERSTOCKING SPEARS AN ENORMOUS FISH.

might hang up all his garments on the branches. Let me see—July is the last month, and the flesh must be getting good." While he was talking, Natty had instinctively employed himself in fastening the inner end of the bark rope, that served him for a cable, to a paddle, and rising suddenly on his legs, he cast this buoy away, and cried: "Strike out, John! let her go. The creater's a fool to tempt a man in this way."

The Mohican threw the fastening of the youth's boat from the canoe, and with one stroke of his paddle sent the light bark over the water like a meteor.

"Hold!" exclaimed Edwards. "Remember the law, my old friends. You are in plain sight of the village, and I know that Judge Temple is determined to prosecute all indiscriminately who kill deer out of season."

The remonstrance came too late; the canoe was already far from the skiff, and the two hunters were too much engaged in the pursuit to listen to his voice.

The buck was now within fifty yards of his pursuers, cutting the water gallantly, and snorting at each breath with terror and his exertions, while the canoe seemed to dance over the waves, as it rose and fell with the undulations made by its own motion. Leatherstocking raised his rifle and freshened the priming, but stood in suspense whether to slay his victim or not.

"Shall I, John, or no?" he said. "It seems but a poor advantage to take of the dumb thing, too. I won't; it has taken to the water on its own nater, which is the reason that God has given to a deer, and I'll give it the lake play; so, John, lay out your arm, and mind the turn of the buck; it's easy to catch them, but they'll turn like a snake."

The Indian laughed at the conceit of his friend, but continued to send the canoe forward with a velocity that proceeded much more from his skill than his strength. Both of the old men now used the language of the Delawares when they spoke.

"Hugh!" exclaimed the Mohican; "the deer turns his head. Hawkeye, lift your spear."

Natty never moved abroad without taking with him every implement that might, by possibility, be of service in his pursuits. From his rifle he never parted; and although intending to fish with the line, the canoe was invariably furnished with all of its utensils, even to its grate. This precaution grew out of the habits of the hunter, who was often led, by his necessities or his sports, far beyond the limits of his original destination. A few years earlier than the date of our tale, the Leatherstocking had left his hut on the shores of the Otsego, with his rifle and his hounds, for a few days' hunting in the hills; but before he returned he had seen the waters of Ontario. One, two, or even three hundred miles had once been nothing to his sinews, which were now a little stiffened by age. The hunter did as the Indian advised, and prepared to strike a blow, with the barbed weapon, into the neck of the buck.

"Lay her more to the left, John," he cried, "lay her more to the left; another stroke of the paddle and I have him."

While speaking, he raised the spear, and darted it from him like an arrow. At that instant the buck turned, the long pole glanced by him, the iron striking against his horns, and buried itself harmlessly in the lake.

"Back water," cried Natty, as the canoe glided over the place where the spear had fallen; "hold water, John."

The pole soon reappeared, shooting upward from the lake, and as the hunter seized it in his hand, the Indian whirled the light canoe around and renewed the chase. But this evolution gave the buck a great advantage, and it also allowed time for Edwards to approach the scene of action.

"Hold your hand, Natty!" cried the youth, "hold your hand; remember it is out of season."

This remonstrance was made as the bateau arrived close to the place where the deer was struggling with the water, his back now rising to the surface, now sinking beneath it, as the waves curled from his neck, the animal still sustaining itself nobly against the odds.

"Hurrah!" shouted Edwards, inflamed beyond prudence at the sight; "mind him as he doubles—mind him as he doubles; sheer more to the right, John, more to the right, and I'll have him by the horns; I'll throw the rope over his antlers."

The dark eye of the old warrior was dancing in his head with a wild animation, and the sluggish repose in which his aged frame had been resting in the canoe was now changed to all the rapid inflections of practised agility. The canoe whirled with each cunning evolution of the chase, like a bubble floating in a whirlpool; and when the direction of the pursuit admitted of a straight course, the little bark skimmed the lake with a velocity that urged the deer to seek its safety in some new turn.

It was the frequency of these circuitous movements that, by confining the action to so small a compass, enabled the youth to keep near his companions. More than twenty times both the pursued and the pursuers glided by him, just without the reach of his oars, until he thought the best way to view the sport was to remain stationary, and by watching a favorable opportunity assist as much as he could in taking the victim.

He was not required to wait long, for no sooner had be adopted this resolution and risen in the boat, than he saw the deer coming bravely toward him, with an apparent intention of pushing for a point of land at some distance from the hounds, who were still barking and howling on the shore. Edwards caught the painter of his skiff, and, making a noose, cast it from him with all his force, and luckily succeeded in drawing its knot close around one of the antlers of the buck.

For one instant the skiff was drawn through the water, but in the next the canoe glided before it, and Natty, bending low, passed his knife across the throat of the animal, whose blood followed the wound, dyeing the waters. The short time that was passed in the last struggles of the animal was spent by the hunters in bringing their boats together and securing them in that position, when Leatherstocking drew the deer from the water and laid its lifeless form in the bottom of the canoe. He placed his hands on the ribs, and on different parts of the body of his prize, and then, raising his head, he laughed in his peculiar manner.

"So much for Marmaduke Temple's law!" he said. "This warms a body's blood, old John. I have n't killed a buck in the lake afore this sin' many a year. I call that good venison, lad ; and I know them that will relish the creater's steaks for all the betterments in the land."

The Indian had long been drooping with his years, and perhaps under the calamities of his race, but this invigorating and exciting sport caused a gleam of sunshine to cross his swarthy face that had long been absent from his features. It was evident the old man enjoyed the chase, more as a memorial of his youthful sports and deeds than with any expectation of profiting by the success. He felt the deer, however, lightly, his hand already trembling with the reaction of his unusual exertions, and smiled, with a nod of approbation, as he said, in the emphatic and sententious manner of his people :

"Good."

"I am afraid, Natty," said Edwards, when the heat of the moment had passed, and his blood began to cool, "that we have all been equally transgressors of the law. But keep your own counsel, and there are none here to betray us. Yet how came those dogs at large ? I left them securely fastened, I know, for I felt the thongs and examined the knots when I was at the hut."

"It has been too much for the poor things," said Natty, "to have such a buck take the wind of them. See, lad, the pieces of the buckskin are hanging from their necks yet. Let us paddle up, John, and I will call them in and look a little into the matter."

When the old hunter landed, and examined the thongs that were yet fast to the hounds, his countenance sensibly changed, and he shook his head doubtingly.

"Here has been a knife at work," he said ; "this skin was never torn, nor is it the work of a hound's tooth. No, no ; Hector is not in fault, as I feared."

"Has the leather been cut ?" cried Edwards.

"No, no—I did n't say it had been cut, lad; but this is a mark that was never made by a jump or a bite."

"Could that rascally constable have dared?"

"Ay! he durst do anything, when there is no danger," said Natty; "he is a curious body, and loves to be helping other people on with their consarns. But he had best not harbor so much near the wigwam!"

In the meantime the Mohican had been examining, with an Indian's sagacity, the place where the leather thong had been separated. After scrutinizing it closely he said, in Delaware:

"It was cut with a knife—a sharp blade and a long handle—the man was afraid of the dogs."

"How is this, John?" exclaimed Edwards: "You saw it not; how can you know these facts?"

"Listen, son," said the warrior. "The knife was sharp, for the cut is smooth; the handle was long, for a man's arm would not reach from this gash to the cut that did not go through the skin: he was a coward, or he would not have cut the thongs around the necks of the hounds."

"On my life," cried Natty, "John is on the scent! It was the constable, and he has got on the rock back of the kennel and let the dogs loose by fastening his knife to a stick. It would be an easy matter to do it, where a man is so minded."

"And why should he do so?" asked Edwards; "who has done him wrong that he should trouble two old men like you?"

"It's a hard matter, lad, to know men's ways, I find, since the settlers have brought in their new fashions. But is there nothing to be found out in the place? and maybe he is troubled with his longings after other people's business, as he often is."

"Your suspicions are just. Give me the canoe: I am young and strong, and will get down there yet, perhaps, in time to interrupt his plans. Heaven forbid that we should be at the mercy of such a man!"

His proposal was accepted, the deer being placed in the skiff in order to lighten the canoe, and in less than five minutes the little vessel of bark was gliding over the glassy lake, and was soon hid by the points of land, as it shot close along the shore.

The Mohican followed slowly with the skiff, while Natty called his hounds to him, bade them keep close, and, shouldering his rifle, ascended the mountain, with the intention of going to the hut by land.

That very day Elizabeth Temple and her friend, the minister's daughter, were strolling over the hills near Templeton. Though the forests were dense, danger at that summer season was not thought of, and the two girls walked and

THE YOUNG HUNTER SAVED THE SLEIGH FROM ITS DANGER.

talked, picked flowers, and admired the green and blue of forest, lake, and sky, thinking it not possible that anything could harm them so long as they had with them Elizabeth's noble and watchful mastiff, Brave.

In this manner they proceeded along the margin of the precipice, catching occasional glimpses of the placid Otsego, or pausing to listen to the rattling of wheels and the sound of hammers, that rose from the valley to mingle the signs of men with the scenes of nature, when Elizabeth suddenly started, and exclaimed:

"Listen! There are the cries of a child on this mountain! Is there a clearing near us, or can some little one have strayed from its parents?"

"Such things frequently happen," replied her companion, Louisa Grant, the minister's pretty daughter. "Let us follow the sounds; it may be a wanderer starving on the hill."

Urged by this consideration, the females pursued the low, mournful sounds that proceeded from the forest with quick and impatient steps. More than once the ardent Elizabeth was on the point of announcing that she saw the sufferer, when Louisa caught her by the arm, and, pointing behind them, cried:

"Look at the dog!"

Brave had been their companion from the time the voice of his young mistress lured him from his kennel to the present moment. His advanced age had long before deprived him of his activity, and when his companions stopped to view the scenery, or to add to the bouquets, the mastiff would lay his huge frame on the ground and await their movements, with his eyes closed and a listlessness in his air that ill accorded with the character of a protector. But when, aroused by this cry from Louisa, Elizabeth Temple turned, she saw the dog with his eyes keenly set on some distant object, his head bent near the ground, and his hair actually rising on his body through fright or anger. It was most probably the latter, for he was growling in a low key, and occasionally showing his teeth, in a manner that would have terrified his mistress had she not so well known his good qualities.

"Brave," she said, "be quiet, Brave! What do you see, fellow?" At the sounds of her voice the rage of the mastiff, instead of being at all diminished, very sensibly increased. He stalked in front of the ladies and seated himself at the feet of his mistress, growling louder than before, and occasionally giving vent to his ire by a short, surly barking.

"What does he see?" said Elizabeth. "There must be some animal in sight."

Hearing no answer from her companion, Miss Temple turned her head, and beheld Louisa, standing with her face whitened to the color of death, and her finger pointing upward, with a sort of flickering, convulsed motion. The quick eye of Elizabeth glanced in the direction indicated by her friend, where she saw the fierce front and glaring eyes of a female panther, fixed on them in horrid malignity, and threatening to leap.

"Let us fly," exclaimed Elizabeth, grasping the arm of Louisa, whose form yielded like melting snow.

There was not a single feeling in the temperament of Elizabeth Temple that could prompt her to desert a companion in such an extremity. She fell on her knees by the side of the inanimate Louisa, tearing from the person of her friend, with instinctive readiness, such parts of her dress as might obstruct her respiration, and encouraging their only safeguard, the dog, at the same time by the sounds of her voice:

"Courage, Brave!" she cried, her own tones beginning to tremble. "Courage, courage, good Brave!"

A quarter-grown cub, that had hitherto been unseen, now appeared, dropping from the branches of a sapling that grew under the shade of the beech which held its dam. This ignorant but vicious creature approached the dog, imitating the actions and sounds of its parent, but exhibiting a strange mixture of the playfulness of a kitten with the ferocity of its race. Standing on its hind legs, it would rend the bark of a tree with its fore paws and play the antics of a cat; and then, by lashing itself with its tail, growling, and scratching the earth, it would attempt the manifestations of anger that rendered its parent so terrific.

All this time Brave stood firm and undaunted, his short tail erect, his body drawn backward on its haunches, and his eyes following the movements of both dam and cub. At every gambol played by the latter, it approached nigher to the dog, the growling of the three becoming more horrid at each moment, until the younger beast, overleaping its intended bound, fell directly before the mastiff. There was a moment of fearful cries and struggles, but they ended almost as soon as commenced by the cub appearing in the air, hurled from the jaws of Brave with a violence that sent it against a tree so forcibly as to render it completely senseless.

Elizabeth witnessed the short struggle, and her blood was warming with the triumph of the dog, when she saw the form of the old panther in the air, springing twenty feet from the branch of the beech to the back of the mastiff. No words of ours can describe the fury of the conflict that followed. It was a confused struggle on the dry leaves, accompanied by loud and terrific cries. Miss Temple continued on her knees, bending over the form of Louisa, her eyes fixed on the animals with an interest so horrid and yet so intense that she almost forgot her own stake in the result. So rapid and vigorous were the bounds of the inhabitant of the forest that its active frame seemed constantly in the air. while the dog nobly faced his foe at each successive leap. When the panther lighted on the shoulders of the mastiff, which was its constant aim, old Brave, though torn with her talons and stained with his own blood, that already flowed from a dozen wounds, would shake off his furious foe like a feather, and, rearing on his hind legs, rush to the fray again with jaws distended and a dauntless eye. But age and his pampered life greatly disqualified the noble mastiff for such a struggle. In everything but courage he was only the vestige of what he had once been. A higher bound than ever raised the wary and furious beast far beyond the reach of the dog, who was making a desperate but fruitless effort to dash at her, and she alighted in a favorable position on the back of her aged foe. For a single moment only could the panther remain there, the great strength of the dog returning with a convulsive effort. But Elizabeth saw, as Brave fastened his teeth in the side of his enemy, that the collar of brass around his neck, which had been glittering throughout the fray, was of the color of blood, and directly, that his frame was sinking to the earth, where it soon lay prostrate and helpless. Several mighty efforts of the wildcat to extricate herself from the jaws of the dog followed, but they were fruitless, until the mastiff turned on his back, his lips collapsed, and his teeth loosened, when the short convulsions and stillness that succeeded announced the death of poor Brave.

Elizabeth now lay wholly at the mercy of the beast. There is said to be something in the front of the image of the Maker that daunts the hearts of the inferior beings of His creation; and it would seem that some such power, in the present instance, suspended the threatened blow. The eyes of the monster and the kneeling maiden met for an instant. when the former stooped to examine her fallen foe; next to scent her luckless cub. From the latter examination it turned, however, with its eyes apparently emitting flashes of fire, its tail lashing its sides furiously, and its claws projecting inches from its broad feet.

Elizabeth Temple did not, or could not, move. Her hands were clasped in the attitude of prayer, but her eyes were still drawn to her terrible enemy— her cheeks were blanched to the whiteness of marble, and her lips were slightly separated with horror.

The moment seemed now to have arrived for the fatal termination, and the beautiful figure of Elizabeth was bowing meekly to the stroke, when a rustling of leaves behind seemed rather to mock the organs than to meet her ears.

"Hist! Hist!" said a low voice. "Stoop lower, gal; your bonnet hides the creater's head."

It was rather the yielding of nature than a compliance with this unexpected order that caused the head of our heroine to sink on her bosom; when she heard the report of the rifle, the whizzing of the bullet, and the enraged cries of the beast, who was rolling over on the earth biting its own flesh and tearing the twigs and branches within its reach. At the next instant the form of Leatherstocking rushed by her, and he called aloud:

"Come in, Hector, come in, old fool; 'tis a hard-lived animal, and may jump ag'in."

Natty fearlessly maintained his position in front of the females, notwithstanding the violent bounds and threatening aspect of the wounded panther, which gave several indications of returning strength and ferocity, until his rifle was again loaded, when he stepped up to the enraged animal, and, placing the muzzle close to its head, every spark of life was extinguished by the discharge.

The death of her terrible enemy appeared to Elizabeth like a resurrection from her own grave. There was an elasticity in the mind of our heroine that rose to meet the pressure of instant danger, and the more direct it had been the more her nature had struggled to overcome them.

A little water that was brought from one of the thousand springs of those mountains in the cap of Leatherstocking restored Louisa Grant to consciousness, and the thanks of both girls were uttered with the warmth that might be expected from the character of Elizabeth. Natty received her vehement protestations of gratitude with a simple expression of good-will, and with indulgence for her present excitement, but with a carelessness that showed how little he thought of the service he had rendered.

"Well, well," he said, "be it so, gal; let it be so, if you wish it; we'll talk the thing over another time. Come, come; let us get into the road, for you've had terror enough to make you wish yourself in your father's house ag'in."

This was uttered as they were proceeding, at a pace that was adapted to the weakness of Louisa, toward the highway; on reaching which the ladies separated from their guide, declaring themselves equal to the remainder of the walk without his assistance, and feeling encouraged by the sight of the village, which lay beneath their feet like a picture, with its limpid lake in front, the winding stream along its margin, and its hundred chimneys of whitened bricks.

The reader need not be told the nature of the emotions which two youthful, ingenuous, and well-educated girls would experience at their escape from a death so horrid as the one which had impended over them, while they pursued their way in silence along the track on the side of the mountain; nor how deep were their mental thanks to that Power which had given them their existence, and which had not deserted them in their extremity; neither how often they pressed each other's arms as the assurance of their present safety came like a healing balm athwart their troubled spirits, when their thoughts were recurring to the recent moments of horror.

Leatherstocking remained on the hill, gazing after their retiring figures until they were hidden by a bend in the road, when he whistled in his dogs, and, shouldering his rifle, returned into the forest.

"Well, it was a skeary thing to the young creaters," said Natty, while he retrod the path toward the plain. " It might frighten an older woman to see a she painter so near her, with a dead cub by its side. I wonder if I had aimed at the varmint's eye if I should n't have touched the life sooner than in the forehead ; but they are hard-lived animals, and it was a good shot, consid'ring that I could see nothing but the head and the peak of its tail. Hah ! who goes there ? "

" How goes it, Natty ? " said Mr. Doolittle, the village constable, stepping out of the bushes with a motion that was a good deal accelerated by the sight of the rifle that was already lowered in his direction. " What ! shooting this warm day ! Mind, old man, the law don't get hold on you."

" The law, squire ! I have shook hands with the law these forty years," returned Natty ; " for what has a man who lives in the wilderness to do with the ways of the law ? "

" Not much, maybe," said Hiram ; " but you sometimes trade in venison. I s'pose you know, Leatherstocking, that there is an act passed to lay a fine of five pounds currency, or twelve dollars and fifty cents, by decimals, on every man who kills deer betwixt January and August. The judge had a great hand in getting the law through."

" I can believe it," returned the old hunter ; " I can believe that or anything of a man who carries on as he does in the country."

" Yes, the law is quite positive, and the judge is bent on putting it in force —five pounds penalty. I thought I heard your hounds out on the scent of so'thing this morning ; I did n't know but they might get you in difficulty."

" They know their manners too well," said Natty, carelessly. " And how much goes to the State's evidence, squire ? "

" How much ! " repeated Hiram, quailing under the honest but sharp look of the hunter ; "the informer gets half, I—I believe—yes, I guess it's half. But there's blood on your sleeve, man—you have n't been shooting anything this morning ? "

" I have, though," said the hunter, nodding his head significantly to the other, " and a good shot I made of it."

" H-e-m ! " ejaculated the magistrate, "and where is the game ? I s'pose it's of a good nater, for your dogs won't hunt at anything that is n't choice."

" They'll hunt anything I tell them to, squire," cried Natty, favoring the other with his laugh. "They'll hunt you, if I say so. He-e-e-re, he-e-e-re, Hector—he-e-e-re,—come this way, pups—come this way—come hither."

"Oh! I have always heard a good character of the dogs," returned Mr. Doolittle, quickening his pace by raising each leg in rapid succession, as the hounds scented around his person. "And where is the game, Leatherstocking?"

During this dialogue the speakers had been walking at a very fast gait, and Natty swung the end of his rifle round, pointing through the bushes, and replied:

"There lies one. How do you like such meat?"

"This!" exclaimed Hiram, "why this is Judge Temple's dog Brave. Take care, Leatherstocking, and do n't make an enemy of the judge. I hope you have n't harmed the animal?"

"Look for yourself, Mr. Doolittle," said Natty, drawing his knife from his girdle, and wiping it, in a knowing manner, once or twice across his garment of buckskin; "does his throat look as if I had cut it with this knife?"

"It is dreadfully torn! It's an awful wound—no knife ever did this deed. Who could have done it?"

"The painters behind you, squire."

"Painters?" echoed Hiram, whirling on his heel with an agility that would have done credit to a dancing-master.

"Be easy, man," said Natty; "there's two of the venomous things; but the dog finished one and I have fastened the other's jaws for her; so do n't be frightened, squire, they won't hurt you."

"And where's the deer?" cried Hiram, staring about him with a bewildered air.

"Anan! deer!" repeated Natty.

"Sartain; ain't there venison here, or did n't you kill a buck?"

"What! when the law forbids the thing, squire?" said the old hunter. "I hope there's no law ag'in killing the painters."

"No; there's a bounty on the scalps—but—will your dogs hunt painters, Natty?"

"Anything; did n't I tell you they'd hunt a man? He-e-e-re, he-e-e-re, pups—"

"Yes, yes, I remember. Well, they are strange dogs, I must say—I am quite in a wonderment."

Natty had seated himself on the ground, and having laid the grim head of his late ferocious enemy in his lap, was drawing his knife with a practised hand around the ears, which he tore from the head of the beast in such a manner as to preserve their connection, when he answered:

"What at, squire? Did you never see a painter's scalp afore? Come, you are a magistrate; I wish you'd make me out an order for the bounty."

"The bounty!" repeated Hiram, holding the ears on the end of his finger for a moment, as if uncertain how to proceed. "Well, let us go down to your hut, where you can take the oath, and I will write out the order. I suppose you have a Bible? All the law wants is the Four Evangelists and the Lord's Prayer."

"I keep no books," said Natty, coldly; "not such a Bible as the law needs."

"Oh! there's but one sort of Bible that's good in law," returned the magistrate, "and your'n will do as well as another's. Come, the carcasses are worth nothing, man; let us go down and take the oath."

"Softly, softly, squire," said the hunter, lifting his trophies very deliberately from the ground and shouldering his rifle. "Why do you want an oath, at all, for a thing that your own eyes have seen? Won't you believe yourself, that another man must swear to a fact that you know to be true? You have seen me scalp the creaters, and if I must swear to it, it shall be before Judge Temple, who needs an oath."

"But we have no pen or paper here, Leatherstocking; we must go to the hut for them, or how can I write the order?"

Natty turned his simple features on the cunning magistrate, with another of his laughs, as he said:

"And what should I be doing with scholars' tools? I want no pens or paper, not knowing the use of either; and I keep none. No, no; I'll bring the scalps into the village, squire, and you can make out the order on one of your law-books, and it will be all the better for it. The deuce take this leather on the neck of the dog, it will strangle the old fool. Can you lend me a knife, squire?"

Hiram, who seemed particularly anxious to be on good terms with his companion, unhesitatingly complied. Natty cut the thong from the neck of the hound, and, as he returned the knife to its owner, carelessly remarked:

"'Tis a good bit of steel, and has cut such leather as this very same before now, I dare say."

"Do you mean to charge me with setting your hounds loose?" exclaimed the other, with a consciousness that disarmed his caution.

"Look you here, Mr. Doolittle," said the hunter, turning on the constable and striking the breech of his rifle violently on the ground, "what there is in the wigwam of a poor man like me that one like you can crave, I don't know; but this I tell you to your face, that you never shall put foot under the roof of my cabin with my consent, and that if you harbor round the spot as you have done lately you will meet with treatment that you will little relish."

"And let me tell you, Mr. Bumpo," said Hiram, retreating, however, with a quick step, "that I know you've broke the law, and that I'm a magistrate, and will make you feel it, too, before you are a day older."

"That for you, and your law, too," cried Natty, snapping his fingers at the justice of the peace. "Away with you, you varmint, before the devil tempts me to give you your desarts. Take care, if I ever catch your prowling face in the woods ag'in, that I do n't shoot it for an owl."

There is something at all times commanding in honest indignation, and Hiram did not stay to provoke the wrath of the old hunter to extremities. When the intruder was out of sight, Natty proceeded to the hut, where he found all quiet as the grave. He fastened his dogs, and, tapping at the door, which was opened by Edwards, asked:

"Is all safe, lad?"

"Everything," returned the youth. "Some one attempted the lock, but it was too strong for him."

"I know the creater," said Natty, "but he'll not trust himself within reach of my rifle very soon—" What more was uttered by the Leatherstocking, in his vexation, was rendered inaudible by the closing of the door of the cabin.

But Natty Bumpo's vexation was destined to grow into real and serious trouble.

For, upon charges being made against him by the constable, that he had killed a deer out of season, Judge Temple was obliged to issue a warrant and order a fine, even though, in his joy at the escape of his daughter from the panther, he was ready at once to pay the fine himself, and also see that Leatherstocking received the bounty promised by the State for the scalp of a panther.

But Leatherstocking was a curious old fellow. He did not understand, and, indeed, openly resisted the law of the frontier, and when Constable Doolittle and Billy Wiley came to his hut to serve the warrant and lay the fine, he not only refused to allow them to do this or to enter his hut, but drove them away with his rifle, the unerring aim of which all the border knew.

This defiance and resistance to the law even Judge Temple could not overlook, and he was forced to issue an order to arrest "Nathaniel Bumpo, sometimes called Leatherstocking," and place him in the village jail.

As for young Edwards, when he knew that his friend was to be arrested, he turned upon Judge Temple with reproach and indignation.

But the Judge had determined to enforce the law and protect its officers. Edwards' plea was of no avail, and after a stormy scene the young man rushed from the house and took his way at once to Leatherstocking's hut.

Meantime the officers had gone to the forest to arrest the old man. So desperate a character was Leatherstocking considered by the pioneers, on account of his obstinacy and his rifle, that it was thought best to send a strong force to arrest him, and so the force that approached the hut was composed of a dozen armed men. The men divided, some plunging deeper into the forest, in order to gain their stations without giving an alarm, and others continuing to advance, at a gait that would allow the whole party to go in order; but all devising the best plan to repulse the attack of a dog, or to escape a rifle-bullet. It was a moment of dread expectation and interest.

When time enough had elapsed for the different divisions of the force to arrive at their stations, the leader raised his voice in the silence of the forest, and shouted the watchword. All was silent in the forest; then, curiosity and impatience getting the complete ascendancy over discretion, the men rushed up the bank, and in a moment stood on the little piece of cleared ground in front of the spot where Natty had so long lived. To their amazement, in place of the hut they saw only its smouldering ruins.

The party gradually drew together about the heap of ashes and the ends of smoking logs; while a dim flame in the center of the ruin, which still found fuel to feed its lingering life, threw its pale light, flickering with the passing currents of the air, around the circle—now showing a face with eyes fixed in astonishment, and then glancing to another countenance, leaving the former shaded in the obscurity of night.

The whole group were yet in the fulness of their surprise, when a tall form stalked from the gloom into the circle, treading down the hot ashes and dying embers with callous feet; and standing over the light, lifted his cap, and exposed the bare head and weather-beaten features of Leatherstocking. For a moment he gazed at the dusky figures who surrounded him, more in sorrow than in anger, before he spoke.

"What would ye with an old and helpless man?" he said. "You've driven God's creaters from the wilderness, where His providence had put them for His own pleasure; and you've brought in the troubles and divilries of the law where no man was ever known to disturb another. You have driven me, that have lived forty long years of my appointed time in this very spot, from my home and the shelter of my head, lest you should put your wicked feet and wasty ways in my cabin. You've driven me to burn these logs, under which I've eaten and drunk—the first of heaven's gifts, and the other of the pure springs—for the half of a hundred years; and to mourn the ashes under my feet as a man would weep and mourn for the children of his body. You've rankled the heart of an old man, that has never harmed you or your'n, with bitter feelings toward his kind, at a time when his thoughts should be on a better world; and you've driven him to wish that the beasts of the forest, who never feast on the blood of their own families, was his kindred and race; and now, when he has come to see the last brand of his hut, before it is melted in ashes, you follow him up, at midnight, like hungry hounds on the track of a worn-out and dying deer. What more would ye have? for I am here—one too many. I come to mourn, not to fight; and, if it is God's pleasure, work your will on me."

When the old man ended, he stood, with the light glimmering around his thinly covered head, looking earnestly at the group, which receded from the pile with an involuntary movement, without the reach of the quivering rays, leaving a free passage for his retreat into the bushes, where pursuit, in the dark, would have been fruitless. Natty seemed not to regard this advantage, but stood facing each individual in the circle in succession, as if to see who would be the first to arrest him. After a pause of a few moments, the leader of the officers of the law began to rally his confused faculties; and, advancing, apologized for his duty, and made Leatherstocking his prisoner. The party now collected; and, preceded by the sheriff, with Natty in their center, they took their way toward the village.

During the walk, divers questions were put to the prisoner concerning his reasons for burning the hut, and whither the Mohican had retreated; but to all of them he observed a profound silence, until, fatigued with their previous duties and the lateness of the hour, the sheriff and his followers reached the village and dispersed to their several places of rest, after turning the key of a jail on the aged and apparently friendless Leatherstocking.

It went badly enough for poor Leatherstocking at his trial. Pioneers are anxious always to uphold the law, and the open resistance made by the old hunter was a crime in the eye of the law that could not be overlooked.

So, when the jury had found him guilty, Judge Temple felt compelled, even though he hated to do so, to impose upon the prisoner the sentence of the law.

"Nathaniel Bumpo," commenced the judge, making the customary pause.

The old hunter, who had been musing again, with his head on the bar, raised himself, and cried, with a prompt, military tone:

"Here!"

The judge waved his hand for silence, and proceeded:

"In forming their sentence the court have been greatly governed as much by the consideration of your ignorance of the laws as by a strict sense of the importance of punishing such outrages as this of which you have been found guilty. They have therefore passed over the obvious punishment of whipping on the bare back, in mercy to your years; but, as the dignity of the law requires an open exhibition of the consequences of your crime, it is ordered that you be conveyed from this room to the public stocks, where you are to be confined for one hour; that you pay a fine to the State of one hundred dollars; and that you be imprisoned in the jail of this county for one calendar month, and, furthermore, that your imprisonment do not cease until the said fine shall be paid. I feel it my duty, Nathaniel Bumpo——"

" And where should I get the money?" interrupted Leatherstocking eagerly. "Where should I get the money? You'll take away the bounty on the painters because I cut the throat of a deer, and how is an old man to find so much gold or silver in the woods? No, no, Judge; think better of it, and don't talk of shutting me up in a jail for the little time I have to stay."

"If you have anything to urge against the passing of the sentence, the court will yet hear you," said the judge mildly.

"I have enough to say ag'in it," cried Natty, grasping the bar on which his fingers were working with a convulsive motion. "Where am I to get the money? Let me out into the woods and hills, where I've been used to breathe the clear air, and, though I'm threescore-and-ten, if you've left game enough in the country I'll travel night and day but I'll make you up the sum afore the season is over. Yes, yes; you see the reason of the thing, and the wickedness of shutting up an old man that has spent his days, as one may say, where he could always look into the windows of Heaven."

"I must be governed by the law——"

"Talk not to me of law, Marmaduke Temple," interrupted the hunter. " Did the beast of the forest mind your laws when it was thirsty and hungering for the blood of your own child? She was kneeling to her God for a greater favor than I ask, and He heard her; and if you now say 'No' to my prayers, do you think He will be deaf?"

"My private feelings must not enter into——"

"Hear me, Marmaduke Temple," interrupted the old man, with melancholy earnestness, "and hear reason. I've traveled these mountains when you was no judge, but an infant in your mother's arms, and I feel as if I had a right and a privilege to travel them ag'in afore I die. Have you forgot the time that you come on to the lake shore, when there wasn't even a jail to lodge in, and didn't I give you my own bearskin to sleep on, and the fat of a noble buck to satisfy the cravings of your hunger? Yes, yes; you thought it no sin then to kill a deer! And this I did, though I had no reason to love you, for you had never done anything but harm to them that loved and sheltered me. And now, will you shut me up in your dungeons to pay me for my kindness? A hundred dollars! Where should I get the money? No, no; there's them that says hard things of you, Marmaduke Temple, but you ain't so bad as to wish to see an old man die in a prison because he stood up for the right. Come, friend, let me pass; it's long sin' I've been used to such crowds, and I crave to be in the woods ag'in. Don't fear me, Judge; I bid you not to fear me, for if there's beaver enough left on the streams, or the buckskins will sell for a shilling apiece, you shall have the last penny of the fine. Where are you, pups? Come away, dogs; come away! We have a grievous toil to do for our years, but it shall be done; yes, yes, I've promised it, and it shall be done."

"There must be an end to this," said the judge, struggling to overcome his feelings. "Constable, lead the prisoner to the stocks. Mr. Clerk, what stands next on the calendar?"

Natty seemed to yield to his destiny, for he sunk his head on his chest and followed the officer from the court room in silence. The crowd moved back for the passage of the prisoner, and when his tall form was seen descending from the outer door a rush of the people for the scene of his disgrace followed.

Without a murmur the old hunter submitted to the punishment of the stocks; and when this was over he was led into the jail and locked up for the night.

But before the close of the day young Oliver Edwards was seen at the window in earnest dialogue with his friend; and after he departed it was thought that he had communicated words of comfort to the hunter, who threw himself on his pallet and was soon in a deep sleep.

The law having been vindicated, Judge Temple determined to show his personal friendship and gratitude to Leatherstocking by paying the fine and promising to care for him after the term of his imprisonment was over. But he bade his daughter act as his messenger.

"You have reason, Bess, and much of it, too, but your heart lies too near your head. But listen: in this pocket-book are two hundred dollars. Go to the prison—there are none in this place to harm you—give this note to the jailer, and when you see Bumpo, say what you please to the poor old man; give scope to the feelings of your warm heart; but try to remember, Elizabeth, that the laws can alone remove us from the condition of the savages; that he has been criminal, and that his judge was your father."

Miss Temple made no reply, but she pressed the hand that held the pocket-book to her bosom, and taking her friend, Louisa Grant, by the arm, they issued together from the inclosure into the principal street of the village.

As they pursued their walk in silence, under the row of houses, where the deeper gloom of the evening effectually concealed their persons, no sound reached them excepting the slow tread of a yoke of oxen, with the rattling of a cart, that were moving along the street in the same direction with themselves. The figure of the teamster was just discernible by the dim light, lounging by the side of his cattle with a listless air, as if fatigued by the toil of the day. At the corner, where the jail stood, the progress of the ladies was impeded for a moment by the oxen, who were turned up to the side of the building, and given a lock of hay, which they carried on their necks, as a reward for their patient labor. The whole of this was so natural and so common that Elizabeth saw nothing to induce a second glance at the team, until she heard the teamster speaking to his cattle in a low voice:

"Mind yourself, Brindle ; will you, sir! will you!"

The language itself was unusual to oxen, with which all who dwell in a new country are familiar; but there was something in the voice also that startled Miss Temple. On turning the corner she necessarily approached the man, and her look was enabled to detect the person of Oliver Edwards concealed under the coarse garb of a teamster. Their eyes met at the same instant, and, notwithstanding the gloom, and the enveloping cloak of Elizabeth, the recognition was mutual.

"Miss Temple!" "Mr. Edwards!" were exclaimed simultaneously, though a feeling that seemed common to both rendered the words nearly inaudible.

"Is it possible!" exclaimed Edwards, after the moment of doubt had passed: "Do I see you so nigh the jail? But you are going to the Rectory. I beg pardon ; Miss Grant, I believe ; I did not recognize you at first."

The sigh which Louisa uttered was so faint that it was only heard by Elizabeth, who replied quickly :

"We are going not only to the jail, Mr. Edwards, but into it. We wish to show the Leatherstocking that we do not forget his services, and that at the same time we must be just, we are also grateful. I suppose you are on a similar errand ; but let me beg that you will give us leave to precede you ten minutes. Good-night, sir ; I—I—am quite sorry, Mr. Edwards, to see you reduced to such labor. I am sure my father would——"

"I shall wait your pleasure, madam," interrupted the youth, coldly. "May I beg that you will not mention my being here?"

Elizabeth promised, and was soon in the presence of the prisoner.

"Leatherstocking!" said Elizabeth, when the key of the door was turned on them again, "my good friend Leatherstocking! I have come on a message of gratitude. Had you submitted to the search, worthy old man, the death of the deer would have been a trifle, and all would have been well——"

"Submit to the sarch!" interrupted Natty, raising his face from resting on his knees, without rising from the corner where he had seated himself; "d'ye think, gal, I would let such a varmint into my hut? No, no—I wouldn't have opened the door to your own sweet countenance then. But they are wilcome to sarch among the coals and ashes now; they'll find only some such heap as is to be seen at every potashery in the mountains."

The old man dropped his face again on one hand, and seemed to be lost in melancholy.

"The hut can be rebuilt and made better than before," returned Miss

Temple, "and it shall be my office to see it done when your imprisonment is ended."

"Can ye raise the dead, child?" said Natty, in a sorrowful voice. "Can ye go into the place where you've laid your fathers, and mothers, and children, and gather together their ashes, and make the same men and women of them as afore? You do not know what 'tis to lay your head for more than forty years under the cover of the same logs, and to look on the same things for the better part of a man's life."

"Other logs and better, though, can be had, and shall be found for you, my old defender," said Elizabeth. "Your confinement will soon be over, and before that time arrives I shall have a house prepared for you, where you may spend the close of your harmless life in ease and plenty."

"Ease and plenty! house!" repeated Natty, slowly. "You mean well, you mean well, and I quite mourn that it can not be; but he has seen me a sight and a laughing-stock, and it can not be."

"Ease and plenty!" he repeated. "What ease can there be for an old man, who must walk a mile across the open fields before he can find a shade to hide him from a scorching sun? Or what plenty is there, where you may hunt a day and not start a buck, or see anything bigger than a mink, or maybe a stray fox? Ah! I shall have a hard time after them very beavers, for this fine. I must go low toward the Pennsylvany line in search of the creaters, maybe a hundred mile, for they are not to be got hereaway. No, no; your betterments and clearings have druv the knowing things out of the country; and instead of beaver-dams, which is the nater of the animal, and according to Providence, you turn back the waters over the low grounds with your mill-dams, as if 'twas in man to stay the drops from going where He wills them to go. But listen!" he said, suddenly.

"The time has come to go," said the hunter, listening; "I hear the horns of the oxen rubbing ag'in the sides of the jail. You won't betray us, gal?" he said, looking simply into the face of Elizabeth. "You won't betray an old man, who craves to breathe the clear air of heaven? I mean no harm, and if the law says that I must pay the hundred dollars, I'll take the season through but that it shall be forthcoming."

"But what mean you?" cried the wondering Elizabeth. "Here you must stay for thirty days; but I have the money for your fine in this purse. Take it; pay it in the morning, and summon patience for your month. I will come often to see you, with my friend; we will make up your clothes with our own hands; indeed, you shall be comfortable."

"Would ye, children?" said Natty, advancing across the floor with an air of kindness, and taking the hand of Elizabeth; "would ye be so kearful of an old man, and just for shooting the beast, which cost him nothing? Such things does n't run in the blood, I believe, for you seem not to forget a favor. Your little fingers could n't do much on a buckskin, nor be you used to such a thread as sinews."

"I grieve, Leatherstocking," continued Elizabeth, "that the law requires that you should be detained here so long; but, after all, it will be only a short month, and——"

"A month!" exclaimed Natty, opening his mouth with his usual laugh; "not a day, nor a night, nor an hour, gal. Judge Temple may sintence, but he can't keep, without a better dungeon than this. I was taken once by the French, and they put sixty-two of us in a blockhouse, nigh hand to old Frontinac; but 't was easy to cut through a pine log to them that was used to timber." The hunter paused and looked cautiously around the room, when, laughing again, he removed the bedclothes, and discovered a hole recently cut in the logs with a mallet and chisel. "It's only a kick, and the outside piece is off, and then——"

"You will not leave us, surely, Leatherstocking," broke in Miss Temple; "I beseech you, reflect that you will be driven to the woods entirely, and that you are fast getting old. Be patient for a little time, when you can go abroad openly, and with honor."

"Is there beaver to be catched here, gal?"

"If not, here is money to discharge the fine, and in a month you are free. See, here it is, in gold."

"Gold!" said Natty, with a kind of childish curiosity; "it's long sin' I've seen a gold piece. We used to get the broad joes in the old war, as plenty as bears be now. I remember there was a man in Dieskau's army that was killed, who had a dozen of the shining things sewed up in his shirt. I did n't handle them myself, but I seen them cut out with my own eyes; they was bigger and brighter than them be."

"These are English guineas, and are yours," said Elizabeth; "an earnest of what shall be done for you."

"Me! Why should you give me this treasure?" said Natty, looking earnestly at the maiden.

"Why! have you not saved my life? Did you not rescue me from the jaws of the beast?" exclaimed Elizabeth, veiling her eyes, as if to hide some hideous object from her view.

The hunter took the money, and continued turning it in his hand for some time, piece by piece, talking aloud during the operation.

"There's a rifle, they say, out on the Cherry Valley, that will carry a hundred rods and kill. I've seen good guns in my day, but none quite equal to that. A hundred rods with any sartainty is great shooting! Well, well; I'm old, and the gun I have will answer my time. Here, child, take back your gold. But the hour has come; I hear him talking to the cattle, and I must be going. You won't tell of us, gal—you won't tell of us, will ye?"

"Tell of you!" echoed Elizabeth. "But take the money, old man; take the money, even if you go into the mountains."

"No, no," said Natty, shaking his head kindly. "I would not rob you so for twenty rifles. But there's one thing you can do for me, if ye will, that no other is at hand to do."

"Name it—name it."

"Why, it's only to buy a canister of powder; 't will cost two silver dollars. Will you get it for me in the town, gal? Say, will you get it for me?"

"Will I? I will bring it to you, Leatherstocking, though I toil a day in quest of you through the woods. But where shall I find you, and how?"

"Where?" said Natty, musing a moment; "to-morrow, on the 'Vision'; on the very top of the 'Vision' I'll meet you, child, just as the sun gets over our heads. See that it's the fine grain; you'll know it by the gloss and the price."

"I will do it," said Elizabeth firmly.

Natty now seated himself, and, placing his feet in the hole, with a slight effort he opened a passage into the street. The ladies heard the rustling of hay, and understood the reason why Edwards was in the capacity of a teamster.

"Let us go," said the hunter; "'twill be no darker to-night, for the moon will rise in an hour."

"Stay!" exclaimed Elizabeth; "it should not be said that you escaped in the presence of the daughter of Judge Temple. Wait, Leatherstocking; let us retire before you execute your plan."

She retired with a cheery "Good night," and the next instant Leatherstocking was outside the jail. Their escape, however, was seen by watchful eyes. At once the chase was on.

"Spread yourselves, men," cried the constable to the crowd, as he passed the ladies, his heavy feet sounding along the street like the tread of a dozen, "spread yourselves. To the mountains; they'll be in the mountain in a quarter of an hour, and then look out for a long rifle."

His cries were echoed from twenty mouths, for not only the jail, but the taverns had sent forth their numbers, some earnest in the pursuit, and others joining it as in sport.

As Elizabeth turned in at her father's gate she saw the two figures stealing cautiously but quickly under the shade of the trees. In a moment Edwards and the hunter crossed their path.

"Miss Temple, I may never see you again," exclaimed the youth; "let me thank you for all your kindness; you do not, can not, know my motives."

"Fly, fly!" cried Elizabeth; "the village is alarmed. Do not be found conversing with me at such a moment, and in these grounds."

"Nay, I must speak, though detection were certain."

"Your retreat to the bridge is already cut off; before you can gain the wood your pursuers will be there." Then she added swiftly: "The street is now silent and vacant; cross it, and you will find my father's boat in the lake. It will be easy to land from it where you please in the hills."

"But Judge Temple might complain of the trespass."

"His daughter shall be accountable, sir."

The youth uttered something in a low voice, that was heard only by Elizabeth, and turned to execute what she had suggested. As they were separating, Natty approached the females, and said:

"You'll remember the canister of powder, children? Them beavers must be had, and I and the pups be getting old; we want the best of ammunition."

"Come, Natty," said Edwards, impatiently.

LEATHERSTOCKING LEADS THE WAY THROUGH THE BURNING FOREST.

"Coming, lad, coming. God bless you, young ones, both of ye, for ye mean well and kindly to the old man."

The ladies paused until they had lost sight of the retreating figures, when they immediately entered the mansion-house.

The next morning, as she had promised, Elizabeth Temple was out in the mountains, bearing the canister of powder. But when she had reached that part of the mountain called for its beautiful view "the Vision," a dreadful thing happened. The forests were on fire!

Elizabeth had another narrow escape from death. Young Oliver Edwards, who was searching for his friend, the Mohican, found her and tried to rescue her. But the fire advancing rapidly almost surrounded them just as they discovered the Mohican almost overcome by the flames. The canister of powder, dropped in the excitement, exploded with a loud report, and, guided by this, Leatherstocking found them. Taking the Indian upon his back, he directed Edwards to wrap Elizabeth in a skin garment of his own, and led them through the burning forest.

It was a narrow escape. Even as they crossed the little terrace of rock, one of the dead trees that had been tottering for several minutes, fell on the spot where they had stood, and filled the air with its cinders.

Such an event quickened the steps of the party, who followed the Leatherstocking with the urgency required by the occasion.

"Tread on the soft ground," he cried, when they were in a gloom where sight availed them but little, and keep in the white smoke; keep the skin close on her, lad; she's a precious one, another will be hard to be found."

Obedient to the hunter's directions, they followed his steps and advice implicitly; and although the narrow passage along the winding of the spring led amid burning logs and falling branches, they happily achieved it in safety. No one but a man long accustomed to the woods could have traced his route through a smoke, in which respiration was difficult and sight nearly useless; but the experience of Natty conducted them to an opening through the rocks, where, with a little difficulty, they soon descended to another terrace, and emerged at once into a tolerably clear atmosphere.

But John, the Mohican, the old warrior, Chingachgook, who had so long been the companion of Leatherstocking, did not survive.

There was loud talk in the village that Leatherstocking and Edwards had set fire to the forest in revenge for the old hunter's imprisonment, and the constable ordered out a party, when the fire had been quenched by rain, to search for and capture the fugitives.

The party was also charged with the recapture of a band of counterfeiters, who, profiting by the example of Leatherstocking, had broken from the village jail, and were now intrenched in a mountain cave. Over this mountain fort, which had long been their retreat, they had, before their arrest, mounted a small cannon for purposes of defense. The gun had, however, never been used. To this cave, when they knew that they were pursued, Leatherstocking and Edwards retreated, with the purpose of defending themselves until they could find an opportunity of escaping. Edwards had also another purpose, connected with the mystery which had surrounded his identity, and which will presently appear. He was temporarily absent when the constable's party advanced, somewhat cautiously, and, after some parley, attacked the cave. A blunder in setting off the cannon fired its charge of bullets into the tree-tops and dismounted the piece, and it seemed likely that much blood would be shed and that the cave would be taken, when Judge Temple suddenly appeared on the scene with Edwards, commanding a cessation of hostilities. The judge was too deeply grateful to Leatherstocking for again saving the life of his daughter to allow him to be further prosecuted, and he now took measures to have all such proceedings abandoned.

While this was going on Edwards appeared from within the cave, carrying, with the aid of Leatherstocking, a rude chair on which rested the form of an aged man, whom Judge Temple presently recognized as the father of an early friend of his own, whom he had lost in the War of the Revolution because they had taken different sides.

To this friend he was indebted for large sums of money, and when he further learned that Oliver was the son of this old-time partner, the grandson of the aged man for whom he had so long cared in secret, he took him again into his family, and made over to him one-half of his fortune and estate.

And so it happened that young Oliver and Elizabeth Temple fell in love with each other, greatly to the joy of Judge Temple ; and at last they were married and lived happily in the great estate at Templeton.

But Leatherstocking would not stay. He had seen enough of the ways of civilization ; a free hunter could not submit to its laws.

"No," he said to Oliver and Elizabeth, as he stood with them beside the slab they had raised to the memory of Chingachgook, the Mohican. "No, it's not all the same here. When I look about me, at these hills, where I used to count sometimes twenty smokes curling over the tree-tops from the Delaware camps, it raises mournful thoughts to think that not a redskin is left of them all, unless it be a drunken vagabond from the Oneidas, or them Eastern Indians, who, they say, be moving up from the seashore, and who belong to none of God's creaters, to my seeming, being, as it were, neither fish nor flesh, neither white man nor savage. Well, well ! the time has come at last, and I must go——"

"Go!" echoed Edwards. " Whither do you go ? "

The Leatherstocking, who had imbibed, unconsciously, many of the Indian qualities, though he always thought of himself as of a civilized being, compared with even the Delawares, averted his face to conceal the workings of his muscles as he stooped to lift a large pack, which he placed deliberately on his shoulders.

"Go!" exclaimed Elizabeth, approaching him with a hurried step. "You should not venture so far in the woods alone at your time of life, Natty; indeed, it is imprudent. He is bent, Oliver, on some distant hunting."

"What Elizabeth tells you is true, Leatherstocking," said Edwards; "there can be no necessity for your submitting to such hardships now! So throw aside your pack, and confine your hunting to the mountains near us, if you will go."

"Hardship! 'Tis a pleasure, children, and the greatest that is left me on this side the grave."

"No, no; you shall not go to such a distance," cried Elizabeth, laying her white hand on his deerskin pack. "I am right! I feel his camp-kettle and a canister of powder! He must not be suffered to wander so far from us, Oliver; remember how suddenly the Mohican dropped away."

"I know'd the parting would come hard, children; I know'd it would," said Natty, "and so I got aside by myself, and thought if I left ye perhaps ye would n't take it unkind, but would know that, let the old man's body go where it might, his feelings stayed behind him."

"This means something more than common," exclaimed the youth. "Where is it, Natty, that you purpose going?"

The hunter drew nigh him with a confident, reasoning air, as if what he had to say would silence all objections, and replied:

"Why, lad, they tell me that on the big lakes there's the best of hunting, and a great range, without a white man on it, unless it may be one like myself. I'm weary of living in clearings, and where the hammer is sounding in my ears from sunrise to sundown. And though I'm much bound to ye both, children,— I would n't say it if it was not true,—I crave to go into the woods ag'in, I do."

"Woods!" echoed Elizabeth, trembling with her feelings. "Do you not call these endless forests woods?"

"Ah! child, these be nothing to a man that's used to the wilderness. I have took but little comfort since your father come on with his settlers; but I would n't go far while the life was in the body that lies under the sod there. But now Chingachgook is gone, and you be both young and happy. Yes, the big house has rung with merriment this month past! And now, I thought, was the time to try to get a little comfort in the close of my days. Woods, indeed! I does n't call these woods, children, where I lose myself every day of my life in the clearings."

"If there be anything wanting to your comfort, name it, Leatherstocking; if it be attainable it is yours," said Oliver.

"You mean all for the best, lad; I know it, and so does the lady, too; but your ways is n't my ways. But somewhere we'll meet at last, children; somewhere. Yes, ind as you've begun, and we shall meet in the land of the just at last."

"This is so new, so unexpected!" said Elizabeth, in almost breathless excitement. "I had thought you meant to live with us and die with us, Natty."

"Words are of no avail," exclaimed her husband; "the habits of forty years are not to be dispossessed by the ties of a day. I know you too well to urge you further, Natty, unless you will let me build you a hut on one of the distant hills, where we can sometimes see you and know that you are comfortable."

"Do n't fear for the Leatherstocking, children; God will see that his days be provided for, and his ind happy. I know you mean all for the best, but our ways does n't agree. I love the woods, and ye relish the face of man; I eat when hungry and drink when a-dry, and ye keep stated hours and rules. Nay, nay; you even overfeed the dogs, lad, from pure kindness; and hounds should be gaunty to run well. The meanest of God's creaters be made for some use, and I'm formed for the wilderness; if ye love me, let me go where my soul craves to be ag'in."

JUDGE TEMPLE RECOGNIZES HIS AGED FRIEND.

The appeal was decisive, and not another word of entreaty for him to remain was then uttered; but Elizabeth bent her head to her bosom and wept, while Oliver dashed away the tears from his eyes; and, with hands that almost refused to perform their office, he produced his pocket-book and extended a parcel of banknotes to the hunter.

"Take these," he said, "at least take these; secure them about your person, and in the hour of need they will do you good service."

The old man took the notes and examined them with a curious eye.

"This, then, is some of the new-fashioned money that they've been making at Albany, out of paper! It can't be worth much to they that has n't larning! No, no, lad; take back the stuff; it will do me no sarvice. I took kear to get all the powder I could carry, and they say lead grows where I'm going. It is n't even fit for wads, seeing that I use none but leather! And now, lady, let an old man kiss your hand, and wish God's choicest blessings on you and your'n."

"Once more, let me beseech you, stay!" cried Elizabeth. "Do not, Leatherstocking, leave me to grieve for the man who has twice rescued me from death, and who has served those I love so faithfully. For my sake, if not for your own, stay. I shall see you in those frightful dreams that still haunt my nights, dying in poverty and age by the side of those terrific beasts you slew. There will be no evil that sickness, want, and solitude can inflict, that my fancy will not conjure as your fate. Stay with us, old man, if not for your own sake, at least for ours."

"Such thoughts and bitter dreams," returned the hunter, solemnly, "will never haunt an innocent parson long. They'll pass away with God's pleasure. And if the catamounts be yet brought to your eyes in sleep, 'tis not for my sake, but to show you the power of Him that led me there to save you. Trust in God, lady, and in your honorable husband, and the thoughts for an old man like me can never be long nor bitter. I pray that the Lord will keep you in mind—the Lord that lives in clearings as well as in the wilderness—and bless you, and all that belong to you, from this time till the great day when the whites shall meet the redskins in judgment, and justice shall be the law, and not power."

Elizabeth raised her head and offered her colorless cheek to his salute, when he lifted his cap and touched it respectfully. His hand was grasped with convulsive fervor by the youth, who continued silent. The hunter prepared himself for his journey, drawing his belt tighter, and wasting his moments in the little reluctant movements of a sorrowful departure. Once or twice he essayed to speak, but a rising in his throat prevented it. At length he shouldered his rifle, and cried, with a clear huntsman's call that echoed through the woods:

"He-e-e-re! he-e-e-re! pups—away dogs, away—ye'll be footsore afore ye see the ind of the journey!"

The hounds leaped from the earth at this cry, and scenting around the graves and the silent pair, as if conscious of their own destination, they followed humbly at the heels of their master. A short pause succeeded, during which even Oliver concealed his face. When the pride of manhood, however, had suppressed the feelings of nature, he turned to renew his entreaties, but saw that the cemetery was occupied only by himself and his wife.

"He is gone!" cried Oliver.

Elizabeth raised her face and saw the old hunter standing looking back for a moment on the verge of the wood. As he caught their glances he drew his hard hand hastily across his eyes, again, waved it on high for an adieu, and uttering a forced cry to his dogs, who were crouching at his feet, he entered the forest.

This was the last that they ever saw of the Leatherstocking, whose rapid movements eluded the pursuit which Judge Temple both ordered and conducted. He had gone far toward the setting sun—the foremost in that band of pioneers who opened the way for the march of the nation across the continent.

THE PRAIRIE.
A TALE OF THE WEST.

BY JAMES FENIMORE COOPER.

SHMAEL BUSH was a squatter. That was, years ago, a roving person who moved with his family and his belongings from place to place over the plains and prairies west of the Mississippi River, settling for a longer or shorter time wherever it suited his fancy or promised a fair living. Then, when tired or dissatisfied with results, he would pull up stakes, load his great wagons, and go further west, hunting for a new camping-ground.

Ishmael was a big man, almost a giant in size and strength. He had a wife, Esther, as strong and rough as he, and six great sons and two daughters. With him also traveled his wife's brother, Abram White, a slouching, evil-faced, surly man, and a young and pretty girl who called Ishmael her uncle, and whose name was Ellen Wade. A funny, little scientific man, hunting specimens, also was of the party. His name was Dr. Bat.

In the sunset light of an autumn day, as these prairie travelers were climbing a swelling rise of land, selecting a good camping-place for the night, they met an old, old man, dressed like one of the hunters of the prairie-land. It was a trapper. His name was Nathaniel Bumpo, and he had had a long and adventurous life, living among Indians, moving westward as civilization followed after him, from the Hudson to the Ohio, from the Ohio to the Mississippi, until now, in his old age, he sought a living on the swelling prairie plains, seeing few white men, and preferring to live alone, a trapper along the western rivers.

The old man met the emigrants, or squatters, and showed them a place to camp; but Ishmael was suspicious, and did not like to have the old trapper stay around. Still, he gave him a surly sort of thanks, and invited him to stay with them all night if he cared to do so. But the trapper declined the invitation,

MAHTOREE SURPRISES THE SLEEPING SENTINEL.

and walked away after the emigrants had chopped down trees on the bank of a stream, for the double purpose of allowing their cattle to browse upon the tops and of using the trunks and large branches to form a slight and irregular defense, and otherwise settled themselves in camp.

But that very night some of the wandering and warlike Indians of the prairies, called the Dacotahs or Tetons, came upon the traces of Ishmael's journey, and followed the trail to the camp.

Then the chief of the tribe, whose name was Mahtoree, proceeded to carefully and silently crawl toward the camp, hoping to escape the notice of the sentinels who he knew would be on guard, and spy into the camp, to see if there was anything there to make it worth his while to surprise and raid the camp of the squatters.

Dragging himself, inch by inch, through the long grass of the prairie, he came suddenly upon the sentinel. It was one of Ishmael's sons, named Asa; but he was asleep. Overcome by the march and work of the day, he had found himself too weary to keep awake, and thus the chief surprised him.

A man of nerves less tried than those of the fierce and conquering Mahtoree would have been keenly sensible of all the hazard he incurred. The reputation of those hardy and powerful white adventurers who so often penetrated the wilds inhabited by his people, was well known to him; but while he drew nigher, with the respect and caution that a brave enemy never fails to inspire, it was with the vindictive animosity of a red man, jealous and resentful of the inroads of the stranger.

Turning from the line of his former route, the Dacotah dragged himself directly toward the margin of the thicket. When this material object was effected in safety, he arose to his feet and took a better survey of his situation. A single moment served to apprise him of the place where the unsuspecting traveler lay.

When certain that he was undiscovered, the Dacotah raised his person again, and, bending forward, he moved his dark visage above the face of the sleeper in that sort of wanton and subtle manner with which the reptile is seen to play about its victim before it strikes. Satisfied at length, not only of the condition but of the character of the stranger, Mahtoree was in the act of withdrawing his head, when a slight movement of the sleeper announced the symptoms of reviving consciousness. The savage seized the knife which hung at his girdle, and in an instant it was poised above the breast of the young emigrant. Then, changing his purpose with an action as rapid as his own flashing thoughts, he sank back behind the trunk of the fallen tree against which the other reclined, and lay in its shadow, as dark, as motionless, and apparently as insensible as the wood itself.

THE PRAIRIE.

The slothful sentinel opened his heavy eyes, and gazing upward for a moment at the hazy heavens, he made an extraordinary exertion, and raised his powerful frame from the support of the log. Then he looked about him, with an air of something like watchfulness, suffering his dull glances to run over the misty objects of the encampment until they finally settled on the distant and dim field of the open prairie. Meeting with nothing more attractive than the same faint outlines of swell and interval which everywhere rose before his drowsy eyes, he changed his position so as completely to turn his back on his dangerous neighbor, and suffered his person to sink sluggishly down into its former recumbent attitude. A long and, on the part of the Teton, an anxious and painful silence succeeded, before the deep breathing of the traveler again announced that he was indulging in his slumbers. The savage was, however, far too jealous of a counterfeit to trust to the first appearance of sleep. But the fatigues of a day of unusual toil lay too heavy on the sentinel to leave the other long in doubt. Still, the motion with which Mahtoree again raised himself to his knees was so noiseless and guarded that even a vigilant observer might have hesitated to believe he stirred. The change was, however, at length effected, and the Dacotah chief then bent

THE RUDE FORTRESS ON THE PRAIRIE.

again over his enemy, without having produced a noise louder than that of the cottonwood leaf which fluttered at his side in the currents of the passing air.

Mahtoree now felt himself master of the sleeper's fate. At the same time that he scanned the vast proportions and athletic limbs of the youth in that sort of admiration which physical excellence seldom fails to excite in the breast of a savage, he coolly prepared to extinguish the principle of vitality which alone could render them formidable. After making himself sure of the seat of life by gently removing the folds of the intervening cloth, he raised his keen weapon, and was about to unite his strength and skill in the impending blow, when the young man threw his brawny arm carelessly backward, exhibiting in the action the vast volume of its muscles.

The sagacious and wary Teton paused. It struck his acute faculties that sleep was even less dangerous to him, at that moment, than even death itself might prove. The smallest noise, the agony of struggling with which such a frame would probably relinquish its hold of life, suggested themselves to his rapid thoughts and were all present to his experienced senses. He looked back into the encampment, turned his head into the thicket, and glanced his glowing eyes abroad into the wild and silent prairies. Bending once more over the respited victim, he assured himself that he was sleeping heavily, and then abandoned his immediate purpose in obedience alone to the suggestions of a more crafty policy.

The retreat of Mahtoree was as still and guarded as had been his approach. He now took the direction of the encampment, stealing along the margin of the brake, as a cover into which he might easily plunge at the smallest alarm. The drapery of a small and solitary hut, which was a part of the squatter's camp, now attracted his notice. After examining the whole of its exterior, and listening with painful intensity, in order to gather counsel from his ears, the savage ventured to raise the cloth at the bottom and to thrust his dark visage beneath. It might have been a minute before the Teton chief drew back, and seated himself with the whole of his form without the linen tenement. Here he ·sat, seemingly brooding over his discovery, for many moments in rigid inaction. Then he resumed his crouching attitude, and once more projected his visage beyond the covering of the tent. His second visit to the interior was longer, and, if possible, more ominous than the first. But it had, like everything else, its termination, and the savage again withdrew his glaring eyes from the secrets of the place.

Mahtoree had drawn his person many yards from the spot in his slow progress toward the cluster of objects which pointed out the center of the position, before he again stopped. He made another pause, and looked back at the solitary little dwelling he had left as if doubtful whether he should not return. But the *chevaux de frise* of branches now lay within reach of his arm, and the very appearance of precaution it presented, as it announced the value of the effects it encircled, tempted his cupidity and induced him to proceed.

The passage of the savage through the tender and brittle limbs of the cottonwood could be likened only to the sinuous and noiseless winding of the reptiles which he imitated. When he had effected his object, and had taken an instant to become acquainted with the nature of the localities within the inclosure, the Teton used the precaution to open a way through which he might make a swift retreat. Then, raising himself on his feet, he stalked through the encampment, like the master of evil, seeking whom and what he should first devote to his fell purposes. He had already ascertained the contents of the lodge in which were collected the woman and her young children, and had passed several gigantic frames, stretched on different piles of brush, which, happily for him, lay in unconscious helplessness, when he reached the spot occupied by Ishmael in person. It could not escape the sagacity of Mahtoree that he had now within his power the principal man among the travelers. He stood long hovering above the recumbent and Herculean form of the emigrant, keenly debating in his own mind the chances of his enterprise and the most effectual means of reaping its richest harvest.

He sheathed the knife, which, under the hasty and burning impulse of his thoughts, he had been tempted to draw, and was passing on, when Ishmael turned in his lair, and demanded roughly who was moving before his half-opened eyes. Nothing short of the readiness and cunning of a savage could have evaded the crisis. Imitating the gruff tones and nearly unintelligible sounds he heard, Mahtoree threw his body heavily on the earth and appeared to dispose himself to sleep. Though the whole movement was seen by Ishmael in a sort of stupid observation, the artifice was too bold and too admirably executed to fail. The drowsy father closed his eyes and slept heavily, with this treacherous inmate in the very bosom of his family.

It was necessary for the Teton to maintain the position he had taken for many long and weary minutes, in order to make sure that he was no longer watched. Though his body lay motionless, his active mind was not idle. He profited by the delay to mature a plan which he intended should put the whole encampment, including both its effects and their proprietors, entirely at his mercy. The instant he could do so with safety, the indefatigable savage was again in motion. He took his way toward the slight pen which contained the domestic animals, worming himself along the ground in his former subtle and guarded manner.

The first animal he encountered among the beasts occasioned a long and hazardous delay. The weary creature, perhaps conscious, through its secret instinct, that in the endless wastes of the prairies its surest protector was to be found in man, was so exceedingly docile as quietly to submit to the close examination it was doomed to undergo. The hand of the wandering Teton passed over the downy coat, the meek countenance, and the slender limbs of the gentle creature with untiring curiosity ; but he finally abandoned his prize, as useless in his predatory expeditions, and offering too little temptation to the appetite. As soon, however, as he found himself among the beasts of burden, his gratification was extreme, and it was with difficulty that he restrained the customary ejaculations of pleasure that were more than once on the point of bursting from his lips. Here he lost sight of the hazards by which he had gained access to his dangerous position ; and the watchfulness of the wary and long-practised warrior was for the moment forgotten in the exultation of the savage.

Meantime the old trapper, Natty Bumpo, and a wandering bee-hunter named Paul Hover, had fallen into the power of the Indians and been captured.

Both knew of the encampment of Ishmael Bush, and when suddenly a long shrill yell rent the air, and was instantly echoed from the surrounding waste, as if a thousand demons opened their throats in common at the summons, Weucha, one of the Indian guards of the white prisoners, uttered a cry of exultation.

"Now!" shouted Paul, unable to control his impatience any longer, "now, old Ishmael, is the time to show the native blood of Kentucky! Fire low, boys —level into the swales, for the redskins are settling to the very earth!"

His voice was, however, lost, or rather unheeded, in the midst of the shrieks, shouts, and yells that were, by this time, bursting from fifty mouths on every side of him. The guards still maintained their posts at the side of the captives, but it was with that sort of difficulty with which steeds are restrained at the starting-post when expecting the signal to commence the trial of speed. They tossed their arms wildly in the air, leaping up and down more like exulting children than sober men, and continued to utter the most frantic cries.

In the midst of this tumultuous disorder a rushing sound was heard, similar to that which might be expected to precede the passage of a flight of buffaloes, and then came the flocks and cattle of Ishmael, in one confused and frightened drove.

"They have robbed the squatter of his beasts!" said the attentive trapper. "The reptiles have left him as hoofless as a beaver!" He was yet speaking, when the whole body of the terrified animals ascended the little acclivity and swept by the place where he stood, followed by a band of dusky and demon-like figures, who pressed madly on their rear.

The impulse was communicated to the Teton horses, long accustomed to sympathize in the untutored passions of their owners, and it was with difficulty that the keepers were enabled to restrain their impatience. At this moment, when all eyes were directed to the passing whirlwind of men and beasts, the trapper caught the knife from the hands of his inattentive keeper, with a power that his age would have seemed to contradict, and, at a single blow, severed the thong of hide which connected the whole drove. The wild animals snorted with joy and terror, and, tearing the earth with their heels, they dashed away into the broad prairies in a dozen different directions.

Weucha turned upon his assailant with the ferocity and agility of a tiger. He felt for the weapon of which he had been so suddenly deprived, fumbled unsuccessfully for the handle of his tomahawk, and then, breaking away, joined in the swift pursuit. The trapper had continued calmly facing his foe during the instant of suspense that succeeded his hardy act, and now that Weucha was seen following his companions, he pointed after the dark train, saying, with his deep and nearly inaudible laugh :

"Red natur' is red natur', let it show itself on a prairie or in a forest. A knock on the head would be the smallest reward to him who would take such a liberty with a Christian sentinel; but there goes the Teton after his horses as if he thought two legs as good as four in such a race! And yet the imps will have every hoof of them afore the day sets in, because its reason ag'in instinct. Poor reason, I allow; but still there is a great deal of the man in the Indian. Ah's me! Your Delawares were the redskins of which America might boast; but few and scattered is that mighty people now. Well, the traveler may just make his pitch where he is; he has plenty of water, though natur' has cheated him of the pleasure of stripping the 'arth of its lawful trees. He has seen the last of his four-footed creatures, or I am but little skilled in Sioux cunning."

"Had we not better join the party of Ishmael?" said the bee-hunter. "There will be a regular fight about this matter, or the old fellow has suddenly grown chicken-hearted."

"Hist! hist! The sound of voices might bring us into danger," said the trapper. "Is your friend," he added, turning to Paul, "a man of spirit enough?"

"Don't call the squatter a friend of mine," interrupted the youth. "I never yet harbored with one who could not show hand and seal for the land which fed him."

"Well, well; let it then be acquaintance. Is he a man to maintain his own, stoutly, by dint of powder and lead?"

"His own! ay, and that which is not his own, too. Can you tell me, old trapper, who held the rifle that did the deed for the sheriff's deputy that thought to rout the unlawful settlers who had gathered nigh the buffalo lick in old Kentucky? I had lined a beautiful swarm that very day into the hollow of a dead beech, and there lay the people's officer at its root, with a hole directly through his heart. Of course, the murder was never strictly brought home to Ishmael Bush, and there were fifty others who had pitches in that neighborhood with just the same authority from the law."

Thoroughly satisfied that he understood the character of the emigrants by the short but comprehensive description conveyed in Paul's reply, the old trapper raised no further question concerning the readiness of Ishmael to avenge his wrongs, but rather followed the train of thought which was suggested to his experience by the occasion.

"Each one knows the ties which bind him to his fellow-creatures best," he answered. "Though it is greatly to be mourned that color, and property, and tongue, and l'arning should make so wide a difference in those who, after all, are but the children of one father. Howsomever," he continued, by a transition not a little characteristic of the pursuits and feelings of the man, "as this is a business in which there is much more likelihood of a fight than need for a sermon, it is best to be prepared for what may follow. Hush! there is a movement below; it is an equal chance that we are seen."

"The family is stirring," said Paul. "What think you, old trapper? How long may it be before these Tetons, as you call them, will be coming for the rest of old Ishmael's goods and chattels?"

"No fear of them," returned the old man, laughing in his own peculiar and silent manner; "I warrant me the rascals will be scampering after their beasts these six hours yet. Listen! you may hear them in the willow bottoms at this very moment; ay, your real Sioux cattle will run like so many long-legged elks. Hist! crouch again into the grass, down with ye both; as I'm a miserable piece of clay, I heard the clicking of a gun-lock!"

The trapper did not allow his companion time to hesitate, but dragging Paul after him, he nearly buried his own person in the fog of the prairie while he was speaking. It was fortunate that the senses of the aged hunter remained so acute, and that he had lost none of his readiness of action. The two men were scarcely bowed to the ground when their ears were saluted with the well-known, sharp, short report of the western rifle, and instantly the whizzing of the ragged lead was heard, buzzing within dangerous proximity of their heads.

"Well done, young chips! well done, old block!" whispered Paul, whose spirits no danger nor situation could entirely depress. "As pretty a volley as one would wish to hear on the wrong end of a rifle! What d'ye say, trapper. Here is likely to be a three-cornered war. Shall I give 'em as good as they send?"

"Give them nothing but fair words," returned the other hastily, "or you are lost."

"I'm not certain it would much mend the matter if I were to speak with my tongue instead of the piece," said Paul, in a tone half jocular, half bitter.

Several shots came in quick succession, each sending its dangerous messenger still nearer than the preceding discharge.

"This must end," said the trapper, rising with the dignity of one bent only on the importance of his object. "I know not what need ye may have, young man, to fear those who come hither, but something must be done to save your life. A few hours more or less can never be missed from the time of one who has already numbered so many days; therefore I will advance. Here is a clear space around you. Profit by it as you need, and may God bless and prosper you as ye deserve!"

Without waiting for any reply the trapper walked boldly down the declivity in his front, taking the direction of the encampment, neither quickening his pace in trepidation nor suffering it to be retarded by fear. The light of the moon fell brighter for a moment on his tall, gaunt form, and served to warn the emigrants of his approach. Indifferent, however, to this unfavorable circumstance, he held his way silently and steadily toward the copse, until a threatening voice met him with the challenge of:

"Who comes—friend or foe?"

"Friend," was the reply; "one who has lived too long to disturb the close of life with quarrels."

"But not so long as to forget the tricks of his youth," said Ishmael, rearing his huge frame from beneath the slight covering of a low bush, and meeting the trapper face to face. "Old man, you have brought this tribe of red rascals upon us, and to-morrow you will be sharing the booty."

"What have you lost?" calmly demanded the trapper.

"Eight as good mares as ever traveled in gears, besides a foal that is worth thirty of the brightest Mexicans that bear the face of the king of Spain. Then the woman has not a cloven hoof for her dairy or her loom, and I believe even the grunters, footsore as they be, are ploughing the prairie. And now, stranger," he added, dropping the butt of his rifle on the hard earth, with a violence and a clatter that would have intimidated one less firm than the man he addressed, "how many of these creatures may fall to you lot?"

"Horses have I never craved, nor even used; though few have journeyed over more of the wide lands of America than myself, old and feeble as I seem. But little use is there for a horse among the hills and woods of York—that is, as York was, but as I greatly fear York is no longer. As for woolen covering and cow's milk, I covet no such womanly fashions. The beasts of the field give me food and raiment. No; I crave no cloth better than the skin of a deer, nor any meat richer than its flesh."

The squatter looked at the old man uncertainly.

"That is no fair answer," he said. "It is, in my judgment, too lawyer-like for a straightforward, fair-weather and foul-weather hunter."

"I claim to be no better than a trapper," the other meekly answered.

"Hunter or trapper—there is little difference. I have come, old man, into these districts because I found the law sitting too tight upon me, and am not over fond of neighbors who can't settle a dispute without troubling a justice and twelve men, but I did n't come to be robbed of my plunder, and then to say thank'ee to the man who did it."

"He who ventures far into the prairie must abide by the ways of its owners."

"Owners!" echoed the squatter, "I am as rightful an owner of the land I stand on as any governor of the States. Can you tell me, stranger, where the law or the reason is to be found which says that one man shall have a section, or a town, or perhaps a country to his use, and another have to beg for earth to make his grave in? This is not nature, and I deny that it is law. That is, your legal law."

"I can not say that you are wrong," returned the trapper, whose opinions on this important topic, though drawn from very different premises, were in singular accordance with those of his companion, "and I have often thought and said as much, when and where I have believed my voice could be heard. But your beasts are stolen by them who claim to be masters of all they find in the deserts."

"They had better not dispute that matter with a man who knows better," said the other in a portentous voice, though it seemed deep and sluggish as he who spoke. "I call myself a fair trader, and one who gives to his chaps as good as he receives. You saw the Indians?"

"I did; they held me a prisoner while they stole into your camp."

"It would have been more like a white man and a Christian to let me have known as much in better season," retorted Ishmael, casting another ominous, sidelong glance at the trapper, as if still meditating evil. "I am not much given to call every man I fall in with "cousin," but color should be something when Christians meet in such a place as this. But what is done is done, and can not be mended by words. Come out of your ambush, boys; here is no one but the old man: he has eaten of my bread and should be our friend, though there is such good reason to suspect him of harboring with our enemies."

The trapper made no reply to the harsh suspicion which the other did not scruple to utter without the smallest delicacy, notwithstanding the explanations and denials to which he had just listened. The summons of the unnurtured squatter brought an immediate accession to their party. Four or five of his sons made their appearance from beneath as many covers, where they had been posted under the impression that the figures they had seen on the swell of the prairie were a part of the Sioux band. As each man approached and dropped his rifle into the hollow of his arm, he cast an indolent but inquiring glance at the stranger, though none of them expressed the least curiosity to know whence he had come or why he was there. This forbearance, however, proceeded only in part from their laziness and indolence. Indeed, the eldest, Asa,—the sleeping sentinel by whose error Mahtoree had profited,—claimed that he had seen some one with the trapper, and asked who it was.

"If you had seen the Tetons racing across the prairies like so many black-looking evil ones on the heels of your cattle, my friend," said the trapper "it would have been an easy matter to have fancied them a thousand."

"Ay, for a town-bred boy or a skeary woman, perhaps. But I'll warrant ye, had your thievish redskins made their push by the light of the sun, my good woman would have been smartly at work among them, and the Sioux would have found she was not given to part with her cheese and her butter without a price. But there'll come a time, stranger, right soon, when justice will have its due, and that, too, without the help of what is called the law. We are of a slow breed, it may be said, and it is often said of us; but slow is sure, and there ar' few men living who can say they ever struck a blow that they did not get one as hard in return from Ishmael Bush."

"Then has Ishmael Bush followed the instinct of the beasts, rather than the principle which ought to belong to his kind," returned the stubborn trapper. "I have struck many a blow myself, but never have I felt the same ease of mind that of right belongs to a man who follows his reason, after slaying even a fawn when there was no call for his meat or hide, as I have felt at leaving a Mingo unburied in the woods, when following the trade of open and honest warfare."

"What! you have been a soldier, have you, trapper? I made a forage or two among the Cherokees, when I was a lad, myself, and I followed Mad Anthony Wayne one season through the beeches; but there was altogether too much tattooing and regulating among his troops for me, so I left him without calling on the paymaster to settle my arrearages. You have heard of such a man as Mad Anthony Wayne, if you tarried long among the soldiers."

"I fou't my last battle, as I hope, under his orders," returned the trapper, a gleam of sunshine shooting from his dim eyes, as if the event was recollected with pleasure, and then a sudden shade of sorrow succeeding, as though he felt a secret admonition against dwelling on the violent scenes in which he had so often been an actor. "I was passing from the States on the seashore into these far regions when I crossed the trail of his army, and I fell in, on his rear, just as a looker-on; but when they got to blows the crack of my rifle was heard among the rest, though, to my shame it may be said, I never knew the right of the quarrel as well as a man of three score and ten should know the reason of his acts afore' he takes mortal life, which is a gift he never can return."

"Come, stranger," said the emigrant, his rugged nature a good deal softened when he found that they had fought on the same side in the wild warfare of the West; "it is of small account what may be the groundwork of the disturbance when it's a Christian ag'in a savage. We shall hear more of this horse-stealing to-morrow; to-night we can do no wiser or safer thing than to sleep."

So saying, Ishmael deliberately led the way back toward his rifled encampment, and ushered the man whose life a few minutes before had been in real jeopardy from his resentment into the presence of his family. Here, with a very few words of explanation, mingled with scarce but ominous denunciations against the plunderers, he made his wife acquainted with the state of things on the prairie, and announced his own determination to compensate himself for his broken rest by devoting the remainder of the night to sleep.

The trapper gave his ready assent to the measure, and adjusted his gaunt form on the pile of brush that was offered him with as much composure as a sovereign could resign himself to sleep in the security of his capital and surrounded by his armed protectors. Paul Hover, he saw, was not about. The bee-hunter, he decided, had observed the caution of keeping himself out of view; and, satisfied as to this, he slept, though with the peculiar watchfulness of one long accustomed to vigilance, even in the hours of deepest night.

In the morning the old trapper, in reply to a direct question from Ishmael, advised him to remove his camp to some safer point.

"The Dacotahs," he said, "will come back here again. Of that you may be sure. What would I advise? Even the female buffalo will fight for her young!"

"It never, then, shall be said that Ishmael Bush has less kindness for his children than the bear for her cubs!"

"And yet this is but a naked spot for a dozen men to make head in, ag'in five hundred."

"Ay, it is so," returned the squatter, glancing his eye toward his humble camp; "but something might be done with the wagons and the cottonwood."

The trapper shook his head incredulously, and pointed across the rolling plain in the direction of the west, as he answered:

"A rifle would send a bullet from these hills into your very sleeping-cabins; nay, arrows from the thicket in your rear would keep you all burrowed, like so many prairie dogs; it would n't do, it would n't do. Three long miles from this spot is a place where, as I have often thought in passing across the desert, a stand might be made for days and weeks together, if there were hearts and hands ready to engage in the bloody work."

Another low, deriding laugh passed among the young men, announcing, in a manner sufficiently intelligible, their readiness to undertake a task even more arduous. The squatter himself eagerly seized the hint which had been so reluctantly extorted from the trapper, who, by some singular process of reasoning, had evidently persuaded himself that it was his duty to be strictly neutral. A few direct and pertinent inquiries served to obtain the little additional information that was necessary, in order to make the contemplated movement, and then Ishmael, who was, in emergencies, as terrifically energetic as he was sluggish in common, set about effecting his object without delay.

Notwithstanding the industry and zeal of all engaged, the task was one of great labor and difficulty. The loaded vehicles were to be drawn by hand across a wide distance of plain, without track or guide of any sort except that which the trapper had furnished. But all bore a hand, and at last the camp was ready to move on. The trapper, however, with the inquisitiveness of the man who lives apart from his fellow-men, watched everything closely. His attention, however, was especially drawn toward the covered hut or tent which the Indian, Mahtoree, had investigated. It seemed to conceal something mysterious, and the old man had almost got his head within the drapery when he was discovered by the surly and evil-faced Abram White.

Dropping the shaft which he had already lifted from the ground preparatory to occupying the place that was usually filled by an animal less reasoning and perhaps less dangerous than himself, Abram bluntly exclaimed:

"I am a fool, as you often say! But look for yourself. If that man is not an enemy I will disgrace father and mother, call myself an Indian, and go hunt with the Sioux."

The cloud, as it is about to discharge the subtle lightning, is not more dark nor threatening than the look with which Ishmael greeted the intruder. He turned his head on every side of him, as if seeking some engine sufficiently terrible to annihilate the offending trapper at a blow; and then, possibly recollecting the further occasion he might have for his counsel, he forced himself to say, with an appearance of moderation that nearly choked him:

"Stranger, I did believe this prying into the concerns of others was the business of women in the towns and settlements, and not the manner in which men who are used to live where each has room for himself deal with the secrets of their neighbors. To what lawyer or sheriff do you calculate to sell your news?"

"I hold but little discourse, except with One, and then chiefly of my own affairs," returned the old man, without the least observable apprehension, and pointing imposingly upward: "a Judge, and Judge of all. Little does He need knowledge from my hands, and but little will your wish to keep anything secret from Him profit you, even in this desert."

The mounting tempers of his untutored listeners were rebuked by the simple, solemn manner of the trapper. Ishmael stood sullen and thoughtful, while his companion stole a furtive and involuntary glance at the placid sky, which spread so wide and blue above his head, as if he expected to see the Almighty eye itself beaming from the heavenly vault. But impressions of a serious character are seldom lasting on minds long indulged in forgetfulness. The hesitation of the squatter was consequently of short duration. The language, however, as well as the firm and collected air of the speaker, were the means of preventing much subsequent abuse, if not violence.

"It would be showing more of the kindness of a friend and comrade," Ishmael returned, in a tone sufficiently sullen to betray his humor, although it was no longer threatening, "had your shoulder been put to the wheel of one of yonder wagons, instead of edging itself in here, where none are wanted but such as are invited."

"I can put the little strength that is left me," returned the trapper, "to this, as well as to another of your loads."

"Do you take us for boys?" exclaimed Ishmael, laughing, half in ferocity and half in derision, applying his powerful strength at the same time to the little vehicle, which rolled over the grass with as much seeming facility as if it were drawn by its usual team.

The trapper paused and followed the departing wagon with his eye, marveling greatly as to the nature of its concealed contents, until it had also gained the summit of the eminence, and in its turn disappeared behind the swell of the land. Then he turned to gaze at the desolation of the scene around him. The absence of human forms would have scarce created a sensation in the bosom of one so long accustomed to solitude, had not the site of the deserted camp furnished such strong memorial of its recent visitors, and, as the old man was quick to detect, of their waste also. He cast his eye upward, with a shake of the head, at the vacant spot in the heavens which had so lately been filled by the branches of those trees that now lay strippèd of their verdure, worthless and deserted logs at his feet.

"Ay," he muttered to himself, "I might have know'd it—I might have know'd it! Often have I seen the same before, and yet I brought them to the spot myself, and have now sent them to the only neighborhood of the kind within many long leagues of the spot where I stand. This is man's wish, and pride, and waste, and sinfulness! He tames the beasts of the field to feed his idle wants, and having robbed the brutes of their natural food, he teaches them to strip the earth of its trees to quiet their hunger."

The squatters bent themselves faithfully to their task, and in an incredibly short time were entrenched in a kind of natural fortress. It was a solitary and ragged rock which rose on the margin of a little watercourse. The few trees which grew about it were soon cut down, and their trunks, with the help of rocks gathered from the sides of the acclivity, were formed into rude and inefficient defenses at the points which offered the fewest natural obstacles to attack. On the apex of the rock was perched the tent which has been already mentioned, and while one of the party, frequently one of the women, kept continual watch on this eminence, the men spent their time for several days in idleness, their unruly tempers and the mystery which surrounded the tent giving rise to frequent quarrels.

After the squatters left him, the trapper remained for some time gazing after them. He continued muttering occasionally to himself until a rustling in the low bushes, which still grew for some distance along the swale that formed the thicket on which the camp of Ishmael had rested, caught his ear, and cut short the soliloquy. The habits of so many years spent in the wilderness caused the old man to bring his rifle to a poise with something like the activity and promptitude of his youth; but, suddenly recovering his recollection, he dropped it into the hollow of his arm again, and resumed his air of melancholy resignation.

"Come forth, come forth!" he said aloud. "Be ye bird or be ye beast, ye are safe from these old hands. I have eaten and I have drunk; why should I take life, when my wants call for no sacrifice. It would not be long afore the birds will peck at eyes that shall not see them, and perhaps light on my very bones; for if things like these are only made to perish, why am I to expect to live forever? Come forth, come forth! You are safe from harm at these weak hands."

"Thank you for the good word, old trapper!" cried Paul Hover, springing actively forward from his place of concealment. "There was an air about you, when you threw forward the muzzle of your piece, that I did not like, for it seemed to say that you were master of all the rest of the motions."

"You are right, you are right!" cried the trapper, laughing with inward self-complacency at the recollection of his former skill. "The day has been when few men knew the virtues of a long rifle, like this I carry, better than myself, old and useless as I now seem. You are right, young man; and the time was when it was dangerous to move a leaf within ear-shot of my stand, or," he added, dropping his voice and looking serious, "for a red

Mingo to show an eyeball from his ambushment. You have heard of the red Mingos?"

"I have heard of minks," said Paul, taking the old man by the arm and gently urging him toward the thicket as he spoke, while at the same time he cast quick and uneasy glances behind him in order to make sure that he was not observed, "of your common black minks, but none of any other color."

"Lord! Lord!" continued the trapper, shaking his head, and still laughing in his deep but quiet manner; "the boy mistakes a brute for a man! Though a Mingo is little better than a beast, or, for that matter, he is worse, when rum and opportunity are placed before his eyes. There was that accursed Huron from the upper lakes, that I knocked from his perch among the rocks in the hills, back of the Hori——"

His voice was lost in the thicket, into which he had suffered himself to be led by Paul while speaking, too much occupied by thoughts which dwelt on scenes and acts that had taken place half a century earlier in the history of the country to offer the smallest resistance.

In the woods Paul and the trapper met another wanderer. He was an officer in the United States army, who was also in search of Ishmael Bush and his camp, for in that camp he was confident was a treasure which he had been tracing and tracking for months.

It so happened that the trapper found out that this young officer was the grandson of an old and dear friend of the trapper in the days when the old man was a great scout and hunter among the New York forests; and when he found what it was that Captain Middleton was searching for, and where he expected to find it, the old man's sympathy and curiosity were at once enlisted in the case.

For Captain Middleton's beautiful young wife, a Mexican lady, had been kidnapped or stolen by Abram White, the evil-faced brother-in-law of Ishmael Bush, to be sold as a slave or held for a ransom, and it was this prize that was kept in the tent-like hut which the Dacotah chief had inspected, which had aroused the trapper's curiosity, and well-nigh brought upon him the wrath and vengeance of Ishmael Bush.

At once a scheme of rescue was decided upon by the trapper, Paul Hover, Captain Middleton, and even funny little Dr. Bat, who did not wish to associate with kidnappers.

Choosing a time when all the men were absent, hunting, or trying to ascertain the whereabouts of the Indians, they approached the fortress, and although the daughters of Ishmael Bush made a fierce resistance, rolling down stones upon the attacking party, and bravely engaging in a hand to hand conflict with their brawny enemies, they succeeded in rescuing the young wife of the captain, while Ellen Wade, who hated her life in the camp and was in love with Paul, the bee-hunter, also escaped.

But meantime Asa, the oldest son of Ishmael Bush, had been killed on the prairie. His father was certain this had been done by the old trapper, in his attempt to get Inez from the camp, and Ishmael vowed revenge.

Falling in with the hostile party of Sioux or Dacotahs, the trapper and his party were compelled to accompany them on a second attack on the Fort, during which they managed to escape, mounted on horses which they did not hesitate to appropriate. At last they reached a place of comparative safety, and disposed themselves to much-needed rest. The sleep of the fugitives lasted for several hours. The trapper was the first to shake off its influence, as he had been the last to court its refreshment. Rising just as the gray light of day began to brighten that portion of the studded vault which rested on the eastern margin of the plain, he summoned his companions from their warm lairs and pointed out the necessity of their being once more on the alert. While Middleton attended to the arrangements necessary to the comforts of Inez and Ellen in the long and painful journey which lay before them, the old man and Paul prepared the meal, which the former had advised them to take before they proceeded to horse. These several dispositions were not long in making, and the little group was soon seated about a repast which, though it might want the elegancies to which the bride of Middleton had been accustomed, was not deficient in the more important requisites of savor and nutriment.

"When we get lower into the hunting-grounds of the Pawnees," said the trapper, laying a morsel of delicate venison before Inez, on a little trencher neatly made of horn and expressly for his own use, "we shall find the buffaloes fatter and sweeter, the deer in more abundance, and all the gifts of the Lord abounding to satisfy our wants. Perhaps we may even strike a beaver and get a morsel from his tail * by way of a rare mouthful."

"What course do you mean to pursue when you have once thrown these bloodhounds from the chase?" demanded Middleton.

"If I might advise," said Paul, "it would be to strike a water course, and get upon its downward current as soon as may be. Give me a cottonwood, and I will turn you out a canoe that shall carry us all, in perhaps the work of a day and night. Ellen is lively enough, but then she is no great race-rider; and it would be far more comfortable to boat six or eight hundred miles than to go loping along like so many elks measuring the prairies; besides, water leaves no trail."

"I will not swear to that," returned the trapper; "I have often thought the eyes of a redskin would find a trail in air."

---

* The American hunters consider the tail of the beaver the most nourishing of all food.

"See, Middleton," exclaimed Inez, in a sudden burst of youthful pleasure, that caused her for a moment to forget her situation, "how lovely is that sky; surely it contains a promise of happier times!"

"It is glorious!" returned her husband. "Glorious and heavenly is that streak of vivid red, and here is a still brighter crimson; rarely have I seen a richer rising of the sun."

"Rising of the sun!" slowly repeated the old man, lifting his tall person from its seat with a deliberate and abstracted air, while he kept his eye riveted on the changing and certainly beautiful tints that were garnishing the vault of heaven. "Rising of the sun! I like not such risings of the sun. Ah's me! the imps have circumvented us with a vengence. The prairie is on fire!"

"God in heaven protect us!" cried Middleton, catching Inez to his bosom, under the instant impression of the imminence of their danger. "There is no time to lose, old man; each instant is a day; let us fly."

"Whither?" demanded the trapper, motioning him with calmness and dignity to arrest his steps. "In this wilderness of grass and reeds you are like a vessel in the broad lakes without a compass. A single step on the wrong course might prove the destruction of us all. It is seldom danger is so pressing that there is not time enough for reason to do its work, young officer; therefore let us await its biddings."

"For my own part," said Paul Hover, looking about him with no equivocal expression of concern, "I acknowledge that should this dry bed of weeds get fairly in a flame, a bee would have to make a flight higher than common to prevent his wings from scorching. Therefore, old trapper, I agree with the captain, and say mount and run."

"Ye are wrong—ye are wrong; man is not a beast to follow the gift of instinct and to snuff up his knowledge by a taint in the air or a rumbling in the sound, but he must see, and reason, and then conclude. So follow me a little to the left, where there is a rise in the ground, whence we may make our reconnoiterings."

The old man waved his hand with authority, and led the way without further parlance to the spot he had indicated, followed by the whole of his alarmed companions. An eye less practised than that of the trapper might have failed in discovering the gentle elevation to which he alluded, and which looked on the surface of the meadow like a growth a little taller than common. When they reached the place, however, the stinted grass itself announced the absence of that moisture which had fed the rank weeds of most of the plain, and furnished a clue to the evidence by which he had judged of the formation of the ground hidden beneath. Here a few minutes were lost in breaking down the tops of the surrounding herbage, which, notwithstanding the advantage of their position, rose even above the heads of Middleton and Paul, and in obtaining a look-out that might command a view of the surrounding sea of fire.

The frightful prospect added nothing to the hopes of those who had so fearful a stake in the result. Although the day was beginning to dawn, the vivid colors of the sky continued to deepen, as if the fierce element were bent on an impious rivalry of the light of the sun. Bright flashes of flame shot up here and there along the margin of the waste like the nimble coruscations of the North, but far more angry and threatening in their color and changes. The anxiety on the rigid features of the trapper sensibly deepened as he leisurely traced these evidences of a conflagration, which spread in a broad belt about their place of refuge, until he had encircled the horizon.

Shaking his head, as he again turned his face to the point where the danger seemed nighest and most rapidly approaching, the old man said,—

"Now have we been cheating ourselves with the belief that we had thrown these Tetons from our trail, while here is proof enough that they not only know where we lie, but that they intend to smoke us out, like so many skulking beasts of prey. See; they have lighted the fire around the whole bottom at the same moment, and we are as completely hemmed in by the devils as an island by its waters."

"Let us mount and ride," cried Middleton; "is life not worth a struggle?"

"Whither would ye go? Is a Teton horse a salamander that can walk amid fiery flames unhurt, or do you think the Lord will show His might in your behalf, as in the days of old, and carry you harmless through such a furnace as you may see glowing beneath yonder red sky? There are Sioux, too, hemming the fire with their arrows and knives on every side, or I am no judge of their murderous deviltries."

"We will ride into the center of the whole tribe," returned the youth fiercely, "and put their manhood to the test."

"Ay, it's well in words, but what would it prove in deeds? Here is a dealer in bees who can teach you wisdom in a matter like this."

"Now, for that matter, old trapper," said Paul, stretching his athletic form like a mastiff conscious of his strength, "I am on the side of the captain, and am clearly for a race against the fire, though it line me into a Teton wigwam. Here is Ellen, who will"—

"Of what use, of what use are your stout hearts, when the element of the Lord is to be conquered as well as human men. Look about you, friends; the wreath of smoke that is rising from the bottoms plainly says that there is no outlet from the spot without crossing a belt of fire. Look for yourselves, my men; look for yourselves; if you can find a single opening I will engage to follow."

The examination which his companions so instantly and so intently made rather served to assure them of their desperate situation than to appease their fears. Huge columns of smoke were rolling up from the plain and thickening in gloomy masses around the horizon. The red glow, which gleamed upon their enormous folds, now lighting their volumes with the glare of the conflagration, and now flashing to another point, as the flame beneath glided ahead, leaving all behind enveloped in awful darkness, and proclaiming louder than words the character of the imminent and approaching danger.

"This is terrible!" exclaimed Middleton, folding the trembling Inez to his heart. "At such a time as this, and in such a manner!"

"The gates of heaven are open to all who truly believe," murmured the pious devotee in his bosom.

"This resignation is maddening! But we are men, and will make a struggle for our lives! How now, my brave and spirited friend, shall we yet mount and push across the flames, or shall we stand here and see those we most love perish in this frightful manner without an effort?"

"I am for a swarming time, and a flight before the hive is too hot to hold us," said the bee-hunter, to whom it will be at once seen that Middleton addressed himself. "Come, old trapper, you must acknowledge this is but a slow way of getting out of danger. If we tarry here much longer it will be in the fashion that the bees lie around the straw after the hive has been smoked for its honey. You may hear the fire begin to roar already, and I know by experience that when the flame once gets fairly into the prairie grass it is no sloth that can outrun it!"

"Think you," returned the old man, pointing scornfully at the mazes of the dry and matted grass which environed them, "that mortal feet can outstrip the speed of fire on such a path? If I knew on which side these miscreants lay!"

"What say you, friend Doctor," cried the bewildered Paul, turning to the naturalist with that sort of helplessness with which the strong are often apt to seek aid of the weak when human power is baffled by the hand of a mightier being,—" what say you; have you no advice to give away, in a case of life and death?"

The naturalist stood, tablets in hand, looking at the awful spectacle with as much composure as if the conflagration had been lighted in order to solve the difficulties of some scientific problem. Aroused by the question of his companion, he turned to his equally calm though differently occupied associate, the trapper, demanding with the most provoking insensibility to the urgent nature of their situation:

"Venerable hunter, you have often witnessed similar prismatic experiments ——"

He was rudely interrupted by Paul, who struck the tablets from his hands, with a violence that betrayed the utter intellectual confusion which had overset the equanimity of his mind. Before time was allowed for remonstrance, the old man, who had continued during the whole scene like one much at a loss how to proceed, though also like one who was rather perplexed than alarmed, suddenly assumed a decided air, as if he no longer doubted on the course it was most advisable to pursue.

"It is time to be doing," he said, interrupting the controversy that was about to ensue between the naturalist and the bee-hunter ; "it is time to leave off books and moanings and to be doing."

"You have come to your recollections too late, miserable old man," cried Middleton ; "the flames are within a quarter of a mile of us, and the wind is bringing them down in this quarter with dreadful rapidity."

"Anan ! the flames ! I care but little for the flames. If I only knew how to circumvent the cunning of the Dacotahs as I know how to cheat the fire of its prey there would be nothing needed but thanks to the Lord for our deliverance. Do you call this a fire ? If you had seen what I have witnessed in the eastern hills, when mighty mountains were like the furnace of a smith, you would have known what it was to fear the flames, and to be thankful that you were spared ! Come, lads, come ; 'tis time to be doing now, and to cease talking ; for yonder curling flame is truly coming on like a trotting moose. Put hands upon this short and withered grass where we stand, and lay bare the 'arth."

"Would you think to deprive the fire of its victims in this childish manner?" exclaimed Middleton.

A faint but solemn smile passed over the features of the old man as he answered :

"Your gran'ther would have said that when the enemy was nigh a soldier could do no better than to obey."

The captain felt the reproof, and instantly began to imitate the industry of Paul, who was tearing the decayed herbage from the ground in a sort of desperate compliance with the trapper's direction. Even Ellen lent her hands to the labor, nor was it long before Inez was seen similarly employed, though none amongst them knew why or wherefore. When life is thought to be the reward of labor, men are wont to be industrious. A very few moments sufficed to lay bare a spot of some twenty feet in diameter. Into one edge of this little area the trapper brought the females, directing Middleton and Paul to cover their light and inflammable dresses with the blankets of the party. So soon as this precaution was observed, the old man approached the opposite margin of the grass, which still environed them in a tall and dangerous circle, and selecting a handful of the driest of the herbage, he placed it over the pan of his rifle.

The light combustible kindled at the flash. Then he placed the little flame in a bed of the standing fog, and withdrawing from the spot to the center of the ring he patiently awaited the result.

The subtle element seized with avidity upon its new fuel, and in a moment forked flames were gliding among the grass, as the tongues of ruminating animals are seen rolling among their food, apparently in quest of its sweetest portions.

"Now," said the old man, holding up a finger and laughing in his peculiarly silent manner, "you shall see fire fight fire! Ah's me! many is the time I have burnt a smooty path from wanton laziness to pick my way across a tangled bottom."

"But is this not fatal?" cried the amazed Middleton; "are you not bringing the enemy nigher to us instead of avoiding it?"

"Do you scorch so easily? your gran'ther had a tougher skin. But we shall live to see; we shall all live to see."

The experience of the trapper was in the right. As the fire gained strength and heat, it began to spread on three sides, dying of itself on the fourth for want of aliment. As it increased, and the sullen roaring announced its power, it cleared everything before it, leaving the black and smoking soil far more naked than if the scythe had swept the place. The situation of the fugitives would have still been hazardous had not the area enlarged as the flame encircled them. But by advancing to the spot where the trapper had kindled the grass, they avoided the heat, and in a very few moments the flames began to recede in every quarter, leaving them enveloped in a cloud of smoke, but perfectly safe from the torrent of fire that was still furiously rolling onward.

The spectators regarded the simple expedient of the trapper with that species of wonder with which the courtiers of Ferdinand are said to have viewed the manner in which Columbus made his egg stand on its end, though with feelings that were filled with gratitude instead of envy.

"That you must have seen many a chopper skimming the cream from the face of the earth, and many a settler getting the very honey of nature, old trapper," said Paul, "no reasonable man can, or, for that matter, shall doubt. But here is Ellen getting uneasy about the Sioux, and now you have opened your mind so freely concerning these matters, if you will just put us on the line of our flight, the swarm will make another move."

"Anan!"

"I say that Ellen is getting uneasy; and as the smoke is lifting from the plain, it may be prudent to take another flight."

"The boy is reasonable. I had forgotten we were in the midst of a raging fire, and that Sioux were round about us like hungry wolves watching a drove of buffaloes. But when memory is at work in my old brain on times long past it is apt to overlook the matters of the day. You say right, my children ; it is time to be moving, and now comes the real nicety of our case. It is easy to outwit a furnace, for it is nothing but a raging element; and it is not always difficult to throw a grizzly bear from his scent, for the creatur' is both enlightened and blinded by his instinct ; but to shut the eyes of a waking Dacotah is a matter of greater judgment, inasmuch as his deviltry is backed by reason."

"Now look off yonder to the east," said the old man, as he began to lead the way across the murky and still smoking plain ; "little fear of cold feet in journeying such a path as this: but look you off to the east, and if you see a sheet of shining white, glistening like a plate of beaten silver through the openings of the smoke, why, that is water. A noble stream is running thereaway, and I thought I got a glimpse of it a while since ; but other thoughts came, and I lost it. It is a broad and swift river, such as the Lord has made many of its fellows in this desert ; for here may natur' be seen in all its richness, trees alone excepted,—trees, which are to the 'arth as fruits are to a garden ; without them nothing can be pleasant or thoroughly useful. Now watch, all of you, with open eyes, for that strip of glittering water; we shall not be safe until it is flowing between our trail and these sharp-sighted Dacotahs."

This latter declaration was enough to insure a vigilant lookout for the desired stream on the part of all the trapper's followers. With this object in view, the party proceeded in profound silence, the old man having admonished them of the necessity of caution as they entered the clouds of smoke, which were rolling like masses of fog along the plain, more particularly over those spots where the fire had encountered occasional pools of stagnant water.

Finally they emerged from the area which had been ravaged by fire, and as they drew near a mass of thicket, Hector, the trapper's old hound, showed signs of uneasiness. "This is foolish, Hector," said the old trapper, "more like an untamed pup than a sensible hound ; one who has got his education by hard experience, and not by nosing over the trails of other dogs, as a boy in the settlements follows on the track of his masters, be it right or wrong. Well, friend," he said to Dr. Bat, "you who can do so much, are you equal to looking into the thicket ; or must I go in myself?"

The doctor assumed an air of resolution, and without further parlance proceeded to do as desired. The dogs were so far restrained by the remonstrances of the old man as to confine their noise to low but often-repeated whinings. When they saw the naturalist advance, however, the pup broke through all restraint and made a swift circuit around his person, scenting the earth as he proceeded ; and, returning to his companion, he howled aloud.

"The squatter and his brood have left a strong scent on the earth," said the old man, watching as he spoke for some signal from his learned pioneer to follow; "I hope yonder school-bred man knows enough to remember the errand on which I have sent him."

Dr. Bat had already disappeared in the bushes, and the trapper was beginning to betray additional evidences of impatience, when the person of the former was seen retiring from the thicket backward, with his face fastened on the place he had just left, as if his look was bound in the thraldom of some charm.

"Here is something skeary, by the wildness of the creatur's countenance!" exclaimed the old man, relinquishing his hold of Hector and moving stoutly to the side of the totally unconscious naturalist. "How is it, friend; have you found a new leaf in your book of wisdom?"

"It is a basilisk?" muttered the doctor, whose altered visage betrayed the utter confusion which beset his faculties. "I had thought its attributes were fabulous, but mighty Nature is equal to all that man can imagine!"

"What is't? What is't? The snakes of the prairies are harmless, unless it be now and then an angered rattler, and he always gives you notice with his tail afore he works his mischief with his fangs. Lord, Lord, what a humbling thing is fear!" said the discontented trapper, who began to grow a little uneasy that his party was all this time neglecting to seek the protection of some cover. "If there is a reptile in the bush, show me the creatur, and should it refuse to depart peaceably, why, there must be a quarrel for the possession of the place."

"There!" said the doctor, pointing into a dense mass of the thicket, to a spot within fifty feet of that where they both stood. The trapper turned his look with perfect composure in the required direction, but the instant his practised glance met the object which had so utterly upset the philosophy of the naturalist, he gave a start himself, threw his rifle rapidly forward and as instantly recovered it, as if a second flash of thought convinced him he was wrong. Neither the instinctive movement nor the sudden recollection was without a sufficient object. At the very margin of the thicket, and in absolute contact with the earth, lay an animate ball that might easily, by the singularity and fierceness of its aspect, have justified the disturbed condition of the naturalist's mind. It were difficult to describe the shape or colors of this extraordinary substance, except to say, in general terms, that it was nearly spherical, and exhibited all the hues of the rainbow, intermingled without reference to harmony, and without any very ostensible design. The predominant hues were a black and bright vermilion. With these, however, the several tints of white, yellow, and crimson were strangely and widely blended. Had this been all it would have been difficult to have pronounced that the object was possessed of life, for it lay as motionless as any stone; but a pair of dark, glaring, and moving eyeballs, which watched with jealousy the smallest movements of the trapper and his companion, sufficiently established the important fact of its possessing vitality.

THE ASSAULT ON THE FORTRESS.

"Your reptile is a scouter, or I'm no judge of Indian paints and Indian deviltries!" muttered the old man, dropping the butt of his weapon to the ground, and gazing with a steady eye at the frightful object, as he leaned on its barrel, in an attitude of great composure. "He wants to face us out of sight and reason, and make us think the head of a redskin is a stone covered with the autumn leaf; or he has some other devilish artifice in his mind!"

"Is the animal human?" demanded the doctor, "of the *genus homo?* I had fancied it a nondescript."

"It's as human, and as mortal, too, as a warrior of these prairies is ever known to be. I have seen the time when a redskin would have shown a foolish daring to peep out of his ambushment in that fashion on a hunter I could name, but who is too old now, and too near his time, to be anything better than a miserable trapper. It will be well to speak to the imp, and to let him know he deals with men whose beards are grown. Come forth from your cover, friend," he continued,

THE PAWNEE AND THE PALEFACES

in the language of the extensive tribes of the Dacotahs; "there is room on the prairie for another warrior."

The eyes appeared to glare more fiercely than before; but the mass which, according to the trapper's opinion, was neither more nor less than a human head, shorn, as usual among the warriors of the West, of its hair, still continued without motion or any other sign of life.

The trapper very deliberately examined the priming of his rifle, taking care to make as great a parade as possible of his hostile intentions, in going through the necessary evolutions with the weapon. When he thought the stranger began to apprehend some danger, he very deliberately presented the piece, and called aloud:

"Now, friend, I am all for peace, or all for war, as you may say. No! well, it *is* no man, as the wiser one here says, and there can be no harm in just firing into a bunch of leaves."

The muzzle of the rifle fell as he concluded, and the weapon was gradually settling into a steady, and what would easily have proved a fatal aim, when a tall Indian sprang from beneath that bed of leaves and brush which he had collected about his person at the approach of the party, and stood upright, uttering the exclamation:

"Wagh!"

The trapper, who had meditated no violence, dropped his rifle again, and laughing at the success of his experiment, with great seeming self-complacency, he drew the astounded gaze of the naturalist from the person of the savage to himself, by saying:

"The imps will lie for hours, like sleeping alligators, brooding their deviltries, in dreams and other craftiness, until such time as they see some real danger is at hand, and then they look to themselves the same as other mortals. But this is a scouter in his war-paint! There should be more of his tribe at no great distance. Let us draw the truth out of him; for an unlucky war party may prove more dangerous to us than a visit from the whole family of the squatter."

"It is truly a desperate and a dangerous species!" said the doctor, relieving his amazement by a breath that seemed to exhaust his lungs of air; "a violent race, and one that is difficult to define or class, within the usual boundaries of definition. Speak to him, therefore; but let thy words be strong in amity."

The old man cast a keen eye on every side of him, to ascertain the important particular whether the stranger was supported by any associates, and then making the usual signs of peace, by exhibiting the palm of his naked hand, he boldly advanced. In the meantime, the Indian betrayed no evidence of uneasiness. He suffered the trapper to draw nigh, maintaining by his own mien and attitude a striking air of dignity and fearlessness. Perhaps the wary warrior also knew that, owing to the difference in their weapons, he should be placed more on an equality, by being brought nearer to the strangers.

FIGHTING FIRE WITH FIRE.

As a descripton of this individual may furnish some idea of the personal appearance of a whole race, it may be well to detain the narrative, in order to present it to the reader in our hasty and imperfect manner. Would the truant eyes of Allston or Greenough turn, but for a time, from their gaze at the models of antiquity to contemplate this wronged and humble people, little would be left for such inferior artists as ourselves to delineate.

The Indian in question was in every particular a warrior of fine stature and admirable proportions. As he cast aside his mask, composed of such party-colored leaves as he had hurriedly collected, his countenance appeared in all the gravity, the dignity, and, it may be added, the terror, of his profession. The outlines of his lineaments were strikingly noble, and nearly approaching to Roman, though the secondary features of his face were slightly marked with the well-known traces of his Asiatic origin. The peculiar tint of the skin, which in itself is so well designed to aid the effect of a martial expression, had received an additional aspect of wild ferocity from the colors of the war-paint. But, as if he disdained the usual artifices of his people, he bore none of those strange and horrid devices with which the children of the forest are accustomed, like the more civilized heroes of the mustache, to back their reputation for courage, contenting himself with a broad and deep shadowing of black, that served as a sufficient and an admirable foil to the brighter gleamings of his native swarthiness. His head was, as usual, shaved to the crown, where a large and gallant scalp-lock seemed to challenge the grasp of his enemies. The ornaments that were ordinarily pendent from the cartilages of his ears had been removed, on account of his present pursuit. His body, notwithstanding the lateness of the season, was nearly naked, and the portion which was clad bore a vestment no warmer than a light robe of the finest dressed deer-skin, beautifully stained with the rude design of some daring exploit, and which was carelessly worn, as if more in pride than from any unmanly regard to comfort. His leggings were of bright scarlet cloth, the only evidence about his person that he had held communion with the traders of the palefaces. But as if to furnish some offset to this solitary submission to a womanish vanity, they were fearfully fringed, from the gartered knee to the bottom of the moccasin, with the hair of human scalps. He leaned lightly with one hand on a short hickory bow, while the other rather touched than sought support from the long, delicate handle of an ashen lance. A quiver made of the cougar-skin, from which the tail of the animal depended, as a characteristic ornament, was slung at his back ; and a shield of hides, quaintly emblazoned with another of his warlike deeds, was suspended from his neck by a thong of sinews.

As the trapper approached, this warrior maintained his calm, upright attitude, discovering neither an eagerness to ascertain the character of those who advanced upon him, nor the smallest wish to avoid a scrutiny in his own person. An eye that was darker and more shining than that of the stag was incessantly glancing, however, from one to another of the stranger party, seemingly never knowing rest for an instant.

"Is my brother far from his village?" demanded the old man in the Pawnee language, after examining the paint and those other little signs by which a practised eye knows the tribe of the warrior he encounters in the American deserts, with the same readiness and by the same sort of mysterious observation as that by which the seaman knows the distant sail.

"It is farther to the town of the Bigknives," was the laconic reply.

"Why is a Pawnee-Loup so far from the fork of his own river, without a horse to journey on, and in a spot empty as this?"

"Can the women and children of a paleface live without the meat of the bison? There was hunger in my lodge."

"My brother is very young to be already the master of a lodge," returned the trapper, looking steadily into the unmoved countenance of the youthful warrior; "but I dare say he is brave, and that many a chief has offered him his daughters for wives. But he is mistaken," pointing to the arrow which was dangling from the hand that held the bow, "in bringing a loose and barbed arrow-head to kill the buffalo. Do the Pawnees wish the wounds they give their game to rankle?"

"It is good to be ready for the Sioux. Though not in sight, a bush may hide him."

"The man is a living proof of the truth of his words," muttered the trapper in English, "and a close-jointed and gallant-looking lad he is, but far too young for a chief of any importance. He is scouting on the track of the Sioux—you may see it by his arrow-heads and his paint; ay, and by his eye, too, for redskin lets his natur' follow the business he is on, be it for peace or be it for war. Quiet, Hector, quiet! Have you never scented a Pawnee afore, pup? Keep down, dog, keep down. My brother is right. The Sioux are thieves. Men of all colors and nations say it of them, and truly."

"The Sioux is a dog. When the Pawnee war-whoop is in their ears the whole nation howls."

"It is true. The imps are on our trail, and I am glad to meet a warrior with the tomahawk in his hand who does not love them. Will my brother lead my children to his village? If the Sioux follow on our path my young men shall help him to strike them."

The young Pawnee turned his face from one to another of the strangers in a keen scrutiny before he saw fit to answer. Then he modestly answered:

"My father shall be welcome. The young men of my nation shall hunt with his sons; the chiefs shall hunt with the grayhead. The Pawnee girls will sing in the ears of his daughters."

"And if we meet the Sioux?" demanded the trapper, who wished to understand thoroughly the more important conditions of this new alliance.

"The enemy of the Bigknives shall feel the blow of the Pawnee."

"It is well. Now let my brother and I meet in council, that we may not go on a crooked path, but that our road to his village may be like the flight of the pigeons."

The young Pawnee made a significant gesture of assent, and followed the other a little apart, in order to be removed from all danger of interruption from the reckless Paul or the abstracted naturalist. Their conference was short, but, as it was conducted in the sententious manner of the natives, it served to make each of the parties acquainted with all the necessary information of the other. When they rejoined their associates the old man saw fit to explain a portion of what had passed between them as follows:

"Ay, I was not mistaken," he said. "It is as I said; this good-looking young warrior—for good-looking and noble-looking he is, though a little horrified perhaps with paint—this good-looking youth, tells me he is out on the scout for these very Sioux. His party was not strong enough to strike the rascals, who are down from their towns in great numbers to hunt the buffalo, and runners have gone to the Pawnee villages for aid. It would seem that this lad is a fearless boy, for he has been hanging on their skirts alone, until, like ourselves, he was driven to the grass for a cover. But he tells me more, my men, and what I am mainly sorry to hear, which is, that the cunning Mahtoree, instead of going to blows with the squatter, has become his friend, and that both broods, red and white, are on our heels, and outlying around this very plain to circumvent us to our destruction."

"How knows he all this to be true?" demanded Middleton.

"What's that?"

"In what manner does he know that these things are so?"

"In what manner? Do you think newspapers and town-criers are needed to tell a scout what is doing on the prairies, as they are in the bosom of the States? No gossiping woman, who hurries from house to house to spread evil of her neighbor, can carry tidings with her tongue so fast as these people will spread their meaning by signs and warnings that they alone understand. 'Tis their l'arning, and what is better, it is got in the open air, and not within the walls of a school. I tell you, captain, that what he says is true."

Assured of the truth of the Indian's statement and awake to their double danger, the fugitives pressed on until they came to the banks of a river.

This they must cross. But how? How could the two girls get over?

"It is a matter of invention," the old trapper declared. "Somehow the river will be crossed." Then he turned to the Pawnee, and explained to him the difficulty which existed in relation to the women. The young warrior listened gravely, and throwing the buffalo skin from his shoulder, he immediately commenced, assisted by the occasional aid of the understanding old man, the preparations necessary to effect this desirable object.

The hide was soon drawn into the shape of an umbrella top, or an inverted parachute, by thongs of deerskin, with which both the laborers were well provided. A few light sticks served to keep the parts from collapsing or falling in. When this simple and natural expedient was arranged, it was placed on the water, the Indian making a sign that it was ready to receive its freight. Both Inez and Ellen hesitated to trust themselves in a bark of so frail a construction, nor would Middleton or Paul consent that they should do so until each had assured himself by actual experiment that the vessel was capable of sustaining a load much heavier than it was destined to receive. Then, indeed, their scruples were reluctantly overcome, and the skin was made to receive its precious burden.

"Now leave the Pawnee to be the pilot," said the trapper; "my hand is not so steady as it used to be; but he has limbs like toughened hickory. Leave all to the wisdom of the Pawnee."

The husband and lover could not well do otherwise, and they were fain to become deeply interested, it is true, but passive spectators of this primitive species of ferrying. The Pawnee selected a beast from among the three horses with a readiness that proved he was far from being ignorant of the properties of that noble animal, and throwing himself upon its back, he rode into the margin of the river. Thrusting an end of his lance into the hide, he bore the light vessel up against the stream, and, giving his steed the rein, they pushed boldly into the current. Middleton and Paul followed, pressing as nigh the bark as prudence would at all warrant. In this manner the young warrior bore his precious cargo to the opposite bank in perfect safety, without the slightest inconvenience to the passengers, and with a steadiness and celerity which proved that both horse and rider were not unused to the operation. When the shore was gained, the young Indian undid his work, threw the skin over his shoulder, placed the sticks under his arm, and returned, without speaking, to transfer the remainder of the party in a similar manner to what was very justly considered the safer side of the river.

"Now, friend Doctor," said the old man, when he saw the Indian plunging into the river a second time, "do I know there is faith in yonder redskin. He is a good-looking, ay, and an honest-looking youth, but the winds of heaven are not more deceitful than these savages, when mischief has fairly beset them. Had the Pawnee been a Sioux, or one of them heartless Mingos that used to be prowling through the woods of York a time back—that is, some sixty years agone—we should have seen his back and not his face turned toward us. But you can see for yourself the boy is true. Once make a redskin your friend, and he is yours as long as you deal honestly by him."

So Dr. Bat and the trapper stepped into the frail craft, to follow their companions across. But even as they did so, a cry rose on the bank and the brutal Dacotah warrior, Weucha, confronted them.

The eyes of the Dacotah and those of the fugitives met. The former raised a long, loud, and piercing yell, in which the notes of exultation were fearfully blended with those of warning. In another instant the steed of the young Pawnee was struggling with the torrent.

The utmost strength of the horse was needed to urge the fugitives beyond the flight of arrows that came sailing through the air at the next moment. The cry of Weucha had brought fifty of his comrades to the shore, but fortunately, among them all there was not one of a rank sufficient to entitle him to the privilege of bearing a gun. One-half the stream, however, was not passed, before the form of Mahtoree himself was seen on its bank, and an ineffectual discharge of firearms announced the rage and disappointment of the chief. More than once the trapper had raised his rifle, as if about to try its power on his enemies, but he as often lowered it without firing. The eyes of the Pawnee warrior glared, like those of the cougar, at the sight of so many of the hostile tribe, and he answered the impotent effort of their chief by tossing a hand into the air in contempt, and raising the war-cry of his nation. The challenge was too taunting to be endured. The Dacotahs dashed into the stream in a body, and the river became dotted with dark forms of beasts and riders.

There was now a fearful struggle for the friendly bank. As the Dacotahs advanced with beasts that had not, like that of the Pawnee, expended their strength in former efforts, and as they moved un-

IN ANOTHER INSTANT THE STEED OF THE YOUNG PAWNEE WAS STRUGGLING WITH THE TORRENT.

encumbered by anything but their riders, the speed of the pursuers greatly outstripped that of the fugitives. But at last the horses of the Dacotahs gained the middle of the current, and their riders were already filling the air with yells of triumph. At this moment Middleton and Paul, who had led the females to a little thicket, appeared again on the margin of the stream, menacing their enemies with the rifle.

"Mount! mount!" shouted the trapper, the instant he beheld them; "mount and fly, if you value those who lean on you for help! Mount, and leave us in the hands of the Lord!"

"Stoop your head, old trapper," returned the voice of Paul; "down with you both into your nest. The Dacotah is in your line; down with your heads, and make room for a Kentucky bullet!"

The old man turned his head and saw that the eager Mahtoree, who preceded his party some distance, had brought himself nearly in a line with the bark and the bee-hunter, who stood perfectly ready to execute his hostile threat. Bending his body low, the rifle was discharged, and the swift lead whizzed harmlessly past him on its more distant errand. But the eye of the Dacotah chief was not less quick and certain than that of his enemy. He threw himself from his horse the moment preceding the report, and sank into the water. The beast snorted with terror and anguish, throwing half his form out of the river in a desperate plunge. Then he was seen drifting away in the torrent, and dyeing the turbid waters with his blood.

The Dacotah chief soon reappeared on the surface, and, understanding the nature of his loss, he swam with vigorous strokes to the nearest of the young men, who relinquished his steed, as a matter of course, to so renowned a warrior. The incident, however, created a confusion in the whole of the Dacotah band, who appeared to await the intention of their leader before they renewed their efforts to reach the shore. In the meantime the vessel of skin had reached the land, and the fugitives were once more united on the margin of the river.

The savages were now swimming about in indecision, as a flock of pigeons is often seen to hover in confusion after receiving a heavy discharge into its leading column, apparently hesitating on the risk of storming a bank so formidably defended. The well-known precaution of Indian warfare prevailed, and Mahtoree, admonished by his recent adventure, led his warriors back to the shore from which they had come, in order to relieve their beasts, which were already becoming unruly.

"Now, mount you with the tender ones, and ride for yonder hillock," said the trapper; "beyond it you will find another stream, into which you must enter, and, turning to the sun, follow its bed for a mile, until you reach a high and sandy plain; there will I meet you. Go; mount; this Pawnee youth and I, and my stout friend, the physician, who is a desperate warrior, are men enough to keep the bank, seeing that show and not use is all that is needed."

Middleton and Paul saw no use in wasting their breath in remonstrances against this proposal. Glad to know that their rear was to be covered even in this imperfect manner, they hastily got their horses in motion, and soon disappeared on the required route. Some twenty or thirty minutes succeeded this movement before the Dacotahs on the opposite shore seemed inclined to enter on any new enterprise. Mahtoree was distinctly visible, in the midst of his warriors, issuing his mandates, and betraying his desire for vengeance by occasionally shaking an arm in the direction of the fugitives; but no step was taken which appeared to threaten any further act of immediate hostility. At length a yell arose among the savages which announced the occurrence of some fresh event. Then Ishmael and his sluggish sons were seen in the distance, and soon the whole of the united force moved down to the very limits of the stream. The squatter proceeded to examine the position of his enemies with his usual coolness, and, as if to try the power of his rifle, he sent a bullet among them, with a force sufficient to do execution even at the distance at which he stood.

"Now let us depart!" exclaimed Dr. Bat, endeavoring to catch a furtive glimpse of the lead, which he fancied whizzing at his very ear; "we have maintained the bank in a gallant manner for a sufficient length of time; quite as much military skill is to be displayed in a retreat as in an advance."

The old man cast a look behind him, and seeing that the equestrians had reached the cover of the hill, he made no objections to the proposal. The remaining horse was given to the doctor, with instructions to pursue the course just taken by Middleton and Paul. When the naturalist was mounted and in full retreat, the trapper and the young Pawnee stole from the spot in such a manner as to leave their enemies for some time in doubt as to their movements. Instead, however, of proceeding across the plain toward the hill, a route on which they must have been in open view, they took a shorter path, covered by the formation of the ground, and intersected the little water-course at the point where Middleton had been directed to leave it, and just in season to join his party. The doctor had used so much diligence in the retreat as to have already overtaken his friends, and of course all the fugitives were again assembled.

The trapper now looked about him for some convenient spot where the whole party might halt, as he expressed it, for some five or six hours.

"Halt!" exclaimed the doctor, when the alarming proposal reached his ears; "why, it would seem that, on the contrary, many days should be passed in industrious flight."

Middleton and Paul were both of this opinion, and, each in his particular manner, expressed as much.

The old man heard them with patience, but shook his head like one who is unconvinced, and then answered all their arguments in one general and positive reply.

"Why should we fly?" he asked. "Can the legs of mortal men outstrip the speed of horses? Do you think the Dacotahs will lie down and sleep, or will they cross the water and nose for our trail? Thanks be to the Lord, we have washed it well in this stream, and, if we leave the place with discretion and wisdom, we may yet throw them off the track. But a prairie is not a wood. There a man may journey long, caring for nothing but the print his moccasin leaves; whereas, on these open plains, a runner placed on yonder hill, for instance, could see far on every side of him, like a hovering hawk looking down on his prey. No, no; night must come and darkness be upon us afore we leave this spot. But listen to the words of the Pawnee; he is a lad of spirit, and many is the hard race that he has run with the Sioux bands. Does my brother think our trail is long enough?" he demanded, in the Indian tongue.

"Is a Dacotah a fish, that he can see it in the river?"

"But my young men think we should stretch it until it reaches across the prairie."

"Mahtoree has eyes; he will see it."

"What does my brother counsel?"

The young warrior studied the heavens a moment, and appeared to hesitate. He mused some time with himself, and then he replied like one whose opinion was fixed.

"The Dacotahs are not asleep," he said; "we must lie in the grass."

"Ah! the lad is of my mind," said the old man, briefly explaining the opinion of his companion to his white friends. Middleton was obliged to acquiesce, and, as it was confessedly dangerous to remain upon their feet, each one set about assisting in the means to be adopted for their security. Inez and Ellen were quickly bestowed beneath the warm and not uncomfortable shelter of the buffalo skins, which formed a thick covering, and tall grass was drawn over the place in such a manner as to evade any examination from a common eye. Paul and the Pawnee fettered the beasts and cast them to the earth, where, after supplying them with food, they were also left concealed in the fog of the prairie. No time was lost when these several arrangements were completed before each of the others sought a place of rest and concealment, and then the plain appeared again deserted in its solitude.

The old man had advised his companions of the absolute necessity of their continuing for hours in this concealment. All their hopes of escape depended on the success of the artifice. If they might elude the cunning of their pursuers by this simple and therefore less suspected expedient, they could renew their flight as the evening approached, and, by changing their course, the chance of final success would be greatly increased. Influenced by these momentous considerations, the whole party lay musing on their situation until thoughts grew weary, and sleep finally settled on them all, one after another.

The deepest silence had prevailed for hours, when the quick ears of the trapper and the Pawnee were startled by a faint cry of surprise from Inez. Springing to their feet, like men who were about to struggle for their lives, they found the vast plain, the rolling swells, the little hillock, and the scattered thickets, covered alike in one white, dazzling sheet of snow.

"The Lord have mercy on ye all!" exclaimed the old man, regarding the prospect with a rueful eye. "Now, Pawnee, do I know the reason why you studied the clouds so closely; but it is too late; it is too late! A squirrel would leave his trail on this light coating of the 'arth. Ha! there comes the imps to a certainty. Down with ye all, down with ye; your chance is but small, and yet it must not be wilfully cast away."

The whole party was instantly concealed again, though many an anxious and stolen glance was directed through the tops of the grass on the movements of their enemies. At the distance of half a mile the Sioux band was seen riding in a circuit, which was gradually contracting itself, and evidently closing upon the very spot where the fugitives lay. There was but little difficulty in solving the mystery of this movement. The snow had fallen in time to assure them that those they sought were in the rear, and they were now employed, with the unwearied perseverance and patience of Indian warriors, in circling the certain boundaries of their place of concealment.

Each minute added to the jeopardy of the fugitives. Paul and Middleton deliberately prepared their rifles, and as Mahtoree came at length within fifty feet of them, keeping his eye riveted on the grass through which he rode, they leveled them together and pulled the triggers. The effort was answered by the mere snapping of the locks.

"Enough," said the old man, rising with dignity; "I have cast away the priming; for certain death would follow your rashness. Now let us meet our fates like men. Cringing and complaining find no favor in Indian eyes."

His appearance was greeted by a yell that spread far and wide over the plain, and in a moment a hundred savages were seen riding madly to the spot. Mahtoree received his prisoners with great self-restraint, though a single gleam of fierce joy broke through his clouded brow.

The exultation of receiving the white captives was so great as for a time to throw the dark and immovable form of their young Indian companion entirely out of view. He stood apart, disdaining to turn an eye on his enemies, as motionless as if he were frozen in that attitude of dignity and composure. But when a little time had passed, even this secondary object attracted the attention of the Dacotahs. Then it was that the trapper first learned, by the shout of triumph and long-drawn yell of delight which burst at once from a hundred throats, as well as by the terrible name which filled the air, that his youthful friend was no other than a redoubtable and hitherto invincible warrior, the open and dreaded foeman of the Dacotahs—the Pawnee chieftain, Hard Heart.

You will remember that Mahtoree, the Dacotah, had peeped into the tent in which the squatter had imprisoned Inez. Now that the chief had her in his power he wished her for his own wife.

But the trapper by his wise and shrewd ways kept the chief from taking Inez away from the other captives, and the attention of the Indians was directed especially toward the torture of the captive Pawnee.

First they tried to get him to give up his Pawnee connections and become a Sioux warrior. But this Hard Heart indignantly refused. "Hard Heart has looked at himself within and without," he said. "He has thought of all he has done in the hunts and in the wars. Everywhere he is the same. There is no change. He is in all things a Pawnee. He has struck so many Dacotahs that he could never eat in their lodges. His arrows would fly backward; the point of his lance would be on the wrong end: their friends would weep at every whoop he gave; their enemies would laugh. Do the Dacotahs know a Loup? Let them look at him again. His head is painted; his arm is flesh; his heart is rock. When the Dacotahs see the sun come from the Rocky Mountains, and move toward the land of the palefaces, the mind of Hard Heart will soften, and his spirit will become Sioux. Until that day he will live and die a Pawnee."

A yell of delight, in which admiration and ferocity were strangely mingled, interrupted the speaker, and but too clearly announced the character of his fate. The captive waited a moment for the commotion to subside, and then he continued.

"See," he added, directing the eyes of the Sioux to the earnest countenance of the attentive trapper; "Hard Heart is not without a grayhead to show him the path to the blessed prairies. If he ever has another father, it shall be that just warrior."

Then Mahtoree, weary of delay, encouraged the tormentors to proceed.

Weucha, the wily Sioux, who, eager for this sanction, had long stood watching the countenance of the chief, bounded forward at the signal like a bloodhound loosened from the leash. Forcing his way into the center of the old squaws, who were already proceeding from abuse to violence, he reproved their impatience, and bade them wait until a warrior had begun to torment, and then they should see their victim shed tears like a woman.

The heartless savage commenced his efforts by flourishing his tomahawk about the head of the captive, in such a manner as to give reason to suppose that each blow would bury the weapon in the flesh, while it was so governed as not to touch the skin. To this customary expedient Hard Heart was perfectly insensible. His eye kept the same steady, riveted look on the air, though the glittering ax described in its evolutions a bright circle of light before his countenance. Frustrated in this attempt, the callous Sioux laid the cold edge on the naked head of his victim, and began to describe the different manners in which a prisoner might be flayed. The women kept time to his cruelties with their taunts, and endeavored to force some expressions of the weakness of nature from the insensible features of the Pawnee. But he evidently reserved himself for the chiefs, and for those moments of extreme anguish when the loftiness of his spirit might evince itself in a manner better becoming his high and untarnished reputation.

The eyes of the trapper followed every movement of the tomahawk with the interest of a real father, until at length, unable to command his indignation, he exclaimed:

"My son has forgotten his cunning. This is a low-minded Indian, and one easily hurried into folly. I can not do the thing myself, for my traditions forbid a dying warrior to revile his persecutors, but the gifts of a redskin are different. Let the Pawnee say the bitter words and purchase an easy death. I will answer for his success, provided he speaks before the grave men set their wisdom to back the folly of this fool."

The savage Sioux, who heard his words without comprehending their meaning, turned to the speaker and menaced him with death for his temerity.

"Ay, work your will," said the unflinching old man ; "I am as ready now as I shall be to-morrow. Though it would be a death that an honest man might not wish to die. Look at that noble Pawnee, Dacotah, and see what a redskin may become who fears the Master of Life and follows His laws. What are you? Can Weucha speak the name of one enemy he has ever struck?"

"Hard Heart!" shouted the Sioux, turning in his fury and aiming a deadly blow at the head of his victim. His arm fell into the hollow of the captive's hand. For a single moment the two stood, as if entranced, in that attitude, the one paralyzed by so unexpected a resistance, and the other bending his head, not to meet his death, but in the act of the most intense attention. The women screamed with triumph, for they thought the nerves of the captive had at length failed him. The trapper trembled for his friend; and Hector, as if conscious of what was passing, raised his nose in the air and uttered a piteous howl.

But the Pawnee hesitated only for that moment. Raising the other hand like lightning, the tomahawk flashed in the air, and Weucha sank at his feet, brained to the eye. Then cutting a way with the bloody weapon, he darted through the opening left by the frightened women, and seemed to descend the declivity at a single bound.

Had a bolt from heaven fallen in the midst of the Dacotah band it would not have occasioned greater consternation than this act of desperate hardihood.

A shrill, plaintive cry burst from the lips of all the women, and there was a moment when even the oldest warriors appeared to have lost their faculties. This stupor endured only for the instant. It was succeeded by a yell of revenge that burst from a hundred throats, while as many warriors started forward at the cry, bent on the most bloody retribution. But a powerful and authoritative call from Mahtoree arrested every foot. The chief, in whose countenance disappointment and rage were struggling with the affected composure of his station, extended an arm toward the river, and the whole mystery was explained.

Hard Heart had already crossed half the bottom which lay between the acclivity and the water. At this precise moment a band of armed and mounted Pawnees turned a swell, and galloped to the margin of the stream, into which the plunge of the fugitive was distinctly heard. A few minutes sufficed for his vigorous arm to conquer the passage, and then the shout from the opposite shore told the humbled Dacotahs the whole extent of the triumph of their adversaries.

Then the surprised Dacotahs, gathering quickly, prepared for the battle. But it became a single combat between the two chiefs. For when Hard Heart had joined his tribesmen and was again armed for the fight, he challenged Mahtoree to single combat upon an island in the river and in full view of both parties.

The Dacotah made the first move. Even before Hard Heart was prepared for the attack Mahtoree, setting an arrow to his bow, sent it, with a sudden and deadly aim, full at the naked bosom of his generous and confiding enemy.

The action of the treacherous Dacotah was too quick and too well-matured to admit of any of the ordinary means of defense on the part of the Pawnee. His shield was hanging at his shoulder, and even the arrow had been suffered to fall from its place, and lay in the hollow of the hand which grasped the bow. But the quick eye of the brave had time to see the movement, and his ready thoughts did not desert him. Pulling hard and with a jerk upon the rein, his steed reared his forward legs into the air, and, as the rider bent his body low, the horse served for a shield against the danger. So true, however, was the aim, and so powerful the force by which it was sent, that the arrow entered the neck of the animal and broke the skin on the opposite side.

Quicker than thought Hard Heart sent back an answering arrow. The shield of the Dacotah was transfixed, but his person was untouched. For a few moments the twang of the bow and the glancing of arrows were incessant, notwithstanding the combatants were compelled to give so large a portion of their care to the means of defense. The quivers were soon exhausted; and though blood had been drawn, it was not in sufficient quantities to impair the energy of the combat.

A series of masterly and rapid evolutions with the horses now commenced.

The wheelings, the charges, the advances, and the circuitous retreats were like the flights of circling swallows. Blows were struck with the lance, the sand was scattered in the air, and the shocks often seemed to be unavoidably fatal; but still each party kept his seat, and still each rein was managed with a steady hand. At length the Dacotah was driven to the necessity of throwing himself from his horse to escape a thrust that would otherwise have proved fatal.

The Pawnee passed his lance through the beast, uttering a shout of triumph as he galloped by. Turning in his tracks, he was about to push the advantage, when his own mettled steed staggered and fell under a burden he could no longer sustain. Mahtoree answered his premature cry of victory, and rushed upon the entangled youth with knife and tomahawk. The utmost agility of Hard Heart had not sufficed to extricate himself in season from the fallen beast. He saw that his case was desperate. Feeling for his knife, he took the blade between a finger and thumb, and cast

MAHTOREE ANSWERED HIS PREMATURE CRY OF VICTORY AND RUSHED UPON THE ENTANGLED YOUTH WITH KNIFE AND TOMAHAWK.

it with admirable coolness at his advancing foe. The keen weapon whirled a few times in the air, and its point meeting the naked breast of the impetuous Dacotah, the blade was buried to the buckhorn haft.

Mahtoree laid his hand on the weapon, and seemed to hesitate whether to withdraw it or not. For a moment his countenance darkened with the most inextinguishable hatred and ferocity, and then, as if inwardly admonished how little time he had to lose, he staggered to the edge of the sands, and halted with his feet in the water. The cunning and duplicity which had so long obscured the brighter and nobler traits of his character were lost in the never-dying sentiment of pride which he had imbibed in youth.

"Boy of the Loups!" he said, with a smile of grim satisfaction, "the scalp of a mighty Dacotah shall never dry in Pawnee smoke!"

Drawing the knife from the wound, he hurled it toward the enemy in disdain. Then, shaking his arm at his successful foe, his swarthy countenance appearing to struggle with volumes of scorn and hatred that he could not utter with the tongue, he cast himself headlong into one of the most rapid veins of the current, his hand still waving in triumph above the fluid even after his body had sunk into the tide forever. Hard Heart was by this time free. The silence which had hitherto reigned in the bands was suddenly broken by general and tumultuous shouts. Fifty of the adverse warriors were already in the river, hastening to destroy or to defend the conqueror; and the combat was rather on the eve of its commencement than near its termination. But to all these signs of danger and need the young victor was insensible. He sprang for the knife, and bounded with the foot of an antelope along the sands, looking for the receding fluid which concealed his prize. A dark, bloody spot indicated the place, and, armed with the knife, he plunged into the stream, resolute to die in the flood or to return with his trophy.

In the meantime the sands became a scene of bloodshed and violence. Better mounted and perhaps more ardent, the Pawnees had, however, reached the spot in sufficient numbers to force their enemies to retire. The visitors pushed their success to the opposite shore, and gained the solid ground in the *mêlée* of the fight. Here they were met by all the unmounted Dacotahs, and, in their turn, they were forced to give way.

The combat now became more careful and Indian-like. As the hot impulses which had driven both parties to mingle in so deadly a struggle began to cool, the chiefs were enabled to exercise their influence, and to temper the assaults with prudence. In consequence of the admonitions of their leaders, the Sioux sought such covers as the grass afforded, or here and there some bush or slight inequality of the ground, and the charges of the Pawnee warriors necessarily became more wary, and of course less fatal.

In this manner the contest continued with varied success, and without much loss. The Sioux had succeeded in forcing themselves into a thick growth of rank grass, where the horses of their enemies could not enter, or where, when entered, they were worse than useless. It became necessary to dislodge the Dacotahs from this cover, or the object of the combat must be abandoned. Several desperate efforts had been repulsed, and the disheartened Pawnees were beginning to think of a retreat, when the well-known war-cry of Hard Heart was heard at hand, and the next instant the chief appeared in their center, flourishing the scalp of the great Sioux, as a banner that would lead to victory.

He was greeted by a shout of delight, and followed into the cover with an impetuosity that for the moment drove all before it. But the bloody trophy in the hand of the partisan served as an incentive to the attacked as well as to the assailants. Mahtoree had left many a daring brave behind him in his band who now exhibited the most generous self-devotion in order to wrest the memorial of the chief from the hands of the avowed enemies of their people.

The result was in favor of numbers. After a severe struggle, in which the finest displays of personal intrepidity were exhibited by all the chiefs, the Pawnees were compelled to retire upon the open bottom, closely pressed by the Sioux, who failed not to seize each foot of ground ceded by their enemies. Had the Sioux stayed their efforts on the margin of the grass, it is probable that the honor of the day would have been theirs, notwithstanding the irretrievable loss they had sustained in the death of Mahtoree. But the more reckless braves of the band were guilty of an indiscretion that entirely changed the fortunes of the fight, and suddenly stripped them of their hard-earned advantages.

A Pawnee chief had sunk under the numerous wounds he had received, and he fell, a target for a dozen arrows, in the very last group of his retiring party. Regardless alike of inflicting further injury on their foes and of the temerity of the act, the Sioux braves bounded forward with a whoop, each man burning with the wish to reap the high renown of striking the body of the dead. They were met by Hard Heart and a chosen knot of warriors, all of whom were just as stoutly bent on saving the honor of their nation from so foul a stain. The struggle was hand to hand, and blood began to flow more freely. As the Pawnees retired with the body, the Sioux pressed upon their footsteps, and at length the whole of the latter broke out of the cover with a common yell, and threatened to bear down all opposition by sheer physical superiority.

The fate of Hard Heart and his companions, all of whom would have died rather than relinquish their object, would have been quickly sealed but for a powerful and unlooked-for interposition in their favor. A shout was heard from a little brake on the left, and a volley from the fatal Western rifle immediately succeeded. Some five or six Sioux leaped forward in the death agony, and every arm among them was as suddenly suspended as if the lightning had flashed from the clouds to aid the cause of the Loups. Then came Ishmael and his stout sons in open view, bearing down upon their late treacherous allies with looks and voices that proclaimed the character of the succor.

THE PRAIRIE.

The shock was too much for the fortitude of the Dacotahs. Several of their bravest chiefs had already fallen, and those that remained were instantly abandoned by the whole of the inferior herd. A few of the most desperate braves still lingered nigh the fatal symbol of their honor, and there nobly met their deaths, under the blows of the re-encouraged Pawnees. A second discharge from the rifles of the squatter and his party completed the victory.

The knife and the lance cut short the retreat of the larger portion of the vanquished. Even the retiring party of the women and children was scattered by the conquerors; and the sun had long sunk behind the rolling outline of the western horizon before the fell business of that disastrous defeat was entirely ended.

The battle was over; but Ishmael, because of his assistance, claimed the captives of the Sioux—Ellen, his niece, Inez, his captive, and the old trapper, who, he believed, had murdered Asa, his son.

"I am called upon this day" said he, "to fill the office which in the settlements you give unto judges, who are set apart to decide on matters that arise between man and man. I have but little knowledge of the ways of the courts, though there is a rule that is known unto all, and which teaches that an 'eye must be returned for an eye,' and 'a tooth for a tooth.' I am no troubler of county-houses, and least of all do I like living on a plantation that the sheriff has surveyed; yet there is a reason in such a law, that makes it a safe rule to journey by, and therefore it ar' a solemn fact that this day shall I abide by it, and give unto all and each that which is his due and no more."

When Ishmael had delivered his mind thus far, he paused and looked about him, as if he would trace the effects in the countenances of his hearers. When his eye met that of Middleton, he was answered by the latter:

"If the evil-doer is to be punished, and he that has offended none to be left to go at large, you must change situations with me, and become a prisoner instead of a judge."

"You mean to say that I have done you wrong in taking the lady from her father's house, and leading her so far against her will into these wild districts," returned the unmoved squatter, who manifested as little resentment as he betrayed compunction at the charge. "I shall not put the lie on the back of an evil deed, and deny your words. Since things have come to this pass between us, I have found time to think the matter over, and though none of your swift thinkers, who can see, or who pretend to see, into the nature of all things by a turn of the eye, yet am I a man open to reason, and, give me my time, one who is not given to deny the truth. Therefore have I mainly concluded that it was a mistake to take a child from its parent, and the lady shall be returned whence she has been brought, as tenderly and as safely as man can do it."

"Ay, ay," added Esther, "the man is right. Poverty and labor bore hard upon him, especially as county officers were getting troublesome, and in a weak moment he did the wicked act ; but he has listened to my words, and his mind has got round again into its honest corner. An awful and a dangerous thing it is to be bringing the daughters of other people into a peaceable and well-governed family."

"And who will thank you for the same, after what has been already done?" muttered Abram, with a grin of disappointed cupidity, in which malignity and terror were disgustingly united. "When the devil has once made out his account, you may look for your receipt in full only at his hands."

"Peace!" said Ishmael, stretching his heavy hand toward his kinsman in a manner that instantly silenced the speaker. "Your voice is like a raven's in my ears. If *you* had never spoken, I should have been spared this shame."

"The matter is settled between us," he continued, turning to Middleton ; "you and your wife are free to go and come, when and how you please. Abner, set the captain at liberty ; and now, if you will tarry until I am ready to draw nigher to the settlements, you shall both have the benefit of carriage ; if not, never say that you did not get a friendly offer."

"Now, may the strong oppress me, and my sins be visited harshly on my own head, if I forget your honesty, however slow it has been in showing itself," cried Middleton, hastening to the side of the weeping Inez the instant he was released ; "and, friend, I pledge you the honor of a soldier that your own part of this transaction shall be forgotten, whatever I may deem fit to have done when I reach a place where the arm of government can make itself felt."

The dull smile with which the squatter answered to this assurance proved how little he valued the pledge that the youth, in the first revulsion of his feelings, was so free to make.

"Neither fear nor favor, but what I call justice, has brought me to this judgment," he said ; "do you that which may seem right in your eyes, and believe that the world is wide enough to hold us both without our crossing each other's path again! If you are content, well ; if you ar' not content, seek to ease your feelings in your own fashion. I shall not ask to be let up when you once put me fairly down. And now, doctor, have I come to your leaf in my accounts. It is time to foot up the small reckoning that has been running on for some time atwixt us. With you I entered into open and manly faith. In what manner have you kept it?"

"That there did exist a certain compactum or agreement between Obed Bat, M. D., and Ishmael Bush, viator, or erratic husbandman," he said, endeavoring to avoid all offense in the use of terms, "I am not disposed to deny. I will admit that it was therein conditioned or stipulated that a certain journey should be performed conjointly, or in company, until so many days had been numbered. But as the said time has fully expired, I presume it fair to infer that the bargain may now be said to be obsolete."

"Ishmael," interrupted the impatient Esther, "make no words with a man who can break your bones as easily as set them, and let the poisoning devil go! He's a cheat from box to phial. Give him half the prairie, and take the other half yourself. He an acclimator! I will engage to get the brats acclimated to a fever-and-ague bottom in a week, and not a word shall be uttered harder to pronounce than the bark of a cherry-tree, with perhaps a drop or two of western comfort. One thing ar' a fact, Ishmael; I like no fellow-travelers who can give a heavy feel to an honest woman's tongue, I—and that without caring whether her household is in order or out of order."

The air of settled gloom which had taken possession of the squatter's countenance lighted for an instant with a look of dull drollery, as he answered:

"Different people might judge differently, Esther, of the virtue of the man's art. But sin' it is your wish to let him depart, I will not plow the prairie to make the walking rough. Friend, you are at liberty to go into the settlements, and there I would advise you to tarry, as men like me, who make but few contracts, do not relish the custom of breaking them so easily."

"And now, young man; you who have so often come into my clearing under the pretense of lining the bee into his hole," resumed Ishmael, after a momentary pause, as if to recover the equilibrium of his mind, "with you there is a heavier account to settle. Not satisfied with rummaging my camp, you have stolen a girl who is akin to my wife, and who I had calculated to make one day a daughter of my own."

A stronger sensation was produced by this than by any of the preceding interrogations. All the young men bent their curious eyes on Paul and Ellen, the former of whom seemed in no small mental confusion, while the latter bent her face on her bosom in shame.

"Harkee, friend Ishmael Bush," returned the bee-hunter, who found that he was expected to answer to the charge of burglary as well as to that of abduction; "that I did not give the most civil treatment to your pots and pails I am not going to gainsay. If you will name the price you put upon the articles, it' is possible the damage may be quietly settled between us, and all hard feelings forgotten. I was not in a church-going humor when we got upon your rock, and it is more than probable there was quite as much kicking as preaching among your wares; but a hole in the best man's coat can be mended by money. As to the matter of Ellen Wade here, it may not be got over so easily. Different people have different opinions on the subject of matrimony. Some think it is enough to say "yes" and "no" to the questions of the magistrate or of the parson, if one happens to be handy, in order to make a quiet house ; but I think that where a young woman's mind is fairly bent on going in a certain direction, it will be quite as prudent to let her body follow. Not that I mean to say Ellen was not altogether forced to what she did, and therefore she is just as innocent in this matter as yonder jackass, who was made to carry her, and greatly against his will, too, as I am ready to swear he would say himself if he could speak as loud as he can bray."

"Nelly," resumed the squatter, who paid very little attention to what Paul considered a highly creditable and ingenious vindication, "Nelly, this is a wide and a wicked world on which you have been in such a hurry to cast yourself. You have fed and you have slept in my camp for a year, and I did hope that you had found the free air of the borders enough to your mind to wish to remain among us."

"Let the girl have her will," muttered Esther from the rear ; "he who might have persuaded her to stay is sleeping in the cold and naked prairie, and little hope is left of changing her humor ; besides, a woman's mind is a wilful thing, and not easily turned from its waywardness, as you know yourself, my man, or I should not be here the mother of your sons and daughters."

"It is quite plain, friend Bush," said Paul, "that there are two opinions in this matter ; yours for your sons, and mine for myself. I see but one amicable way of settling this dispute, which is as follows : Do you make a choice among your boys of any you will, and let us walk off together for the matter of a few miles into the prairies ; the one who stays behind can never trouble any man's house or his fixen, and the one who comes back may make the best of his way he can in the good wishes of the young woman."

"Paul!" exclaimed the reproachful but smothered voice of Ellen.

"Never fear, Nelly," whispered the literal bee-hunter, whose straightgoing mind suggested no other motive of uneasiness on the part of his mistress than concern for herself; "I have taken the measure of them all, and you may trust an eye that has seen to line many a bee into his hole."

"I am not about to set myself up as a ruler of inclinations," observed the squatter. "If the heart of the child is truly in the settlements, let her declare it ; she shall have no let or hindrance from me. Speak, Nelly, and let what you say come from your wishes, without fear or favor. Would you leave us to go with this young man into the settled countries, or will you tarry and share the little we have to give, but which to you we give so freely ?"

Thus called upon to decide, Ellen could no longer hesitate. The glance of her eye was at first timid and furtive. But as the color flushed her features, and her breathing became quick and excited, it was apparent that the native spirit of the girl was gaining the ascendency over the bashfulness of sex.

"You took me a fatherless, impoverished, and friendless orphan," she said, struggling to command her voice, "when others, who live in what may be called affluence compared to your state, chose to forget me ; and may Heaven in its goodness bless you for it ! The little I have done will never pay you for that one act of kindness. I like not your manner of life ; it is different from the ways of my childhood, and it is different from my wishes ; still, had you not led this sweet and unoffending lady from her friends, I should never have quitted you until you yourself had said, ' Go, and the blessing of God go with you ! ' "

" The act was not wise, but it is repented of ; and so far as it can be done in safety, it shall be repaired. Now, speak freely : will you tarry or will you go ? "

" I have promised the lady," said Ellen, dropping her eyes again to the earth, " not to leave her ; and after she has received so much wrong from our hands, she may have a right to claim that I keep my word."

" Take the cords from the young man," said Ishmael. When the order was obeyed, he motioned for all his sons to advance, and he placed them in a row before the eyes of Ellen. " Now, let there be no trifling, but open your heart. Here ar' all I have to offer besides a hearty welcome."

The distressed girl turned her abashed look from the countenance of one of the young men to that of another until her eye met the troubled and working features of Paul. Then nature got the better of forms. She threw herself into the arms of the bee-hunter, and sufficiently proclaimed her choice by sobbing aloud. Ishmael signed to his sons to fall back, and, evidently mortified, though perhaps not disappointed by the result, he no longer hesitated.

" Take her," he said, " and deal honestly and kindly by her. The girl has that in her which should make her welcome in any man's house, and I should be loth to hear she ever came to harm."

And when he learned, too, that not the old trapper but his own brother-in-law, Abram White, was the murderer of Asa, Ishmael released the old man and worked his revenge on the criminal Abram.

Released thus from all their troubles, the captives went with Hard Heart and the friendly Pawnees to their distant village.

Then, with words of friendship and of farewell, they left Hard Heart and his band. The soldiers of Captain Middleton joined him, and the white travelers embarked to go down the river.

" They are a valiant and an honest tribe," said the old trapper, as he looked back at his Pawnee friends ; " that will I say boldly in their favor ; and second only do I take them to be to that once mighty but now scattered people, the Delawares of the Hills. Ah's me, Captain, if you had seen as much good and evil as I have seen in these nations of redskins you would know of how much value was a brave and simple-minded warrior. I know that some are to be found who both think and say that an Indian is but little better than the beasts of these naked plains. But it is needful to be honest in one's self to be a fitting judge of honesty in others. No doubt, no doubt, they know their enemies, and little do they care to show to such any great confidence or love."

"It is the way of man," returned Captain Middleton, "and it is probable they are not wanting in any of his natural qualities."

"No, no; it is little that they want that natur' has had to give. But as little does he know of the temper of a redskin who has seen but one Indian or one tribe, as he knows of the color of feathers who has only looked upon a crow. Now, friend steersman, just give the boat a sheer toward yonder low sandy point, and a favor will be granted at a short asking."

The steersman did so, and then, much against the wishes of the rest, the old trapper parted from them.

The old man whistled his dogs to the land, and then he proceeded to the final adieux. Little was said on either side. The trapper took each person solemnly by the hand, and uttered something friendly and kind to all. Middleton was perfectly speechless, and was driven to affect busying himself among the baggage. Paul whistled with all his might, and even

THE DEATH OF THE OLD TRAPPER.

Dr. Bat took his leave with an effort that bore the appearance of desperate philosophical resolution. When he had made the circuit of the whole, the old trapper with his own hands shoved the boat into the current, wishing God to speed them. Not a word was spoken, nor a stroke of the oar given, until the travelers had floated past a knoll that hid the trapper from their view. He was last seen standing on the low point, leaning on his rifle, with Hector crouched at his feet and the younger dog frisking along the sands in the playfulness of youth and vigor.

The very next year Captain Middleton was again called to the West by his military duties.

These concluded, he and Paul Hover determined to cross the country to visit the Pawnee, Hard Heart, and to inquire into the fate of his friend the trapper. As his train was suited to his functions and rank, the journey was effected with privations and hardships that are the accompaniments of all traveling in a wild, but without any of those dangers and alarms that marked his former passage through the same regions. When within a proper distance, he dispatched an Indian runner belonging to a friendly tribe to announce the approach of himself and party, continuing his route at a deliberate pace in order that the intelligence might, as was customary, precede his arrival. At length the cavalcade, at whose head rode Middleton and Paul, descended from the elevated plain on which they had long been journeying to a luxuriant bottom, that brought them to the level of the village of the Pawnees. The sun was beginning to fall, and a sheet of golden light was spread over the placid plain, lending to its even surface those glorious tints and hues that the human imagination is apt to conceive from the embellishment of still more imposing scenes. Suddenly Paul said: "See! we are not altogether slighted, for here comes a party at last to meet us, though it is a little pitiful as to show and numbers."

Paul was right in both particulars. A group of horsemen were at length seen wheeling round a little copse and advancing across the plain directly toward them. The advance of this party was slow and dignified. As it drew nigh, the chieftain of the Pawnees was seen at its head, followed by a dozen younger warriors of his tribe. They were all unarmed, nor did they even wear any of those ornaments or feathers which are considered testimonials of respect to the guest an Indian receives, as well as evidence of his own importance.

The meeting was friendly, and soon, in silence, they entered the town. Its inhabitants were seen collected in an open space, where they were arranged with the customary deference to age and rank. The whole formed a large circle, in the center of which were perhaps a dozen of the principal chiefs. Hard Heart waved his hand as he approached, and, as the mass of bodies opened, he rode through, followed by his companions. Here they dismounted;

and as the beasts were led apart, the strangers found themselves environed by a thousand grave, composed, but solicitous faces.

Middleton gazed about him in growing concern, for no cry, no song, no shout, welcomed him among a people from whom he had so lately parted with regret. But there was no symptom of hostility on the part of their hosts. Hard Heart beckoned for Middleton and Paul to follow, leading the way toward the cluster of forms that occupied the center of the circle. Here the visitors found the cause of all this silence and ceremony—the old trapper was dying.

He was placed on a rude seat, which had been made with studied care to support his frame in an upright and easy attitude. His eye was glazed, and apparently as devoid of sight as of expression. His features were a little more sunken and strongly marked than formerly; but there all change, so far as exterior was concerned, might be said to have ceased. His approaching end was not to be ascribed to any positive disease, but had been a gradual and mild sinking away.

His body was placed so as to let the light of the setting sun fall full upon the solemn features. His head was bare, the long, thin locks of gray fluttering lightly in the evening breeze. His rifle lay upon his knee, and the other accoutrements of the chase were placed at his side, within reach of his hand. Between his feet lay the figure of a hound, with its head crouching to the earth, as if it slumbered; and so perfectly easy and natural was its position that a second glance was necessary to tell Middleton he saw only the skin of Hector, stuffed, by Indian tenderness and ingenuity, in a manner to represent the living animal. The younger dog was playing at a distance. Near at hand stood the wife of Hard Heart, holding in her arms a little child that might boast of a parentage no less honorable than that which belonged to the son of Hard Heart. The rest of those immediately in the center were aged men, who had apparently drawn near in order to observe the manner in which a just and fearless warrior would depart on the greatest of his journeys.

The old trapper was reaping the reward of a life remarkable for temperance and activity, in a tranquil and placid death. His vigor in a manner endured to the very last. He had hunted with the tribe in the spring, and even throughout most of the summer, when his limbs suddenly refused to perform their customary offices. A sympathizing weakness took possession of all his faculties, and the Pawnees believed that they were going to lose, in this unexpected manner, a sage and counselor whom they had begun both to love and respect.

When he had placed his guests in front of the dying man, Hard Heart, after a pause that proceeded as much from sorrow as decorum leaned a little forward, and demanded:

"Does my father hear the words of his son?"

"Speak," returned the trapper, in tones that issued from his chest, but which were rendered awfully distinct by the stillness that reigned in the place. "I am about to depart from the village of the Pawnees, and shortly shall be beyond the reach of your voice."

"See, here is a friend," said the chief, beckoning to Middleton to approach. Middleton took one of the meagre hands of the trapper, and struggling to command his voice, he succeeded in announcing his presence.

The old man listened like one whose thoughts were dwelling on a very different subject; but, when the other had succeeded in making him understand that he was present, an expression of joyful recognition passed over his faded features.

"I hope you have not so soon forgotten those whom you so materially served," said Middleton. "It would pain me to think my hold on your memory was so light."

"Little that I have ever seen is forgotten," returned the trapper: "I am at the close of many weary days, but there is not one among them all I could wish to overlook. I remember you, with the whole of your company; ay, and your gran'ther, that went before you. I am glad that you have come back upon these plains, for I had need of one who speaks English, since little faith can be put in the traders of these regions. Will you do a favor to an old and dying man?"

"Name it," said Middleton; "it shall be done."

"It is a far journey to send such trifles," resumed the old man, who spoke at short intervals, as strength and breath permitted; "a far and weary journey is the same; but kindnesses and friendships are things not to be forgotten. There is a settlement among the Ostego hills——"

"I know the place," interrupted Middleton, observing that he spoke with increasing difficulty; "proceed to tell me what you would have done."

"Take this rifle, pouch, and horn, and send them to the person whose name is graven on the plates of the stock,—a trader cut the letters with his knife,—for it is long that I have intended to send him such a token of my love!"

"It shall be so. Is there more that you could wish?"

"Little else have I to bestow. My traps I give to Hard Heart, my Indian son; for honestly and kindly has he kept his faith. Let him stand before me."

Middleton explained to the chief what the trapper had said, and relinquished his own place to the other.

"Pawnee," continued the old man, always changing his language to suit the person he addressed, and not infrequently according to the ideas he expressed, "it is a custom of my people for the father to leave his blessing with the son before he shuts his eyes forever. This blessing I give to you; take it, for the prayers of a Christian man will never make the path of a just warrior to the blessed prairies either longer or more tangled. May the God of a white man look on your deeds with friendly eyes, and may you never commit an act that shall cause Him to darken His face. I know not whether we shall ever meet again. There are many traditions concerning the place of Good Spirits. It is not for one like me, old and experienced though I am, to set up my opinions against a nation's. You believe in the blessed prairies, and I have faith in the sayings of my fathers. If both are true, our parting will be final; but if it should prove that the same meaning is hid under different words, we shall yet stand together, Pawnee, before the face of your Great Spirit, who will then be no other than my God. I fear I have not altogether followed the gifts of my color, inasmuch as I find it a little painful to give up forever the use of the rifle and the comforts of the chase. But then, the fault has been my own, seeing that it could not have been His."

The old man made a long and apparently a musing pause. At times he raised his eyes wistfully, as if he would again address Middleton, but some innate feeling appeared always to suppress his words. The other, who observed his hesitation, inquired, in a way most likely to encourage him to proceed, whether there was aught else that he could wish to have done.

"I am without kith or kin in the wide world," the trapper answered; "when I am gone there will be an end of my race. We have never been chiefs; but honest, and useful in our way I hope it can not be denied, we have always proved ourselves. My father lies buried near the sea, and the bones of his son will whiten on the prairies——"

"Name the spot, and your remains shall be placed by the side of your father," interrupted Middleton.

"Not so, not so, Captain. Let me sleep where I have lived—beyond the din of the settlements! Still I see no need why the grave of an honest man should be hid, like a redskin in his ambushment. I paid a man in the settlements to make and put a graven stone at the head of my father's resting-place. It was of the value of twelve beaver-skins, and cunningly and curiously was it carved. Then it told to all comers that the body of a Christian lay beneath; and it spoke of his manner of life, of his years, and of his honesty. When we had done with the Frenchers in the old war I made a journey to the spot, in order to see that all was rightly performed, and glad I am to say, the workman had not forgotten his faith."

"And such a stone you would have at your grave!"

"I? No, no; I have no son but Hard Heart, and it is little that an Indian knows of white fashions and usages. Besides, I am his debtor already, seeing it is so little I have done since I have lived in his tribe. The rifle might bring the value of such a thing—but then I know it will give the boy pleasure to hang the piece in his hall, for many is the deer and the bird that he has seen it

THE PRAIRIE.

destroy. No, no; the gun must be sent to him whose name is graven on the stock."

"But there is one who would gladly prove his affection in the way you wish; he who owes you not only his own deliverance from so many dangers, but who inherits a heavy debt of gratitude from his ancestors. The stone shall be put at the head of your grave."

The old man extended his emaciated hand, and gave the other a squeeze of thanks.

"I thought you might be willing to do it, but I was backward in asking the favor," he said, "seeing that you are not of my kin. Put no boastful words on the same, but just the name, the age, and the time of the death, with something from the Holy Book; no more, no more. My name will then not be altogether lost on 'arth; I need no more."

Middleton intimated his assent, and then followed a pause that was only broken by distant and broken sentences from the dying man. He appeared now to have closed his accounts with the world, and to wait merely for the final summons to quit it. Middleton and Hard Heart placed themselves on the opposite sides of his seat, and watched with melancholy solicitude the variations of his countenance. For two hours there was no very sensible alteration. The expression of his faded and time-worn features was that of a calm and dignified repose. Then he turned quietly, gave one last look at the glorious sunset across the prairies, half-raised himself, and dropped back. When Middleton and Hard Heart, each of whom had involuntarily extended a hand to support the form of the old man, turned to him again they found that the subject of their interest was removed forever beyond the necessity of their care. They mournfully placed the body in its seat, and the oldest chief of the Pawnees arose to announce the termination of the scene to the tribe. The voice of the old Indian seemed a sort of echo from that invisible world to which the meek spirit of the trapper had just departed.

"A valiant, a just, and a wise warrior, has gone on the path which will lead him to the blessed grounds of his people!" he said. "When the voice of the Great Spirit called him, he was ready to answer. Go, my children; remember the just chief of the palefaces, and clear your own tracks from briers!"

The grave was made beneath the shade of some noble oaks. It was long and carefully watched by the Pawnees of the Loups, and was often shown to the traveler and the trader as a spot where a just white man slept. In due time the stone was placed at its head, with the simple inscription which the trapper had himself requested. The only liberty taken by Middleton was to add: "May no wanton hand ever disturb his remains."

www.ingramcontent.com/pod-product-compliance
Lightning Source LLC
Chambersburg PA
CBHW030819230426
43667CB00008B/1285